COGNITIVE STRATEGIES FOR
SPECIAL EDUCATION

Research on training programs for students with learning difficulties has usually focused on the development of social and behavioral skills and the acquisition of cognitive interventions and procedures. This book attempts to apply the methods validated by research and synthesize the discoveries made in the psychological laboratory for the benefit of teachers in regular classrooms. It reviews the literature relevant to special needs teaching and traces the development of cognitive research as it applies to education.

The authors propose a specific and practical teaching strategy which has been successfully used by those working with students with special needs. Starting from the basic belief that education is an interactive process between the participants, Ashman and Conway have emphasized the role and responsibility both of the teacher and the learner. Their book should be of value to researchers and practitioners in psychology and special education.

Adrian F. Ashman is Senior Lecturer at the Schonell Special Education Research Centre, University of Queensland. Robert N.F. Conway lectures at the Special Education Centre, Hunter Institute of Higher Education, Waratah, New South Wales.

Cognitive Strategies for Special Education

Process-based instruction

Adrian F. Ashman
and Robert N.F. Conway

R

ROUTLEDGE
London and New York

First published 1989
by Routledge
11 New Fetter Lane, London EC4P 4EE
29 West 35th Street, New York, NY 10001

© 1989 A.F. Ashman and R.N.F. Conway

Printed and bound in Great Britain by
Biddles Ltd, Guildford and King's Lynn

British Library Cataloguing in Publication Data

Ashman, Adrian, F.
  Cognitive strategies for special education:
  processed-based instruction.
  1. Educational institutions. Students with
  special educational needs. Cognitive
  development. Teaching methods
  I. Title   II. Conway, Robert F., *1949-*
  371.9

  ISBN 0-415-00594-9
  ISBN 0-415-00595-7 Pbk

Library of Congress Cataloging-in-Publication Data

Ashman, A.F. (Adrian F.)
    Cognitive strategies for special education : process-based
    instruction / Adrian F. Ashman and Robert N.F. Conway.
       p.   cm.
    Bibliography: p.
    Includes indexes.
    ISBN 0-415-00594-9. ISBN 0-415-00595-7 (pbk.)
    1. Special education. 2. Learning, Psychology of. 3. Teaching.
  4. Cognitive learning. I. Conway, Robert N.F., 1949–
  II. Title.
  LC3969.A83   1989
  371.9—dc19   88-26453
                                                     CIP

Contents

List of Figures

List of Tables

Preface

Research on academic training programs for students with learning difficulties and intellectual disabilities has proliferated over the past three decades. In the past twenty years, a substantial portion of this research has dealt with investigations that have focused upon how students learn rather than how much they know or are able to learn. Such approaches deal with activities occurring within the brain and thus fall within the domain of cognitive educational psychology.

With this change in emphasis toward cognition, the focus of research has reflected the move from simple and somewhat naive approaches to memory training, to the inclusion of memory aids (strategies), and knowledge of the use of these aids that lead to insight and understanding (meta-strategies or metacognition). Much of the cognitive research has been undertaken as teaching interventions within the context of the educational or psychological laboratory, though teachers have seen few benefits accrue to students within regular or special classrooms.

Many of the books on cognitive interventions and procedures have been written by researchers, for researchers, about research. A relatively small number of them have been written by researchers, for teachers about research, and a smaller number again have been written about teaching. This volume is an attempt to blend the last two categories: It reviews the literature relevant to teaching, and describes an instructional method that synthesizes and applies methods validated by research.

As the title implies, the book traces the development of cognitive research as it applies to education. It reviews and critiques the cognitive literature, and might be seen as a resource volume for beginning or experienced teachers, for teacher trainees, or for students of educational psychology. While we have not aimed specifically to produce a "how-to" book, we have developed an argument proposing a specific and practical teaching strategy which has been, and is being used by teachers working with special needs students.

The format of this volume differs from many of the books that are based upon behavioral teaching principles. We do not deal specifically with ways of remediating reading, mathematics, psychomotor, or language difficulties in a step-by-step fashion. We have not included charts or task analyses of academic skills. Rather, we have focused upon the development of a teaching strategy that emphasizes the role and responsibilities of the teacher, and the role and responsibilities of the learner. It is our belief that education is a interactive process between the participants.

The book has 10 chapters. The first provides a background stage for research into interventions for students with learning difficulties and intellectual disabilities. The second chapter traces the influence of cognition in special education from the time of Itard and the Wild Boy of Aveyron to present research developments. Chapters 3 and 4 describe contemporary attempts to teach information processing skills as a prerequisite for the development of academic achievement. Specifically, Chapter 3 outlines general themes adopted by researchers, and the following chapter evaluates the strengths and deficits in many of the investigations.

Chapter 5 draws together the results of a decade of intervention research into a coherent foundation for information processing training that can be applied to the classroom. This chapter essentially provides the framework for the development of instruction that is process-, rather than product-based. Chapter 6 explores the relationship between academic achievement and cognitive processing and describes the generation of an instructional model that has been used in a laboratory setting.

Chapter 7 describes the transition of the laboratory model to the classroom and Chapter 8 details how Process-Based Instruction can be incorporated in current classroom practices. Chapter 9 deals with the extension of Process-Based Instruction beyond the classroom. The chapter deals with change within the classoom, within the school, and across educational systems. Chapter 10 is a retrospective. It provides comment upon education from a personal, professional, and institutional perspective.

The authors wish to acknowledge the skilful, dedicated assistance of the many individuals who have assisted with the preparation of this book. We are most grateful to those who have reviewed drafts including Dr. Susan Wright, Professor John Elkins, Helen Brazel, Barbara Crickmore, and Gordon Smith. We wish to acknowledge the substantial contribution made by Lyndall Hopton to the project over the past two years. She was involved in one of the classroom studies of Process-Based Instruction as the cooperating teacher, and has been closely associated with all aspects of the preparation of the manuscript, including the drawing of figures. We also express our gratitude to Sannie Pritchard who prepared several of the tables. Finally, we thank our wives, Susan and Helen for their patience during the preparation of this book.

1

The Learning Process

In the eighteenth century, the philosopher Helvetius suggested that the differences between individuals were due entirely to differences in education. Many may question such a simple claim though there would be few, who upon thinking back to their school days, would not agree that the process of education had a substantial impact upon them. Some may recall with delight the friendships that were made and the acclamations that came with academic success. Others may remember little that was positive, having only the closed wounds of emotional, and sometimes physical violence on which to reflect.

This book is about education and educational practice. It is about change and innovation. It addresses individual differences in learning, particularly when they are related to learning difficulties or intellectual disabilities.

DEFINING EDUCATION

In its broadest sense, education derives from general life experiences and involves the initiation of people into their culture or society. It involves aspects of their upbringing, the learning of values and social mores, and the development of knowledge about the way in which society operates. Ideally, education allows the person to participate in society in a meaningful and effective way. It begins with foetal interactions within the womb, and ends with the clinical death of the brain.

Education is an integral part of society and involves the transmission of knowledge and the activation of learning through the experience of life and formal education. Education, then, includes planned and unplanned experiences that expand a person's information storehouse, promote learning, and lead to problem solving behavior.

Formal education refers to *systematic* instruction or training that young people and adults receive in preparation for life. For most of us, formal education begins with the learning of socially appropriate behaviors under parents' direction. It continues with our enrolment into school, and perhaps into college or university.

The implicit (though sometimes explicit) agenda of education is social adaptation. It is the impact of our formal and informal learning which provides the basis for interactions with those about us. With the infinite number of permutations and combinations of experiences that direct our learning, education takes on a unique and private meaning. There are those members of society who have learned to adapt easily to change, while others require specific guidance and extended learning experiences to develop living skills and competence in problem solving. It is toward this latter group that this book primarily is directed.

SPECIAL EDUCATION

From our philosophical point of view, all individuals are unique, and hence, special. However, there are those in our community who, by virtue of their physical and intellectual abilities, require a more relevant or appropriate instruction than is usually available within formal and informal educational structures. We call these people exceptional or special, and we have constructed a domain of education to satisfy their learning requirements and a social philosophy to justify it (Laura & Ashman, 1985). This domain is called Special Education.

For some teachers, the theory and the practice of instruction developed within special education settings seems to have little relevance to the regular classroom. For teachers holding such a view, there is no need for a flow of information between these two teaching contexts. It was this viewpoint that led to the segregation of special classes from the mainstream in the belief that teaching within these classes required different instructional techniques. Consequently, special education classes have continued to be isolated physically, politically, and socially.

In contrast, other teachers have recognized that the principles of development and learning are the same for all and have viewed special education as the testing ground for pedagogical change. This disposition implies a two-way flow of information between special and regular education. What special education has to offer regular education comes primarily from teachers' experiences with individuals and with small groups of children who have special needs. These needs demand persistence and imagination and often involve the sensitive application of behavioral and psychological principles. On the other hand, special educators have much to learn from regular classroom teachers, for instance, on how to organize, motivate, pace instruction, and assess outcomes for large groups of students (Hobbs, Bartel, Dokecki, Gallagher, & Reynolds, 1977).

The division between special and regular education for students with mild learning and developmental disabilities is becoming increasingly indistinct with the current emphasis on the integration of exceptional learners into mainstream classes. As a consequence, there is a growing demand for instructional methods and techniques that best meet the diversity of students' abilities and competencies that are to be found within mainstream and special classrooms.

THE PSYCHOLOGY OF EDUCATION

Innovation and change in education generally, and in special education particularly, has not been a series of random events or discoveries. Most developments have been the products of review, preparation, and testing. In simple terms, they have been the products of research and classroom practice.

It is difficult to consider instructional and educational practice without entering into the field of educational psychology. While psychology refers to the study of behavior, educational psychology is concerned with the systematic study of human behavior as it relates to learning. Educational psychology is a discipline in its own right with theory, procedures, and a research heritage rooted in scientific method.

The province of educational psychology is expansive. It is not simply a catalogue of prescriptions that tell teachers how to teach. It is a knowledge base that allows for the generation of hypotheses and solutions that apply to the activity of learning. It deals with the nature of learning and to the many factors that influence learning. These include the study of:

3

1. human growth and development, including individual differences, aptitude, physical and developmental disabilities;
2. the nature of cognition and intellectual activities, including reasoning, problem solving, and intellectual disabilities;
3. personality and adjustment, including social influences on learning, emotions, human interactions, communication, and behavioral disorders;
4. measurement and evaluation, including test construction and administration;
5. school psychology and counseling, including inter-professional activities, affective components of learning; and,
6. the study of academic content and skills, including teaching practice and methods, classroom dynamics, motivation, cognitive style, and learning difficulties.

Thus, educational psychology spans the range of activities that occur both inside and outside the classroom. It directs attention toward the complex interplay between classroom and interpersonal dynamics, teaching methods and techniques, the nature of learning and cognition, and learner characteristics. Hence, the development of any "new" instructional approach for use with regular or special students would, by necessity, involve the study of educational psychology. As a starting point for our discussion, we now turn to several issues that will set the framework for our discussion of instruction and learning.

LEARNING AND INFORMATION PROCESSING

As a general statement, human learning is concerned with the acquisition of knowledge or skills. We talk about learning how to communicate with others, how to read, how to remember, and how to drive a car. We learn prejudices, moral standards, and "about things", that is, the relationships between objects and events. Moreover, we know that there are vast individual differences in the ability to learn and to reason.

Defining Learning

Some writers have suggested that it is very difficult to write an entirely satisfactory definition of learning (Hilgard & Bower, 1966). From a behavioral viewpoint, learning is a relatively permanent process that results from practice, and is reflected in a change in performance. Of course, this explanation of how learning occurs is based upon the consequences of a specific behavior, and its value as an adaptive response to the environment. Within this conceptual framework of learning there is little room for individual differences: given prescribed environmental conditions, learning must occur.

From a different theoretical perspective, learning can be described in terms of the thought processes that occur within our brains. From this information processing viewpoint, learning becomes the *process of learning* which involves:

* paying attention to what is to be learned;
* learning by rote or by understanding concepts and processes;
* controlling the rate or the quality of learning; and,
* being aware that learning has taken place.

Using an information processing approach, the notion of individual differences in learning becomes a relevant and important concept. Moreover, we can examine the automatic or conscious processing of information by students and catalogue their strengths and weaknesses, not in terms of learning outcomes, but by reference to the cognitive systems that mediate learning.

Defining Information Processing

Information processing is a major theoretical and practical framework that describes how humans think. It describes the attainment of concepts and reasoning skills in terms of how we acquire, organize, store, and retrieve information. Typically, these cognitive activities involve a series of stages through which information passes and this passage of information through the system involves active, constructive processes rather than passive reception of knowledge.

Although these stages of information processing are not directly observable, researchers and theoreticians have isolated and defined component parts and have developed formal models and theories of human cognition that can be tested experimentally (Burton, 1982; Klausmeier, 1979). In essence, these models describe the cognitive skills possessed and being acquired by the learner, and also the manner in which they are used in problem solving activities.

While the description of information processing sounds somewhat mechanistic, the application of the theory provides for a thoroughly humanistic view of learning. It describes how an individual actually deals with information being presented, and how new information is integrated with knowledge already held by the individual. Information processing theory allows for the diagnosis of learning difficulties in terms of both cognitive and affective variables.

Individual Differences and Learning Styles

Individual differences are found in both intellectual abilities and motivation. Teachers are well aware that these two factors interact and can identify students who are:

* academically bright, highly motivated and highly successful;
* bright, but impulsive and less successful in their problem solving activities; and,
* of low academic ability, but determined to do the best they can, and who finally succeed through determination and effort.

Intellectual ability is predominantly a function of an individual's genetic endowment, but how that person responds in a learning situation will affect the degree to which the genetic potential is realized. Moreover, it has been suggested that individual differences may also be related to one's life goals and style in interpersonal interactions (Tyler, 1974).

Cognitive style is the term that refers to an individual's characteristic approach to learning and problem solving. Several cognitive styles have been identified. The Theory of Psychological Differentiation (Witkin, Moore, Goodenough, & Cox, 1977) distinguishes between learners who are passive, have low self-esteem, poor impulse control and need structure and direction (field-dependent) and those who are self-reliant, assured and approach learning tasks with a flexible viewpoint (field-independent). A second approach concerns the concepts of reflection and impulsivity in which individuals trade-off fast responses for accurate responses (Kagan, Rosman, Day, Albert, & Phillips, 1964).

While the literature on cognitive style has not grown at the same prodigious rate as it did in the 1960s and early 1970s, the importance of the subjective aspects of emotion as components of the learning process has remained. Moreover, educators have become sensitive to the need to match instructional techniques and programs to students' personal learning styles. This approach is based upon the assumption that the way in which information is presented to a person is not necessarily the way in which that individual would normally process the information (Blackman & Goldstein, 1982). While support for this proposition may not be overwhelming, it is an important consideration in the development of instructional theories and practices and has direct relevance to classroom behavior.

THE NATURE OF CLASSROOM INSTRUCTION

Formal education involves the interplay of many variables. Some writers have emphasized language, human interactions and the socialization process that occurs within the classroom (Turnure, 1986). Others have considered interactions between teaching styles and methods, learner variables, and the nature of the situation in which learning takes place. A useful framework in which classroom instruction can be considered includes three clusters of variables: ecological variables, curriculum variables, and direct teaching variables (Marsh, Price, & Smith, 1983). We will look at each of these in turn.

Ecological Variables

Learning is not simply the acquisition of content and outcomes. It is also a function of the environment in which learning takes place (Fraser, 1986).

There are three variables that are related to the learning environment: classroom climate; use of space and time; and, participation-interaction. *Classroom climate*, is particularly

7

important as it may restrict or facilitate interactions within the classroom and students' acquisition of skills. In Fraser's terms, it is the "quality of life" within the classroom that governs outcomes. There are several factors which contribute to this quality of life within the classroom. These include the cohesiveness or friction within the class group, the degree of student involvement in the learning process, teacher support, clarity of class and school rules, teacher control, and innovation.

While a positive classroom climate may not lead directly to an increase in student's performance, it can contribute to the development of positive student attitudes and feelings (such as self-concept and perception of school). These subjective aspects of emotion have a greater influence on academic achievement than is commonly accepted (Morsink, Soar, Soar, & Thomas, 1986; Soar & Soar, 1983). Alternatively, a classroom climate can be negative as a result of teacher attitudes or actions. Not surprisingly, this type of climate will limit the gains obtainable from teaching activities.

Optimum use of classroom space and time ensures that students have the chance to maximize learning skills. In-class time needs to be allocated carefully. Through preparation of teaching activities and materials, together with organization of classroom space, the teacher can ensure that students are involved in the learning process throughout the day and that time is not wasted or used inappropriately.

Participation-interaction describes the students' involvement in the instructional process. It focuses on the concept of the student as an active modifier of instruction rather than a passive recipient of it. Many students learn to passively accept education. That is, they are reinforced to wait passively for teacher initiated, monitored, and reinforced learning rather than taking an active role in the learning process. This variable focuses attention upon the setting in which learning occurs, for example, in large or small groups, in individualized instruction, or during independent learning activities. It also involves the concept of social reciprocity which refers to student-initiated interactions (Conway & Gow, in press).

Studies of social reciprocity have been directed toward the enhancement of students' participation through the use of such teaching strategies as asking questions, peer tutoring, and offering support to peers. Although social reciprocity training is still in an early stage of development, it appears to have direct applications to

8

mainstream or mixed ability classes (Ladd, 1981; Strain, Odom, & McConnell, 1985).

Student participation and interaction has special implications in teaching practices with students with intellectual disabilities, particularly in the area of problem solving. Having students develop their own solutions to problems reduces their reliance on the suggestions or solutions of others (Ellis, 1986). Students may learn to express ideas in their own words and discuss both processes and solutions with other students, enhancing the "natural dialogue" within the classroom (Meichenbaum, 1980).

Curriculum Variables

While ecological variables deal with the social context in which learning occurs, curriculum variables relate to the way in which information is presented. Curriculum variables include both the sequence in which skill-related material is presented, and the use and adaptation of materials and equipment for children who have diverse educational needs. The sequencing of instruction, in particular, has been a major focus of educational research in many curriculum areas for several decades. Analysis of reading, mathematics and language skills (task analysis) remains as one of the positive contributions of curriculum research undertaken during the 1960s and 1970s.

In spite of the positive attributes of task analysis through the focus on curriculum design and sequencing, an over-reliance on task analysis has the effect of constraining educational innovation. The result has been a rigid application of prescriptive teaching procedures which has in turn led to the development of curriculum documents that have tended to make teaching tasks functionally and developmentally irrelevant. Care with, and attention to what is presented and how it is presented is a vital issue in the development of effective teaching strategies.

Direct Teaching Variables

Direct teaching variables relate to the way in which information is actually presented to the learner and the management of learning behavior. Specifically, these variables include the means by which the students' attention and time on-task may be extended, the

9

organization of input, how they respond to instruction, and the quality and quantity of feedback given.

Each of the variables above emphasizes the importance of goal-directed teaching procedures. In the first instance, students' attention and time on-task can be maximized through the use of explicit, motivating activities: These will help students to understand the relevance of the task, what is required of them, and how they can solve the problem. Second, how an answer is to be given may affect the way in which a student attempts the task. For example, consider the different demands of writing a word or spelling it aloud. Finally, reinforcement of learning behavior is well known to classroom teachers as a vital ingredient in the learning process as it enhances the possibility of further learning. If reinforcement comes only from the teacher, then higher level problem solving skills may be constrained. The use and development of these teaching variables facilitates learner responsibility for monitoring and evaluating learning outcomes (McGraw, 1978; Deci & Porac, 1978).

INTRODUCING COGNITIVE THEORY INTO THE CLASSROOM

Teachers are continually deluged by new ideas, methods, techniques, curriculum documents, and administrative directives. In proposing any educational innovation, the onus is upon the advocate of change to demonstrate its application and practical value to teachers and students alike. While cognitive theorists have argued for the introduction of information processing into classroom practice, there have been few serious attempts to court the interest of teachers. Rather than assume the obvious advantages of any one approach over another, we offer several points that agents-of-change need to consider.

First, educators must be mindful of early attempts to adapt what were essentially theoretical notions of the learning process to classroom practice. The inclusion of novel and different content in training programs may lead teachers to consider contemporary information processing training as being a re-run of perceptual training programs (such as the Frostig program for the development of visual perception, Frostig & Horne, 1964), that were hailed as innovations in the 1960s, but later discredited.

Second, teachers are justified in being sceptical of training approaches if the tasks and teaching practices proposed cannot be related to the curriculum content taught in the classroom. A perusal of special education and educational psychology journals will show that many studies aimed at improvement in teaching practice have been undertaken in what is termed a laboratory situation. That is, the study of instruction and learning behavior is conducted in isolation from the usual learning context, namely, the classroom. Moreover, many of these studies have used learning and memory tasks that were theoretically rational, but which were seen by teachers as being unrelated to the learning activities that occur in school.

Third, teachers are unlikely to implement training programs that require substantial alteration to the current curriculum. This may be a function of the lack of time available to them to make appropriate adaptations, or they may not believe that they have the expertise necessary to integrate new techniques and procedures into their particular settings (Lovitt, Rudsit, Jenkins, Pious, & Benedetti, 1986). In addition, teachers may be concerned about student disorientation if changes in curriculum presentation are major, or occur frequently.

Finally, teachers must not be expected to abandon known and effective teaching methods merely because a new approach or strategy has been made available (Sheinker, Sheinker, & Stevens, 1984). Methods perceived by teachers as being efficient in terms of preparation time and consistency of presentation will not be abandoned unless compelling technical (rather than educational) reasons can be demonstrated.

The four points mentioned above are valid, but in no way preclude the successful incorporation of cognitive theory into classroom practice. The most important concern for educators is that adequate background, knowledge, and training is provided so that teachers understand clearly how to implement new strategies that are integrated into, but not a substitution for academic tasks. Change must not be made for the sake of change, but because there are relevant and compelling reasons for it. Moreover, teachers must be aware that an information processing approach to instruction may not be as effective with students who are below the concrete operations stage of cognitive development. They also must recognize that mastery of basic skills is a prerequisite to acquisition and use of generalized cognitive strategies.

It is our view that there is a real need to reconsider the instructional methods that are used within regular and special classrooms. It is toward this end that we have undertaken the study of information processing and the development of cognitive theories as a substantive base upon which teaching practice can rest.

PROCESS-BASED INTERVENTIONS

The term process-based intervention refers to a genus of educational programs that have been developed from cognitive theory. In Chapter 7, we have identified *Process-Based Instruction* (PBI) as a specific example of a process-based intervention.

PBI is one method of integrating cognitive theory within the regular curricula topics of the classroom. As such, it is a *cognitive curriculum* that assists students and teachers to work systematically toward solving curriculum tasks by providing a pedagogical framework. It combines good teaching practice with procedures derived from sound educational and psychological research.

In the chapters to follow, we have undertaken a review of the emergence of cognitive theory in the literature pertaining to special education. We provide not only a case for redefining instruction in information processing terms, but also a practical guide to the introduction of teaching strategies which incorporate cognitive theory. In our presentation, we have attempted to ensure that the approach is relevant, practical, and consistent with common teaching practice.

2

From Sensory Stimulation to Cognition

For those who underwent teacher training in the 1960s and 1970s, educational psychology was assigned a high priority. Emphasis was given to learning theories in various forms such as humanism, the developmental theory of Piaget and others, and to issues such as creativity, intelligence, and motivation.

From the mid 1970s, the influence of cognitive psychology began to appear. Cognition dealt with the processes involved in acquiring, storing, transforming, creating, evaluating, and using knowledge. Authors became generous in their discussion of aspects of cognition, dealing with issues such as memory, problem solving and cognitive style and the manner in which information processing influenced practically every facet of learning. Teacher trainees, no doubt dutifully read their texts, learned the new terminology of cognition and information processing, and possibly allowed most of this information to decay once the academic component of their training had been completed successfully.

From a practical point of view, the training in educational psychology has provided little more than background information. More important has been the acquisition of those fundamental teaching skills that enable the student teacher, and (later) the newly certified teacher, to transfer knowledge and skills to their pupils in the most efficient manner. One could argue that the knowledge gained from the educational psychology texts had been relegated to the most distant corner of the brain, where it was buried in a shallow grave marked "Pure and Impractical".

In special education training, students have been exposed to a new set of textbooks that have provided what appears to be a more acceptable form of information than is found in the general psychology texts. The new collection includes those volumes with titles such as *Teaching Children with Learning Problems*, *Teaching Handicapped Children*, *Strategies for Teaching* ...; the list is extensive. In these books, the content makes sense to the new and experienced teacher alike. Chapters with recognizable headings such as "Improving spelling skills", "Arranging the classroom environment", "Reading", "Arithmetic", "Principles of behavior management", and "Social-emotional problems" relate to the reality we call the classroom.

The material contained in most of the new collection is presented in a straightforward way. It has to do with task analysis, behavioral objective, assessment, skill development, and a profusion of exercises that can be translated into classroom practice across the curriculum. The foundation for many of these approaches might best be seen as the knowledge and application of sound learning principles to increase the teacher's practical performance. Instructional sequences and basic learning theory have become the primary foundation for special education. Indeed, the research and theory in information processing has had little impact upon contemporary special education practice. However, the vast majority of specialist texts fail to include a discussion of cognitive theory, and certainly have not shown how information processing can be applied to teaching and learning.

From our perspective, the minor influence of cognitive theory on teaching practice is understandable though disappointing. The strong influence of behavioral technologies for teaching specific skills has tended to over-shadow the importance of cognitive psychology. Although information processing has been an under-utilized and misunderstood body of knowledge, it has the potential to provide an evolving and substantial teaching-learning framework. Within a model of instruction based upon information processing, behavioral "splinter" skills can be replaced by a curriculum in which processing and curriculum content are taught as one. Such a view is shared by other contemporary writers.

In this chapter, we sketch the development of psychological influences in the area of special education. We provide an outline of historical events, touch upon the influences of behaviorism and consider students' preparation for post-school life. It is a sketch drawn with the broadest and most coarse pencil, but it is intended to outline how initial educational provisions for students with intellectual and learning disabilities were the causal and logical antecedents of contemporary process-based interventions.

As will become evident, there has been a cyclical pattern within the conceptual foundations of special education teaching practice. The rise and fall and rise again of cognitive influences was punctuated by the influence of the behavioral approach in the 1960s. As the impetus and impact of special education grew, there came a movement toward behavioral concerns, which now is giving way, once again, to the study of learning as a cognitive rather then behavioral activity.

THE BEGINNING OF SPECIAL EDUCATION

Since the earliest recorded writings of the human species, differences between individuals' skills and competencies have been observed. It was not until the publication of *Emile* by Rousseau in 1762 that educators recognized that the learning environment and children's unique abilities need to be congruent.

The German educator Johann Herbart also had a major influence upon educational practice through his attempt to describe the learning process in psychological terms. His approach to teaching and learning extended into the 19th century and exerted a considerable influence on the programs adopted by several of the pioneer workers in the field of intellectual disability.

The educational climate during the second half of the 18th century was characterized by rapid development, and the application of the scientific method based upon observation and experimentation. By 1800, educators had addressed the issues of hearing and visual impairment, and turned to a consideration of intellectual disability, and consequently, the raising of the educational curtain on the work of Itard, Seguin and Montessori.

Scientific Methods and Pedagogy

The name, Itard, is associated with the often-reported story of the Wild Boy of Aveyron. In 1799, it must have been hard to imagine why an 11 or 12-year-old would be wandering the desolate countryside in the French Department of Aveyron (about midway between Marseilles and Bordeaux). It's not surprising that scientific minds, ripe with nativist and sensationalist ideas would have accepted that the boy had been raised in the wild, in much the same way as we fantasize how Tarzan was nurtured by apes. Indeed, documentation had been gathered on ten such characters who had been found between 1544 and 1767 living among wolves, bears, wild sheep, and oxen. Itard, at that time a young physician, was supremely confident that the wild boy could be transformed from his animal state to a noble and civilized person through appropriate instruction (Pygmalion ideals did not have to wait for George Bernard Shaw).

Victor, as the boy became known, was taken to Paris in 1801 where he was examined by a noted psychiatrist, Philippe Pinel. Pinel was far from convinced that Victor was a noble savage. He pronounced him an abandoned idiot, but Itard accepted the educational challenge presented by Victor and began intensive work with the boy which was to extend over nearly a decade.

Several descriptions of Victor revealed behavior that was more akin to an animal than a human. Victor selected food by smell, but was indifferent to either fragrant or foul odors. He drank while lying flat on the ground, immersing his mouth in the water. He often walked on all fours or fell into a running gait. He fought with his teeth, tore off his garments and was unresponsive to sounds even when pistol shots were fired directly behind him (Wallin, 1917).

At the end of five years of training, Itard had been far from successful. He had neither restored Victor to normality nor demonstrated that simple ideas were the result of sensations alone. Though frustrated, he had achieved some notable successes. Humphreys, the first translator of Itard's book dealing with Victor's education, claimed that the boy's social and emotional development had been impressive. He was clean, affectionate, able to read a few words and capable of understanding much of what was said to him. From an educational point of view, Itard had been the first teacher to observe and study his pupils in a clinical manner by focusing upon intellectual development. In essence, he had been the first special educator to prescribe teaching practices based upon psychological principles.

Where Itard finished, Seguin began, initiating the first school for children with intellectual disabilities in the mid-1830s. His book dealing with his pedagogical theory and practice, *The Moral Treatment, Hygiene and Education of Idiots and Other Backward Children*, was received with great enthusiasm in France. It encapsulated an educational science by providing philosophical premises, an enabling theory, a description of instructional procedures, the presentation of records, and evidence of results.

The political unrest in the mid 1800s prompted Seguin to emigrate to the United States where he settled in Ohio and set up a general medical practice. Several schools based upon Seguin's Parisian model were in operation in the United States and it wasn't long before he was involved in the management of several schools for children with intellectual disabilities and in extending his already rich literary legacy in educational practice.

In her treatise on Seguin's pedagogy, Talbot (1964) drew attention to the interplay of medical and psychological techniques that led to the development of Seguin's theory of human learning. Activity was the basis for, and the means of learning, and included the use of real objects and varying experiences. Seguin's educational procedures emulated Itard's by focusing upon action, specifically imitative postures, gross and fine motor movements, the use and handling of tools, and sensory and vocal activities. He included imitative writing, word-matching, object to word matching, comparison and judgments, attention to memory, and moral training which dealt with affection, gratitude, anger, personal justice. These broad dimensions provided the foundation for an extension of the then contemporary principles of teaching.

Itard and Seguin had a wide-ranging impact upon the development of educational provisions for children with learning and intellectual disabilities at a time when enlightened governments were beginning to accept responsibility for the education of children with special needs. In the United States, Seguin's impact was profound. The first school based upon Seguin's methods was established in Massachusetts in 1848, with others following in New York in 1851, Philadelphia in 1854, and Ohio and Connecticut in the closing years of the 1850s. The first European school for children with intellectual disabilities was established as a special class within a school at Halle (about 15 kilometers south-east of Brussels) in 1859.

A class similar to that at Halle which focused upon practical issues of everyday living was established in Dresden in 1867. This was classified as a day auxiliary school as it was intended to supplement the parent's work with preschool age children. Over the ensuing years, schools and special classes were established in several towns in Germany following a proclamation by the then minister for Education, Von Grossler, that all towns having over 20,000 residents should open auxiliary schools. By 1894, 32 schools had been established catering for nearly 2,500 children.

The fame of these classes was far-reaching and parents in England and even the United States acted to gain a place for their children in the German schools, regardless of the increasing number of similar schools appearing in their own countries. In 1890, the German Government made education compulsory for all children between ages 6 and 14 years and, as a result, the number of children with intellectual disabilities attending special programs rose sharply. German auxiliary schools became the models for progressive education during the latter part of the 19th century and the early years of the 20th century (Preen, 1976).

In England, special provisions for children with intellectual disabilities were not forthcoming until the 1890s. The Education Act of 1880 made school compulsory for all children between the ages of 6 and 12 years, causing concern for parents whose children were unable to cope with regular school programs. It was Francis Warner's report in 1892 that provided the impetus for improvement in education for children with disabilities. Warner had conducted a census of children in the London area and found that some 500 of the estimated 50,000 required special schooling. However, it was not until the government inquiry in 1904 that substantial changes in the educational system in favor of children with intellectual disabilities became a reality.

Special Education Around the Turn of the Century

While Seguin had been an inspiration to many, his influence on Maria Montessori was profound: She was inspired to hand copy his 600 page book on the treatment, hygiene and education of backward children. While contemporary publishers might have something to say to Maria about copyright, her justification was that she would have time to consider each word and comprehend Seguin's spirit completely.

Montessori was attracted to the physiological foundation of learning and she believed that intellectual disability was an educational, rather than a medical problem. While that was somewhat contrary to popular belief, Montessori convinced the Italian Government of her views in 1898 and she was invited to open a school for children with intellectual disabilities and was given complete authority to institute pedagogical and organizational policies.

18

Montessori's ideas were not new (having been emphasized by Locke, Rousseau, Froebel and Seguin), but she was dedicated, innovative and enthusiastic. It was not long before she was renowned as an educator across Europe and Great Britain. Today, Montessori is best known for the didactic materials that are used to develop children's sensitivity to their environment. Her contribution to the study of children with learning and intellectual disabilities rests in her conviction that these students can learn through discovery. While Montessori moved away from working with special students, the consequence of her efforts was to provide further awakening of the educational and scientific worlds to the needs of educationally disabled children (Preen, 1976).

Expansion of Special Education Provisions

From 1900, schools for children with intellectual and learning disabilities grew from a similar heritage to that of the large institutions that provided homes for many thousands of adults with severe and profound disabilities. The primary motivation behind special school placement was the provision of an appropriate learning environment in which consideration could be given to individual differences in learning. Moreover, the goal of academic training was the eventual return of students to the educational mainstream where their training could be completed. With the expansion of special classes and an increase in students' academic performances, there developed a realization that many other children experiencing difficulties might also benefit from small group instruction.

Withdrawal of slow learners from the mainstream of education found support in the growing public acceptance of the principle of equal opportunity in education. This led to a growth in the number of special classes and the development of remedial programs in language arts and mathematics. Following some early educational successes with intellectually disabled students in special schools and classes, it was not long before many children were being labeled as exceptional on the basis of learning difficulties, social or cultural disadvantage, physical handicap, intellectual disability or deviant behavior and provided with special class placement.

Some children benefited from special programs, though gains were often less significant than were claimed by the advocates of special education. Grouping according to the various disability

19

categories may have provided more efficient instruction for some students, but variation between pupils in learning capacity and motivation made categorization of children more arbitrary than discrete (Ashman, 1980).

One of the first arguments against special class placement for disabled learners came in the much quoted work of Dunn (1968). His article was the stimulus for the reintegration of children with disabilities into regular classes. The advocates of mainstreaming claimed that academic and social learning is undertaken more efficiently in regular classes leading to more rapid social development and less stereotyping than would occur in isolated special classes.

The Education for all Handicapped Children Act of 1975 in the United States, provided a focus for integration advocates and the literature dealing with this important issue has expanded dramatically over the past decade. Not all the literature supports the concept of integration or mainstreaming. A reasoned account of mainstreaming by Strain and Kerr (1981), using evidence compiled from 40 years of research, concluded that the arguments for and against special class *versus* regular class placement was equivocal.

The development of special education practice from the early work of Itard up to the turn of the 20th century was dominated by contemporary views of human physiology. Considerable emphasis was placed upon mental training through the stimulation of the senses. This was consistent with the medical discoveries of the time that brought the identification of the central and peripheral nervous systems. While remaining convinced that sensory stimulation and activity was the fundamental principle underlying learning, Montessori was to change the emphasis of learning from one that was primarily medical, to one that was pedagogical, that is, mental development would occur if the teaching techniques were correct.

In the first half of the 20th century, experimental and Gestalt psychology and the writings of Dewey and James were beginning to influence the conceptualization of the process of learning. Imagery, perception, motivation, habit, intelligence, memory, instincts, personality and psychoanalytic theory were issues designated as important to the understanding of how knowledge was acquired, and forgotten (McRae, 1929). Moreover, individual differences were being considered. Far from being deplored as an inevitable and disturbing factor of human nature, individual differences were held to be at least as important as the general laws concerning learning.

20

However, perhaps the most significant contribution to education in the 20th century was the application of learning theory (behaviorism) to teaching practice. The developing interest of educators in learning theory marked the decline in the modest impact of cognition on special education.

THE RISE OF BEHAVIORISM IN SPECIAL EDUCATION

From the late 1940s to the mid-1970s, behaviorism played a major role in the advancement of psychological and educational practices. Fundamental to this approach is the premise that most human behavior is acquired or modified through learning procedures or environmental influences. Although it could be argued that it is more correctly a procedure or a problem solving strategy than a theoretical model, behaviorism makes a number of important assumptions about the way in which learning occurs. In brief:

* Behaviors can be defined in instructional terms;
* Behaviors can be learned and modified; and,
* Behaviors are environmentally determined and reinforced.

Initially, behaviorists severed their association from prevailing psychological theory by rejecting the inferred motives, hypothesized needs, impulses and drives which were used commonly as explanations for human behavior. This can be seen in the work of Skinner, whose books, *Walden Two* (1948) and *Beyond Freedom and Dignity* (1971) provided clear examples of the powers of behavioral procedures.

Teaching within a Behavioral Framework

Behavior management has had a profound effect on the organization of classroom teaching strategies, particularly in the areas of moderate, severe and profound intellectual disabilities. The development of highly task-analyzed curricula have provided teachers with sequences of learning events that ensure the success of instruction (Koorland, 1986; Rose, Koorland, & Epstein, 1982). Such analyses incorporate discrete and systematic steps for instruction that, although designed to ensure the development of

21

specific knowledge, have often led to the teaching of many discrete splinter skills without any real need on the part of the learner to understand the learning process.

Thousands of individual programs, based upon behavioral principles, have focused upon curriculum content from mathematics and reading to social and vocational skills. However, an analysis of the contemporary literature suggests there have been few studies related specifically to the development of cognitive skills other than those dealing with self-instruction training. Clinical studies have tended to focus upon the application of behavioral theory to various forms of neurosis including the reduction of fear, anxiety, weight reduction and eating behavior rather than school achievement (Koorland, 1986). The majority of educational studies have dealt with the manipulation of the learning environment (for example, Boyd, Skedsvold, & Rossiter, 1986; McGee, Krantz, & McClannahan, 1986; Phillips, 1985; Pigott, Fatuzzo, & Clement, 1986).

There is no question that behavior management techniques are important practical skills that justify consideration in most teaching situations. Good teaching practice involves the almost unconscious use of shaping, positive reinforcement, extinction, and the fading of prompts to enhance the student's independence in learning, and apply newly acquired skills. While the overt status of the behavioral approach may have been reduced, its continuted presence within teachers' instructional repertoires is assured.

Behavior modification is evolving to meet this changing status. The concept of cognitive behavior modification has emerged to reflect the interaction between unseen events which occur within the individual's brain and environmental factors (Nelson & Polsgrove, 1984). The notion of psychology without the brain now has assumed reduced importance in the study of human learning and development (Greenberg, 1983).

The Influence of Thought Processes on Behaviorism

The current issues concerning the role of information processing in behavioral theory are exemplified in Figure 2.1 by an updated model of behavior change described by Molloy (1985). The major departure of Molloy's approach from the traditional cause-behavior-consequences model is the inclusion of cognitive and physiological components that have two-way interactions with the environment.

Figure 2.1: A Model of Behavior Analysis (after Molloy, 1985)

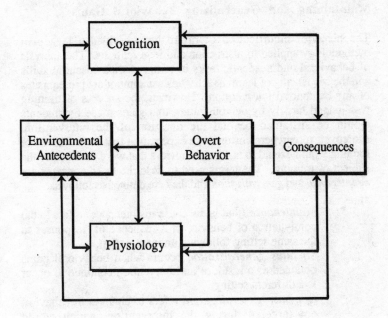

The introduction of cognition to a behavioral model assists in the explanation of behavior when observable responses are not obvious. For example, various life events may be registered and retained in memory by the learner for use long after the original learning has taken place. Beliefs and expectations may influence what we notice around us as a result of our awareness or conscious thought. In much the same way, external events may have a direct influence on our behavior and physiology. A poor diet that produces hypoglycemia, for instance, may be the direct cause of the irritability shown by a child in the classroom.

Molloy's model, which reflects a cognitive-behavioral approach, is a concession to the thinking nature of the human species. Importantly, it reflects the disquiet with the radical behaviorist's approach that excludes any cognitive influences on behavior. This uneasiness is implicit in the comments of practitioners and educational researchers, other than those who work with populations having severe and profound disabilities (Cullari & Ferguson, 1981).

Maintaining and Generalizing Behavioral Gains

The behavior modification literature has provided a legacy in methodology applied to instruction and interventions. The analysis of behavioral and academic tasks in terms of their essential skills and the sequencing of learning activities were important prerequisites of any behavioral intervention. However, the success of training was judged largely by demonstrating that gains made by students would be sustained beyond the duration of the intervention. Moreover, researchers nurtured the expectation that the influence of training would extend to tasks or behaviors that were not directly the subject of training. The terms used to describe these concepts are *maintenance* and *generalization* and they are defined as follows:

* *Maintenance* (that is, response maintenance) refers to the continuation of behavior or a sequence of responses in the same setting following an intervention.
* *Stimulus generalization* occurs when behavioral gains obtained as a result of an intervention continue to occur in a different setting.
* *Response generalization*, refers to changes in behavior, not targeted during the intervention, which would typically be ignored or reported only in anecdotal records (Campbell & Stanley, 1963).

The main concern with maintenance and generalization was providing hard evidence of their existence. For example, if a behavior continued for a week following the end of an intervention, would this constitute maintenance, and hence, be satisfactory evidence of program success? Since no methodological precedent existed, researchers applied the "rule of thumb" which prescribed that maintenance periods be of equal duration to the treatment periods (Levine, Fasnacht, Funabiki, & Burkart, 1979).

Concurrently, behavioral researchers were confronting the baffling problem of stimulus generalization. In some cases, the failure to achieve generalization meant failure to obtain long-term

24

generalization, though researchers often neglected to provide sufficient evidence for generalization. In contrast, response generalization has been of less concern though some changes can be anticipated in social or academic behaviors as a result of training in one or the other (Keeley, Shamberg, & Carbonell, 1976; McLaskey, Rieth, & Polsgrove, 1980; Wasserman & Vogrin, 1979).

Failure of behavioral researchers to achieve generalization was attributed to inadequate planning and to weaknesses in research design. These methodological deficiencies included inadequate evaluation of the effects of time, drop-out rates, maturation, the uncontrolled use of social reinforcers, and the lack of consistent data recording by multiple observers.

There are three questions that need consideration before behavioral researchers can claim successful generalization:

1. Is the degree of variation in performance (quality and quantity) between the training and generalization phases of the intervention sufficient to permit the claim of generalization?
2. If a brief re-training program is introduced between the treatment and the generalization testing phase, does this constitute true stimulus generalization, or does the skill need reactivation to be generalized?
3. Is the occurrence of maintenance and generalization clearly defined?

(Conway, 1981)

Debate and conjecture over issues such as those above have not been limited to behavioral research. While the use of terminology is different in the cognitive literature, the problem of obtaining maintenance and generalization certainly is not restricted to behavioral interventions. The difficulty in achieving generalization, in particular, has been the Achilles' heel of cognitive researchers. The troubles have not been limited to laboratory or classroom interventions, but extend well beyond school into adulthood.

In the next section, we consider the relevance of secondary programs for students with learning and intellectual disabilities to their post-school life. This directly addresses the issue of generalization of school learning to problem solving within the career or vocational options available to adults with special needs.

INFORMATION PROCESSING AT THE HIGH SCHOOL LEVEL

Most school-based interventions and remedial programs have focused on young children; often those between ages 6 and 12 years. This may reflect parental or educational priorities, or it may have stemmed from the more diversified training presented to teachers of elementary and primary school children (including a focus on developmental learning stages and individual differences). In contrast, training for regular high school teachers concentrates upon the complexities of the subject content and the accurate transfer of this information to the class. There appears to be little concern for the range of students' information processing and academic competence or the adaptation of materials and techniques to meet students' needs.

Contemporary High School Programs

It has only been in the recent past that teacher training institutions have addressed the needs of the broad range of students in the high school, recognizing that there are many adolescents who reach school-leaving age without functional reading or arithmetic skills. This means that there is a substantial group of students in high schools who are experiencing learning difficulties or mild intellectual disabilities. The educational provisions for disabled students often involve the development of what we euphemistically call "life-skills", but which in some schools means no more than running errands, assisting the maintenance man, or gardening.

There is one issue that needs to be raised concerning the high school curriculum in particular. Special educators have questioned the appropriateness of the traditional curriculum for many students with educational disabilities. The traditional curriculum is based upon a developmental model in which teachers build upon previously taught skills within discrete subject areas, frequently as a foundation for entry into tertiary education. As an alternative, a functional curriculum deals with the preparation of students for the post-school environment. Many special education programs have opted for the latter, distancing themselves from mainstream curriculum approaches. Functional curriculum advocates believe

26

that subject content, instructional practices, grouping, teaching materials, and assessment procedures currently used in mainstream education are inappropriate.

Mandell and Gold (1984), for example, argued that teaching approaches commonly used with students up to grade 6 are inappropriate for high school students. The many adolescents functioning below grade 6 level will not gain the academic and social skills required for successful integration into adult society before leaving school. The acquisition of relevant knowledge and skills may be accomplished through a combination of regular secondary and vocational education with supplemental special education support in both prevocational and traditional curriculum areas.

Program options for adolescents with mild to moderate learning and behavior problems have commonly been provided in self-contained special classes or special vocational training centres. Mandell and Gold advocated several alternative models:

1. *Resource Model.* The primary goal of the resource teacher is to provide remedial instruction in academic areas in which the student is weak, provide career education, and act as an advocate for the disabled students;

2. *Tutorial Model.* The primary goal of the tutor is to help the students make the transition from the resource model to the regular class by developing study, organizational, and attending skills required in mainstream classes;

3. *Teacher Consultant Model.* The consultant works more with the teacher than with the students directly;

4. *Work-Study Programs.* The purpose of these programs is to provide students with on-the-job training and classroom instruction that emphasizes basic academic skill. Students spend part of the day learning a vocational skill and another part in a special class.

5. *Vocational Programs.* These are macro-programs operated in a vocational high school, though students with intellectual disabilities often are unable to gain entry as preference is given to higher functioning students.

Models such as those described by Mandell and Gold demonstrate that teachers and researchers have not come to terms with the educational needs of adolescent students with learning and intellectual disabilities. Although their alternative service delivery models provide a range of instructional approaches, Mandell and Gold failed to address adequately the importance of selecting appropriate curriculum content. For example, the *Resource Model* reinforces the principle of teaching students strategies to cope with the complexity of the regular curriculum. This principle assumes that the content is appropriate and meaningful to the students and that inability (or unwillingness) to deal with it is the students' fault. The model fails to acknowledge that the content presented in regular (mainstream) classes continues to be inappropriate for special students.

Teachers who have students with mild intellectual disabilities in their classses need to modify aspects of the teaching program because such students do not have adequate fundamental reading, listening, and note-taking skills and are frequently not motivated (Lovitt, Rudsit, Jenkins, Pious, & Beneditti, 1986).

As a broader concern, special students need a functional curriculum that is both ecologically and developmentally appropriate. At the same time, such a curriculum must provide the opportunity for active student participation in the acquisition of processing skills that will generalize beyond formal schooling.

The Need for Functional Cognitive Skills

In many cases, adolescents with special needs have had little experience in developing skills associated with problem solving beyond basic self-care and management skills. Teachers might argue that students acquire these higher order, problem solving skills through general educational experience, and through trial-and-error learning. Yet in many cases, provisions are not made within the curricula for such learning experiences. There are few curricula that emphasize problem solving and analytical skills (Bloom, 1984; Swanson, 1984), and few studies have dealt with the usefulness of alternative curricula specifically aimed at successful transitions from school to employment. Typically, the results of these efficacy studies draw attention to the positive relationship between years of schooling, the quality of social skills possessed by students, and the students' academic competence in areas such as reading and mathematics (Fardig, Algozzine, Schwartz, Hensel, & Westling, 1985; Mithaug, Horiuchi, & Fanning, 1985). However, there is little emphasis placed upon the more important, general skills that support planning and problem solving.

One report that made reference to a functional curriculum in a secondary special education program was prepared by Wehman, Kregel, and Barcus (1985). Their document emphasized the need to include skills required by students in actual local employment situations, and the importance of ensuring that the content would generalize to potential jobs and facilitate eventual movement into the labor force. Wehman et al. claimed that vocational training must begin to develop skills early, with increasing emphasis being given to the skill development as students become older. This is decidedly true, but the need to emphasize problem solving must not simply be included by implication only. Educators must ensure that problem solving is incorporated into basic academic and vocational training that is functionally appropriate.

AN ARGUMENT FOR COGNITIVE INTERVENTIONS

Education involves the acquisition of knowledge and adaptation to the environment. It involves extending our knowledge base and restructuring our knowledge about the world in which we live. This is generally called learning. However, learning involves more than the traditional behaviorists would have us believe. It is more than the precise management of the environment and the establishment of the contiguity between a behavior and its consequences. There is something else that causes the human species (and some of our fellow animals) to construct a view of the world that we might call subjective reality.

Regardless of the type of being, existence is fraught with a multitude of problems. Success in overcoming these difficulties is the challenge of survival. The systematic, goal-directed pursuit of solutions to the many problems we confront is the characteristic feature of human activity. Moreover, the quality of the solutions to life problems depends upon the perceiving, reasoning, conceiving, and judging behavior of the individual. This suggests that the quality of one's learning (for learning is just one form of problem) is intimately bound to cognitive competence. If we accept that learning is not random and is derived from our experiences, then the development of intellectual skills that enable us to organize and to store information must become a central feature of instruction.

29

The Influence of Cognition on Learning

Examination of the literature related to instruction and remediation over the past ten years reveals a growing interest in cognitive issues, not only with regular students, but with a broad range of special students. There have been literally hundreds of studies that have investigated the effectiveness of training children to use specific information processing skills to enhance their learning.

The study of cognitive psychology has drawn attention to several interrelated factors that influence learning performance. While there are numerous ways in which these factors can be described, we favor a simple division into three rather general factors, namely, knowledge, motivation, and organizational competence. These can be represented by a Venn diagram (Figure 2.2 on the following page). The relevance of each factor can be shown fairly easily.

Knowledge

Knowledge in this context does not simply refer to "units" of information such as the distance between London and New York, the number of gold medals won by Chilean runners since the inception of the first modern Olympic Games, or the current market value of the US dollar in Yen.

Knowledge also refers to the existing automatic routines and plans that have been stored away in memory to be retrieved, when required, as a means of achieving certain goals. For instance, Christmas is a unit of information to the extent that it:

* occurs on the 25th of December;
* represents the day on which Jesus Christ was born; and,
* occurs 7 days before the end of the Julian calender year.

Christmas also implies plans and strategies. These might include:

* our method of dealing with holidays;
* which relatives are expected to appear on our doorstep looking for expensive presents;
* a search for, and purchase of large free range birds and other culinary delicacies;

* the purchase of presents of appropriate prices for those who gave us presents last year; plus,
* any number of other important and unimportant details.

Some writers have made the distinction between knowing how to perform some action, and knowing something about the relationship between objects or events (Tharp & Gallimore, 1985). Knowledge, then, is both an integrated collection of facts, and a set of procedures for knowing.

Figure 2.2: Three General Factors Associated with Learning Performance

Motivation

Motivation refers to the learner's desire to become involved in the specific events being undertaken. It has to do with the learner's arousal and the relevance or importance of the task to the individual. Motivation energizes and directs behavior and includes such behavioral properties as intensity, effort, and persistence (Ferguson, 1976).

Motivation is also related to achievement through learning or cognitive style and attribution patterns. For instance, students who believe they are in control of their environment, and who are intrinsically motivated to achieve mastery or success are generally those students who are most successful. In contrast, students with learning and intellectual disabilities often have a long history of failure that has eroded away confidence and the desire to persist and achieve (Chapman, Silva, & Williams, 1984). This history of failure leads to passive learning responses.

Organization

Organization refers to planning and decision making. In the general sense, planning is the process that begins with the recognition that a problem exists requiring action or thought. It then involves selecting plans that exist within the knowledge base or generating new plans that may lead to a solution. The second component, decision making, is an integral part of the planning process through the setting of priorities, determining appropriate methods for solving the problem, and the monitoring and varying of performance to achieve the goal.

The other important issue related to organization is our awareness of how we deal with learning or problem solving situations. For example, our experience with long lines at supermarket check-outs may encourage us to shop at less popular times, thereby avoiding a problem situation. The organizational unit, then, also includes what have been called *executive* strategies (or control functions).

The three factors in action

Consider the once popular parlor game, "Trivial Pursuit". It is easy to see that the knowledge base can let a player down in this quiz game. For example, if you don't know the names of the dwarves captured and hung in trees by the spiders in Tolkien's *The Hobbit,* it won't matter how much motivation or organizational competence you have. You cannot hope to answer the question correctly and add another pie-piece to your collection.

If you find Trivial Pursuit far too trivial for imagination (as some people do), then your lack of application, enthusiasm, and competitive spirit will leave your competitors exasperated. Moreover, poor motivation may cause you to be inefficient in your choice of subject area and may discourage the use of information you already possess. One additional consequence can be attributing your failure to the stupidity of the game, rather than to personal deficiencies.

If you have only one pie-piece left to collect and your inadequate planning skills have you moving around the board randomly, you may never win. You may never consider maximizing your chances by evaluating the types of questions available and your potential for good fortune in selecting subject areas in which your knowledge is substantial.

While this is a fairly simple example, the same conditions apply in the classroom. Each of these cognitive domains (knowledge, motivation, organization) has been shown to have an important impact on students' learning and successful problem solving.

The beginning of cognitive research

By the early 1960s, researchers had come to realize the important role of memory in all intellectual pursuits, and that by unraveling the mysteries of memory, they would also expose the secrets of learning and intellectual disabilities. The intensive study of memory and memory aids had began. From the research, came numerous models of memory (such as the basic example shown in Figure 2.3). However, it was soon recognized that how memory developed was a far more complex mental process than portrayed by early memory models.

One of the most important contributions of early cognitive psychology research was the generation of a research framework for investigating the acquisition of information, strategies to aid recollection, and the organizational features of cognition. Consequently, by the 1970s, the study of cognition was having a clear impact upon our understanding of the problems experienced by special students, especially those with intellectual disabilities, in terms of their effective use of memory aids.

By the middle of the 1980s, multi-component models of information had begun to appear. Several dealt specifically with the relationship between factors similar to those described in Figure 2.2 (that is, knowledge, motivation, organization), while others included personality variables. These are exemplified by the three listed below:

Figure 2.3: A Multi-component Memory Model

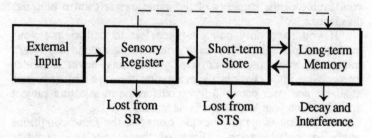

(After Atkinson & Shiffrin, 1968)

1. *Dispositional State* (personality, values, cognitive style), *Knowledge State* (content, processes, strategies), and *Structural State* (speed of processing, capacity) (Lawson, 1986);
2. *Arousal* (maintaining cortical control), *Coding* (input, storage and retrieval), and *Planning and Decision-Making* (Das, Kirby, & Jarman, 1979);
3. *Performance Components* (enabling action of plans), *Knowledge-Acquisition Components* (learning new information and generalization), and *Meta-Components* (decisions, strategy selection) (Sternberg, 1985).

In summary, the use of cognitive psychology as the theoretical foundation for instruction has been based upon the ability of this approach to explain observable behavior and to account for those aspects of learning that are peculiarly human. To a large extent, our decision to pursue the development of a teaching model for use with students having learning and intellectual disabilities was predicated upon the wealth of literature that has become available over the past two decades. Moreover, it has come from the perception of many writers, researchers, and educators who have recognized that there is

34

value in training information processing concepts to encourage changes in learning and problem solving.

We have directed attention to several information processing approaches, beginning with the memory models of Atkinson and Shiffrin (1968) and leading to the triarchic synthesis presented by Sternberg (1985). Our review of models has caused us some dismay as a result of the seeming lack of relevance to the classroom of many theoretical presentations. What has been presented and debated at scientific conferences and in the multitude of special education journals, seems to bear little resemblance to the teaching practice in classes with or without disabled students. The literature is rife with idealized views of how children learn and how information processing operates in children. The translation of these ideals and theories, however, is often left to some mystical intermediary who will cause this knowledge and wisdom to be spread throughout the land. It just seems that nobody knows how or when this will occur.

Indeed, we are not alone in this view, others have claimed that contemporary information processing theory has very little to do with educational practice (Swanson, 1984; Wong, 1986a). Hence, our cautions to researchers and teachers at the beginning of this chapter were not made without foundation.

3

Cognitive Instruction

In the last chapter, we drew attention to the role of cognition in the learning and teaching process over the past century. By the end of the 1970s, researchers had come to recognize that inefficiencies in learning and problem solving could not be removed simply by teaching students to use memory aids. More complex processes appeared to be involved and it was not long before the study of memory strategies became the study of strategic behavior. With this transition, came the emphasis on the monitoring and regulatory activities of cognition and the introduction of these higher-order operations into strategy training studies.

In this chapter, we review the major influences that have shaped the development of instruction based upon information processing theory. In brief, the purpose of the chapter is to familiarize the reader with the terms and concepts of information processing theory. We deal with interventions that have concentrated on specific cognitive strategies (for example, rehearsal, mnemonics and verbal self-instruction) and more general cognitive re-orientation strategies. Here then, are the precursors or antecedents of contemporary process-based intervention methods.

COGNITIVE BEHAVIORAL INSTRUCTION

Learning and problem solving involves a change in behavior, or at least, a change in the student's tendency to behave in a certain way. While behaviorists claim that environmental factors account for this behavior change, advocates of information processing theory believe that control ultimately rests with the individual. This belief led to the development of teaching strategies that emphasized both cognitive and behavioral aspects of the learning process.

Cognitive behavioral instruction attempts to modify behavior through changes to an individual's intellectual or social cognitions. The term cognitive-behavioral excludes interventions that are strictly behavioral. It also excludes those that are extremely cognitive in nature and which place little emphasis on environmental adaptation (Sternberg, 1981). These exclusions serve to remind us of three points: First, learning is not strictly a behavioral or cognitive activity; second, learning typically occurs within a social framework (that is, cognitive development occurs in the company of others); and, third, instruction is directed toward the demands of a changing environment (that is, we must use existing intellectual skills to deal with the many tasks and learning events that confront us).

The beginning of cognitive behavioral studies can be traced to the early 1970s when the previously strong influence of behavior modification began to wane. Researchers moved away from a primary focus on students' behaviors and from the belief that the teacher's role was to organize the environment to evoke a specific response. Whereas behavioral interventions focused on the condition of learning and content, cognitive approaches dealt with the internal processing strategies available to the learner. In other words, the focus of cognitive training was on how learners acquired knowledge, and how they dealt with (or processed) that knowledge (Shuell, 1986).

Cognitive behavioral interventions were based on a general acceptance that both environmental and internal (person) factors are independently and interdependently important to the process of learning. Training was based on four core assertions:

1. The human organism responds primarily to cognitive representations of its environment rather than to the real aspects of those environments;
2. These cognitive representations are functionally related to the processes and dimensions of learning;
3. Most human learning is cognitively mediated; and,
4. Thoughts, feelings, and behaviors are causally interactive.

These assertions are important because of their emphasis on the learner's responsibility for the learning process rather than on the efforts of an outside trainer (Mahoney, 1977). Developing the movement from dependence to independence in learning using cognitive and behavioral principles was the primary goal of early cognitive interventions. The mechanisms for promoting this change were the mental activities of self-monitoring, self-checking and self-evaluation; in short, self-instruction techniques.

Verbal Self-instruction

The earliest cognitive behavioral studies were attributed to the work of Meichenbaum and his colleagues (Meichenbaum, 1972, 1974, 1977; Meichenbaum & Goodman, 1971; Meichenbaum & Asarnow, 1978). His verbal self-instruction model was based on the premise that a teacher can instruct students to work through a series of self-instruction steps to facilitate learning and problem solving. For example, the student would learn to verbalize the process involved in spelling a new word as: "First, I will look at the word. Then I will try to break it into smaller parts ..." and so on. Through systematic training, these self-instructions become internalized by students as part of their repertoire of learning strategies, and the teacher's role becomes less directive and more supportive.

The Meichenbaum five-step training sequence included:

1. *Cognitive modelling* - the instructor models the self-instructions aloud whilst completing a task;
2. *Overt external guidance* - students perform the tasks while the teacher provides the self-instructions;
3. *Overt self-guidance* - the students perform the task while instructing themselves aloud;
4. *Faded overt guidance* - the students whisper the instructions while completing the task; and,
5. *Covert self-instruction* - the students perform the task while using internal language (that is, private speech).

Both cognitive and behavioral influences can be seen within this model. Modelling, the movement from external (teacher) to internal (student) responsibility for self-instructions, and the fading of external cues are distinctly behavioral. Strategy training is a cognitive influence that allows students to learn an appropriate strategy to deal with specific problems. More recently, cognitive behavioral theorists have placed more emphasis on the generation of strategies by students rather than by the teacher.

The verbal self-instruction model has been used widely as the basis of many studies and has been modified to meet the needs of special groups such as students experiencing difficulties in mathematics and reading (for example, Malamuth, 1979; Whitman & Johnson, 1983). Verbal self-instruction has also been applied to small group teaching of students with intellectual disabilities, though many of these applications have incorporated general self-instructions (such as self-checking) that can be used in a variety of situations rather being limited to a specific task (Brown, Campione, & Barclay, 1979).

The effectiveness of verbal self-instruction approaches has not been overwhelming despite the strong theoretical arguments for its use. In a review of verbal self-instruction studies, Ryan, Short, and Weed (1986) claimed that the approach has been effective in improving students' learning behavior and in maintaining their performance gains after training had ceased. However, students did not appear to transfer their newly-acquired skills from the training locations to the classroom. Other writers also have been critical of verbal self-instruction. For example, Leon and Pepe (1983) used verbal self-instruction to remediate arithmetic skills in students with either learning difficulties or mild intellectual disabilities. Although they found self-instruction training superior to traditional arithmetic training, they identified a number of issues needing clarification. These included:

1. the necessity of including all five stages of training;
2. the degree of elaboration necessary in the dialogues between teacher and students; and,
3. the effectiveness of verbal self-instruction for use with all exceptionalities across a wide age range.

Perhaps the major criticism of existing verbal self-instruction approaches is the reliance on teacher-designed instructional sequences. These instructor-imposed learning strategies pay little attention to how students would describe the learning activity in their own words, or how they would prefer to tackle the problem (that is, the student's processing preference). The success of this model of instruction appears to depend upon the ability of the student to interpret the demands of the verbal self-instructions so that the meaning becomes personal.

Following the early work of Meichenbaum, cognitive researchers began to realize that training self-instruction skills alone did not immediately transform students into functional learners (Mahoney & Nezworski, 1985). Their recognition that a more complex relationship existed between cognitive activities and performance directed educators' attention toward a genre of research that had been developing concurrently with verbal self-instruction, namely, the study of memory strategies and strategic behavior.

STRATEGY TRAINING

Information processing theory grew from research concerned with the understanding of memory and memory deficiencies. With the development of the new knowledge base came the creation of a set of terms to describe information processing concepts and activities. Before we proceed further, it would be useful to clarify the relationship between several of these concepts. We do this by using an analogy. Though we are aware that analogies often are not completely satisfactory they can be useful for showing the relationships between concepts.

Skills, Strategies, Processes and the Brain

We can think of the brain as a highly complex lattice of wires, akin to a large telephone exchange. This wiring forms the *architectural structure of the brain*. Assuming that there is no organic impairment, one person's brain will conform to the same architectural pattern of brain cells (or neurons) as that of another.

In the telephone exchange, certain equipment (such as switching equipment, transmitters and receivers) allows for the passage of electrical currents along various pathways. This equipment is analogous to the *cognitive processes* that operate within the brain allowing for the movement and integration of information from one part of the brain to another. These processes enable thoughts, insights, dreams, plan development, and action. In fact, as you read this text, your brain will be taking in the words through the medium of your eyes, transmitting these visual stimuli to the brain so that the word symbols are transformed into thoughts and meaning.

Access to the telephone system is also needed. This means that we must know how to make the switching devices work for us by using prescribed routines. We need to push the buttons (or spin the dial) in the accepted way to make the machine operate. *Information processing strategies* work in a similar way. They provide the initial organization that allows information to enter the system (the brain) in the most effective way. In other words, a strategy is a conscious or automatic cognitive act or systematic routine that enables information to be stored in, or retrieved from memory. Strategies organize information into usable, meaningful units, although the repertoire of stored and available strategies may differ from person to person. For example, the telephone number 6961000 may be organized as 696 one thousand by one person, and as 69 61, triple O by another.

Psychologists and educators also refer to *skills*. These are knowledge-based practices. In our telephone example, the ability to push or dial specific numbers to reach our home, office, and friends is a skill we have learned. It has little to do with the operation of the technology, or with what happens inside the colored case we call the telephone, but it does relate to the routines and the operation of the switching gear. In the case of intellectual skills, human beings have devised a means of dealing with symbols. For example, reading is a very important skill. The ability to make sense out of the words you are reading now is based upon your knowledge of shapes, and how letters combine into words, phrases, clauses, sentences, and paragraphs. Ultimately, this knowledge leads to meaning once the translation has taken place in the brain.

There are many analogies that could exemplify the relationship between the architecture of the brain and the various cognitive activities that take place within it. We could talk about locks and keys, about computer hardware, software and keyboard skills. Like all analogies, the telephone exchange example may be prone to over-generalization though it serves to exemplify a highly complex structure.

One could argue from the discussion of the brain and its functions, that the effectiveness of our information processing is an indicator of intellectual competence. In other words, intelligence is a function of how effective we are in storing, retrieving, and integrating information.

Intelligence and Information Processing

An extensive discussion of intelligence is really outside the scope of this book, but it will be useful to consider the differences between the concepts of intelligence and information processing to draw attention to the differences between their respective foci. Intelligence is supposed, rather than being something that is real. In short, it is a hypothetical construct (MacCorquodale & Meehl, 1948). We can refer to intelligence as though it exists, but we can't touch, feel or see it. We can, of course, measure it by inferring that intelligent behavior has certain quantifiable characteristics. The vague nature of intelligence is exemplified by the many descriptions of the nature of intelligence such as those of Spearman, Guilford, Eysenck, Vernon, Burt, Cattell, Thurstone, and more recently Gardner, and the range of measures that have been generated such as the Wechsler scales, Stanford-Binet, Lorge-Thorndike, Peabody, and Raven's Matrices.

Intelligence is bound to the psychometric measurement that provides an indication of the amount of knowledge a person possesses based upon selected items. The test score (an IQ) is a "product" but it gives no indication of how the score was achieved. For example, a child might get 7 out of 10 items correct in a mathematics test but many others might receive the same score. What does this tell us about the children or their intelligence? There are over a hundred ways that children can achieve a score of 7. So, the score doesn't tell us by what means the children achieved the result, only that such a result was obtained. The same argument holds true for IQ scores.

In contrast to the concept of intelligence, information processing theory strives to describe the way in which learning and problem solving takes place. Functionally, cognitive theorists have studied the processing of information using two systems of internal organization, namely:

* *the representational system*, concerned with the organizing, attending to, and interpreting information being received by the senses or acting as input within the thinking process; and,
* *the executive system*, concerned with processes such as planning, monitoring, checking and evaluating which manage the representational system (Anderson, 1975).

43

The unique contribution of information processing comes from the identification of individual strengths and weaknesses in the use of the storage, retrieval and organizational mechanisms (that is, the processes, strategies, and skills) that operate as cognition.

The Systematic Study of Strategic Behavior

Early information processing studies traced the development of memory across childhood, and in doing so, identified the role of memory (or coding) strategies in recall. It seemed as though a natural extension of this work with the developmentally young was to compare the memory characteristics and performance of disabled children with their non-disabled peers. It came as little surprise that differences between these groups were primarily due to the effectiveness of strategy use (see for example, Cohen & Nealon, 1979).

The study of the representational system, and in particular the effect of strategy training, became a major research focus in the mid 1960s. Early projects tended to concentrate upon the development of memory aids, such as rehearsing lists of numbers or letters for learning and later recall, and the relationship between strategy use and memory performance. The most prominent characteristic of these research efforts was the use of a narrow range of training activities within a laboratory setting. This approach provided for the isolation of specific training effects through tight experimental control and limited interference from curriculum content.

Rehearsal strategies

Rehearsal has been a commonly studied memory strategy. Notable among this literature is the study of cumulative rehearsal, clustering, rote recall, and self-interrogative activities of students with mild intellectual disabilities (Belmont, Ferretti & Mitchell, 1982; Borkowski & Buchel, 1983; Reid, 1980; Turner & Bray, 1985).

Typically, early and recent studies alike have shown that significant gains in recall can be obtained through training. Students have learned to use the rehearsal strategies successfully during the intervention phase but have experienced varying degrees of success in maintaining these gains and in generalizing the newly acquired skill to other rehearsal tasks. In some cases, even the

44

strategy training has not been beneficial. Glidden and Warner (1983), for instance, found no differences following training between adolescents with mild intellectual disabilities who were taught a cumulative rehearsal strategy and others who were not. They reported that members of the first group apparently failed to use the cumulative rehearsal strategy in favor of existing, less efficient strategies. Clearly, these students saw no value in the teacher-imposed strategy.

The Glidden and Warner report sounds at least two warnings. First, one can question the value of teaching only one *input* strategy, such as rehearsal. When only one strategy is taught, students with intellectual disabilities may develop competence in their use of that strategy at the time of presentation, but it is possible that they may fail to acquire the vital *retrieval* strategies necessary for completion of the task.

A second caution relates to the failure of students to rehearse if they are not prompted to do so. This may stem from their inability to perceive that the same strategic behavior can apply to a different though related task. For example, an individual may learn to rehearse numbers, but fail to rehearse if the stimuli are combinations of letters and numbers. This rigidity in applying strategies only to the training task has been called *welding* (Shif, 1969), and it has become recognized as an important barrier to overcome in strategy training interventions.

More recent studies have shown the effects of removing some of the experimental constraints on students in strategy training studies. Turner and Bray (1985), for instance, taught rehearsal strategies to children and adolescents with mild intellectual disabilities. They allowed the students to use the rehearsal strategy in whatever manner they thought appropriate. That is, they could study the individual pictures in any order and they could look at the sequence as many times as they wish. When ready to attempt to recall, the student notified the researcher. Turner and Bray argued that students with a mild intellectual disability may have been mislabeled as strategy deficient on the basis of experiments in which investigators used highly constraining rehearsal tasks. In their study, they showed that the children and adolescents were able to use spontaneous rehearsal strategies as demanded by the task.

While rehearsal and sequencing strategies are important skills, there are other memory aids (called mnemonics) that can be added to students' repertoires of strategies. We will describe several of these in the next section.

45

Mnemonics

Mnemonics allow personally relevant meaning to be assigned to incoming stimuli. These organizational strategies include the following:

* *Visualization* involves creating an image in the mind so that it can be "seen" and described. When asked to remember four objects (such as tree, cheese, boy, desk), the person may create images of these real objects in the mind.

* *Chunking* refers to the recoding of two or more nominally independent items of information into a single familiar unit. Chunking is a knowledge-specific strategy that depends upon familiarity with the stimuli. Information presented in chunks (for example, 4,3,2,1 - 3,5,7,9, - 8,6,4,2) is more easily recalled by students than unchunked numbers (though not always at the first attempt).

* *Verbal elaboration* also involves the recoding of material into meaningful units. This occurs by making up a sentence to help recall items, by asking questions about the information being presented, or by drawing implications or inferences about the stimuli. For example, if a person is given the words "boot, chalk, bus" to recall, making up a sentence, such as "My boot had chalk on it which I rubbed off when I got on the bus", might aid recall.

* *Categorization* is a method of expanding on, or integrating information into an existing knowledge base. It is a chunking strategy that allows for the collection of elements into a suitable and meaningful group. For instance, "bus, potato, truck, peas, car, aircraft" would be recalled more easily when collected under the categories of vehicles and food, than when considered in isolation.

The value of using the strategies such as those listed above was demonstrated early in the evolution of cognitive research (Winschel & Lawrence, 1975).

In a review of mnemonic strategy training, Kramer, Nagle, and Engle (1980) stressed the need to make strategies relevant to the individual, particularly in classroom studies. They argued that although a strategy may be of value, it will be of limited use until we know how to teach the mnemonic so that students will apply them to tasks outside the training context. Moreover, the successful use of strategies requires a knowledge of when and how to apply them in learning and problem solving situations. This became the second focus of intervention research dealing with the executive system.

Executive strategies

Most information processing models of cognition include a component that is called the executive. The executive refers to a controlling agent or process that is capable of performing an intelligent assessment of the activities occurring within the brain. The executive has several functions: predicting limitations in information processing capacity, maintaining an awareness of the self-instruction activities and their value, maintaining awareness of both problems being faced and strategies being applied, and monitoring of problem solving operations. In brief, the executive acts to control our information processing activities (Brown, Bransford, Ferrara, & Campione, 1983).

One important executive strategy refers to our knowledge of how our thinking processes operate. The term used to describe this understanding is *metacognition*. Brown et al. (1983) suggested that metacognition requires not only an awareness of cognition (that is, an understanding of the information processing involved in complex skills) but also competence in planning, monitoring, self-questioning and self-directing. Terms commonly associated with metacognition include "planning to make a plan", "stop-check" and "knowing when, where, and how to remember". Hence, metacognition relates to all stages of problem solving and academic endeavors, for instance:

* recognizing the need for a strategy;
* evaluating the task requirements and searching for the availability of an appropriate strategy within their repertoire; and,
* executing the strategy and monitoring its effectiveness (Campione & Brown, 1978).

Many of the early memory studies involving executive processes were based upon the presumed need to make the student's

47

information processing more efficient through memory control processes called metamemory. Studies by Brown and her colleagues in the late 1970s saw the first attempts at metamemory training with students with a mild intellectual disability (Brown & Barclay, 1976; Brown, et al., 1979). A major feature of these interventions was the emphasis on general skills such as planning, checking, and self-monitoring. Hence, training focused not only on the task but on providing information about the activity and its effects. The results of these studies showed obvious age-related differences. For instance, comparison of students having a mental age of around 8 years with others having a mental age around 6 years demonstrated that the older children were able to incorporate general strategy training skills in their problem solving activities related to transfer tasks, while the younger children were not (Brown et al., 1979).

Many of the early metacognition studies are of historical importance as they reported students' failure to transfer training. They emphasized the need for students to be involved actively in learning, informed of the value of using the strategy, and to be given the opportunity to apply the strategy in alternative tasks (Brown & Palincsar, 1982). Moreover, they led to a reevaluation of teaching materials to be included in strategy training. Teaching materials such as stories, picture sequences and expository text became more common as a consequence of the belief that strategy use would only occur if the student perceived the task to be meaningful and relevant.

COMPREHENSIVE TRAINING MODELS

Numerous studies have focused upon the development of memory strategies and the use of executive strategies such as metacognition. Most of these have been concerned with specific issues, or specific training procedures such as metamemory. Few investigations have been associated with the development or evaluation of general cognitive training models.

There have been two notable exceptions. To be completely unbiased, they have not been widely accepted though the developers of these two broadly-based instructional models have relatively high status in the area of intellectual disabilities (Snart, 1985). The better known of the two approaches, Instrumental Enrichment, was developed by Feuerstein and his colleagues in Israel and the United States. The second approach proceeded from a model of information processing developed by Das and his colleagues in Canada. We will describe these approaches below to highlight the information processing foundation of each.

Instrumental Enrichment

Feuerstein developed a training program designed to improve the reasoning skills of culturally deprived and educationally disadvantaged adolescents, though in practice, it has been used most frequently with adolescents with intellectual disabilities (Feuerstein, Rand, & Hoffman, 1979; Feuerstein, Rand, Hoffman & Miller, 1980). Feuerstein argued strongly that instruction must discourage students from being "passive acceptance learners", waiting for teachers to tell them what to do next. Feuerstein claimed that students needed to become active modifiers of their environment so that they could move towards increasingly higher levels of intellectual functioning.

The Feuerstein Instrumental Enrichment (FIE) program is based upon a set of goals that relate directly to the proposition that students can increase their capacity to benefit from experiences in formal and informal learning settings. Some of the goals include:

1. the acquisition of vocabulary, concepts, operations and relationships relevant to problem solving;
2. the development of insight and understanding of one's own thought processes, that is, metacognition;
3. the formation of proper study habits so that they become spontaneous and automatic;
4. the development of motivation based upon the intrinsic interest generated by the task; and,
5. the transition of the student from a passive recipient, to an active generator of information.

The training program is based around a set of fourteen paper-and-pencil exercises that provide structured practice in specific cognitive skills. These materials are not related to current academic tasks: Feuerstein claimed that to make them so would distract the student from the cognitive focus of the task. Each lesson follows a standard format in which the teacher guides the performance of the students and relates the exercises to current learning problems. A lesson sequence would typically include:

1. an introductory discussion to motivate students to work on the specific exercise for that lesson (10 minutes);
2. a period in which the students work on paper and pencil exercises independently, in pairs or small groups (25 minutes);
3. a discussion of methods used and problems encountered in the lesson to develop insight and to bridge the gap between principles and processes in real-life situations (10 minutes); and,
4. a summary of the lesson given in the students' words.

The concept of *bridging* is important in FIE. It refers to attempts to ensure that students recognize the relevance of strategy application in their regular class work. However, this is a relatively minor component in terms of duration and emphasis of the lessons which focus predominantly on the cognitive aspects of the FIE training tasks. Another feature of FIE is the length of training. In contrast to the vast majority of cognitive training studies, FIE involves a number of weekly sessions that extend over a prolonged period, frequently measured in years.

Instrumental Enrichment has been applied in a variety of educational environments, predominantly in Israel and in North and South America. Research has included culturally disadvantaged adolescents, post-secondary students, educationally delayed adolescents, and adolescents with intellectual disabilities. All studies have reported improved cognitive performance by students (Feuerstein et al., 1980; Howie, Thickpenny, Leaf, & Absolum, 1985; Messerer, Hunt, Meyers, & Lerner, 1984; Narrol, Silverman, & Waksman, 1982).

An example of Instrumental Enrichment

A study reported by Howie et al. (1985) is typical of the application of FIE within special classes for adolescents with mild intellectual disabilities. Eight students undertook 158 hours of instruction over a two year period though this was less than half of the recommended 400 hours. Lessons occurred for three hours (Year 1) or two hours (Year 2) per week in small groups following the format outlined above. In the first year, FIE lessons complemented the classroom curriculum and involved the class teacher, while in the second year, one group was taught in a withdrawal (that is, laboratory type) situation with no class teacher involvement. Only five of the eighteen FIE tasks were used.

The posttest results demonstrated an improvement in IQ over pretest scores with a further increase being recorded 6 months after the program had ended. In contrast to many other cognitive training studies that concentrate on group performances, Howie et al. used a single-subject research design that demonstrated the variability and inconsistency in individual student attainments, both within the training tasks and in transfer tasks.

The results obtained by Howie et al. are indicative of those reported in other projects over the past decade. These data also demonstrate that performance gains in general ability can be maintained, and in fact, improved subsequent to the termination of the teaching program.

Some criticisms of Instrumental Enrichment

In a definitive review, Savell, Twohig, and Rachford (1986) concluded that although statistically significant results have been obtained in many of the FIE studies, it is difficult to compare effects across studies due to the use of a wide range of pre and posttest measures. Savell et al. raised a number of questions relating to the inconsistency across FIE programs. The variability in length of training, the failure of researchers to use more than a few of the 14 paper and pencil tasks, and the vague description of how bridging may occur have not helped to make the evaluation exercise an easy one.

Regardless of the methodological differences between FIE studies, Savell et al. drew attention to common differences reported between experimental and control groups. These included a minimum of one week of training for the teaching staff (as required by Feuerstein), at least 80 hours of intervention for students over one or two years, and the presentation of the program in conjunction with subject matter of interest or importance to the students.

In an article more critical of FIE than Savell et al., Bradley (1983) challenged many of the significant results reported in FIE research on the basis of design weaknesses. He concluded that while there have been some statistically significant results, the importance of the data is diminished by inadequate methodology, a lack of educational significance of the results, and the failure of improvement in general intellectual ability to be reflected in specific school-based academic performance.

While FIE may not satisfy the demands of some scholars and practitioners, it is an important landmark in the field of educational innovation. It has provided a stimulus for cognitive training within the classroom, and continues to motivate educators to amend traditional teaching practices. Significant among its contributions are the notions of students as active learners, the need for a link or bridge between cognitive skills and academic tasks, and the need for prolonged in-depth training in the use of information processing skills. We turn our attention now to the second approach which has several features in common with Instrumental Enrichment.

A Neurological Foundation for Instruction

Neuropsychological theory has brought a new dimension to the discipline of education. One theory of brain functions to be popularized within literature deals with left-right hemispherical dominance, in which language and reasoning activities were assigned to the left side of the brain, and creativity to the right. While the evidence in support of different intellectual functions being located in different hemispheres is generally accepted, it is far from conclusive. There is greater support in the research literature for the concept of front-back than left-right organization of the brain.

The diligent student of neuropsychology will find a rich field in which to generate debate and assumption about learning and problem solving. For our purposes, we are concerned with the applications of brain function research to the development of cognitive interventions, and the work of Soviet psychologist, Alexander Luria, has been a prominent stimulus. Luria (1973) viewed the brain as a complete system of coordinated behavioral and neurological activities. Thus, the interaction between several areas of the cerebral cortex is essential in undertaking any behavioral task.

In defining the working brain, Luria was in conflict with the two extremist views of neurological functions: strict localization of thought processes to specific parts of the brain, and the holistic, un-differentiated neurological functioning. The former has been criticized for its lack of scope and failure to explain general cognitive deficits that often accompany specific brain damage or lesions. Criticisms of the latter concern the failure of that view to account for the common finding of pervasive disruption of even simple thought functions arising from minor brain damage.

Luria acknowledged the importance of regions of the brain but emphasized that different neurological activities were capable of achieving the same end-product. Conversely, at the lower levels of behavior, similar neurological systems may give rise to very different end-product behaviors.

The importance of working zones within the brain is acknowledged in Luria's discussion of arousal, coding, and planning. The importance of these three concepts in contemporary cognitive theory has been highlighted by many writers and researchers. One information processing model in particular has used these three basic units as the foundation (Das et al., 1979).

The Information-Integration Model

The Information-Integration Model is a representation of Luria's hypotheses concerning brain functions in information processing terms. The model describes cognition as an interaction between input, storage, and retrieval activities (called coding), and planning. These cognitive processes are similar to those described earlier as the representational and executive systems. The unique contribution of the Das et al. approach is the link between cognitive theory and the prescribed way in which the brain organizes information so that meaning can be derived.

The model is represented in Figure 3.1 (over the page) and has four components:

Sensory Input. This component of the model refers to the transmission of information to any of the sensory receptors, such as the eyes, ears, or kinesthetic receptors. Information may come to the person as a whole unit (for example, when we see the British "Union Jack" flag or the French "Tricolor"), or as a series of stimuli (for example, the description of a football game on the radio).

The Sensory Register. Originally, the sensory register was thought to be a buffer, able to either block information from reaching the central processor or interrupt the central processor by forcing it to accept the information. In a later explanation, the decision on what information is transmitted by the Sensory Register to the Central Processor was thought to be determined by the interaction between states of arousal and attention, information processing, and planning. This description brings the whole model into play rather than simply the Sensory Register (Das & Varnhagen, 1986).

Figure 3.1: A Representation of the Information-Integration Model

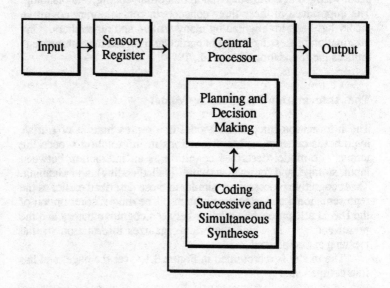

The Central Processor. There are two main central processor components: simultaneous and successive coding (or syntheses), together with planning and decision making. The two coding options, simultaneous and successive, are central to both assessment and training.

   Simultaneous synthesis is defined as the synthesis of separate elements into groups. The essential nature of this sort of processing is that any portion is surveyable as a whole. In contrast, *successive synthesis* refers to the processing of information in a serial fashion. During the presentation, the content is not surveyable as a whole unit (Das et al., 1979). The difference between surveying as a whole or in sequenced sections is the fundamental difference between the two forms of coding. Both forms of coding can be perceptual, conceptual or related to memory.

The type of coding that takes place within the Central Processor is independent of the manner in which the information is received at the sensory receptor. How an individual chooses to code the information within the central processor depends on two main factors: the person's habitual form of coding which is directly related to development and prior learning experiences; and, the requirements of the task. Both forms of coding are available to the individual, assuming there is no neurological damage, though a person may not use the most appropriate form when faced with a particular task.

The second part of the central processor involves the use of planning and decision making. Planning is certainly not a new cognitive concept (as will be shown later) but the role of planning was not considered fully until Ashman (1978) examined the various dimensions of planning within this processing model. A person's planning competence is thought now to be a major factor in the selection of the correct coding form, as it ensures that the individual applies coding strategies within a meaningful frame of reference.

Output. The output demanded by any task can be either simultaneous or successive. It may be a specific behavior or action, or it might be the resolution of a mental activity that involves no observable behavior.

Assessment in the Integration-Information Model

The psychometric evaluation of the coding and the planning aspects of the model has been a prominent feature of Das' research. Up to the present time, the measurement of simultaneous and successive syntheses has been based upon tests drawn from various sources including those developed by Luria (1966; 1980). Many of the tests were developed by others as measures of intellectual ability (such as Raven's Progressive Matrices), or as diagnostic tests aimed at specific deficiencies (such as Memory-for-Designs). These were adopted by Das et al. as measures of simultaneous coding. Other tasks such as Digit Span and several verbal and nonverbal experimental tests have been used as measures of successive coding.

Although Das et al. have claimed that the simultaneous-successive dichotomy was not simply another way to describe the nonmemory-memory division, successive coding tests traditionally have been memory based. Simultaneous coding tasks have included both memory (Memory-for-Designs) and nonmemory (Figure Copying) tests. The failure of Das and his colleagues to include

55

nonmemory tests of successive coding and aural tests of simultaneous coding regularly has weakened the validity of the model in the eyes of some theoreticians. Following the confirmation and measurement of planning as a conceptually independent component of the information integration model, several tests were added to the test pool. These were drawn largely from the neuropsychological domain and included measures such as Trail Making and Visual Search (see Ashman, 1982).

In 1983, the Kaufman Assessment Battery for Children (K-ABC) provided the first normative battery of information processing tests (Kaufman & Kaufman, 1983). This battery focused specifically upon the evaluation of information processing competence using the simultaneous and sequential (successive) coding dichotomy, producing both a Processing Scale for each and a Mental Processing Composite Score. While there has not been unequivocal support for this new measurement device, the K-ABC has provided a valid alternative to the traditional Wechsler and Stanford-Binet tests of intelligence, as well as a normative alternative to the Das battery.

Numerous studies have been reported using simultaneous and successive synthesis as the research base. Studies have examined the relationship between coding competence and intellectual functioning levels (Jarman, 1978), scholastic ability levels (Robinson, 1984), cultural and racial groups and socio-economic levels (Molloy, 1973). Measurement of simultaneous and successive coding by students and adults with mild intellectual disabilities have covered elementary/primary school-aged students (Jarman & Das, 1977), adolescents (Ashman, 1984), and adults (Snart & Swann, 1982). In all cases the presence of the two coding strategies was clearly demonstrated though there have been some anomalies in the apparent demands of some coding tests across groups.

Training based on the Information-Integration Model

Training studies began soon after the development of the Information-Integration Model. Early studies tended to focus on teaching only one coding strategy though more recent interventions have introduced both simultaneous and successive coding strategies in the belief that both strategies are essential for successful completion of a wide range of academic tasks.

A distinctive feature of the various training studies using students with learning disabilities has been the use of what might be called preacademic training tasks (called "context-free" by Das) in which the content is clearly understood by the learners. The task is one that students already know, and hence, they understand how a coding strategy can assist in solving the task. The use of these laboratory tasks was based upon the argument that a root cause of poor academic performance is the failure of students to apply coding strategies appropriately to the specific academic task being learned. Moreover, strategic behavior was considered to be integrated more effectively by the learner when trained in isolation from academic content. The major fallacy in this argument is its presupposition that an information processing strategy learned on a simple, known task will be transferred by the student to current academic content.

Three studies with elementary students with learning difficulties have demonstrated improvement on coding tests and on some academic measures (Brailsford, 1981; Kaufman, 1978; Krywaniuk, 1974). All studies employed teaching materials that were either familiar to the students, or which were easily learned by them.

A common feature of these investigations was the provision of some evidence for the transfer of strategies use to coding tasks that required the use of one or the other coding strategy. Thus, the generalization obtained could be clearly argued as generalization rather than task maintenance. Moreover, generalization was reported to reading tasks, demonstrating that the students recognized the need to use the strategies to solve academic tasks.

In contrast, training studies involving students with mild intellectual disabilities have not achieved generalization. Parmenter (1984), for example, trained late adolescents to use successive coding strategies in tasks that had previously been used by Krywaniuk or Kaufman. Parmenter explained the lack of generalization in terms of his participants' inability to use the new strategy in preference to their existing inefficient or inappropriate strategies. He suggested that the students' failure to develop an appropriate level of proficiency may have been a function of the design of the intervention.

In another study, Conway (1985) incorporated both simultaneous and successive tasks in a training program for elementary special class students with mild intellectual disabilities. Training emphasized discrimination between the two coding strategies and used group teaching strategies that reflected usual classroom teaching techniques. Again, the failure to obtain generalization was explained in terms of the students' inability to perceive the necessity to apply the newly acquired strategies to nontraining tasks.

The results of the Parmenter and Conway studies led Das (1985) to suggest that the failure of intellectually disabled students to generalize to untrained academic tasks was a specific limiting characteristic not found in students with learning difficulties or a cultural disadvantage. This could mean that far generalization may not be a realistic expectation for students with intellectual disabilities. However, an alternative explanation may implicate instructional procedures that failed to reinforce strategic behavior in a manner appropriate for the students used in the studies.

Criticisms of the Information-Integration Model

Theories and models are always open to criticisms, regardless of their scientific discipline. The Information-Integration Model also has attracted harsh evaluation on conceptual and methodological grounds. Carroll (1978), for instance, challenged the use of certain statistical techniques (namely, factor analysis) on which the division of the coding processes was based. Carroll argued that in breaking certain statistical conventions, interpretation of the relationship between components could be challenged, and by implication, the validity of the model was questioned. Humphreys (1978) likewise challenged the methodology employed in a study dealing with the relationship between simultaneous and successive syntheses and reading achievement.

In response to these criticisms, Das and his colleagues have reported several psychometric replication studies and have argued that there is consistency in the divisions between the two coding dimensions and planning. However, careful examination of the body of literature related to the model will reveal numerous anomalies as a result of test substitutions in studies across age, ability, and experimental conditions. In other words, some simultaneous tests act like successive tests when given to certain groups, notably those with low ability. This makes the identity of processes seem somewhat fluid when one would want them to be static. Vernon, Ryba, and Lang (1978) exemplified this problem when they were unable to replicate early studies using a battery of tests different to those reported by Das.

The structure of the training studies based upon the model leaves much to be desired. There are three major weaknesses inherent in this intervention approach. First, there was a heavy reliance on student motivation and ability. Typically, students were required to recognize that coding strategies taught using novel tasks and materials could be applied to other (usually academic) tasks. Second, the students' classroom teachers were not involved in the intervention projects. Consequently, they were neither able to demonstrate the application of the trained strategies to current curriculum topics nor were they required to orient their teaching toward coding strategies. Third, training was provided as an additional learning activity, remote from the students' usual classroom activities.

Notwithstanding these criticisms, the Information-Integration Model constitutes one of the few comprehensive models of information processing to be found in the literature to date. It satisfies some important requirements in addition to its cognitive basis for remediation and instruction. For instance, it allows for comparison between individuals and groups of children and adults with and without cognitive disabilities; it emphasizes the interdependence of coding and planning components; and, it cuts across the traditional sensory modality boundaries (such as visual-perceptual, and auditory-visual). As such, the model has much to recommend it.

Strengths and Shortcomings of Existing Training

The various approaches outlined in this chapter constitute a selective overview of the development of cognition as a basis for educational interventions. Researchers working within the area have demonstrated the value of information processing as a means of explaining the nature of learning, especially as it applies to complex intellectual endeavors. Moreover, the various research activities undertaken over the past two decades have provided a plethora of information relating to the cognitive competence of individuals having either learning or intellectual disabilities, notably in the areas of attention, memory, strategic behavior, planning, and problem solving.

One of the important contributions of information processing theory to the study of developmental disabilities has been the examination of aptitude by treatment interactions (called ATIs). This concept refers to the way in which one treatment or instructional procedure will work well with some students and poorly with others as a result of specific aptitude competence. If the type of intervention changes, so might the level of performance change (perhaps even reverse) for the same group of students (Cronbach & Snow, 1977). Thus, one advantage of information processing theory is the opportunity to explore the relationship between concepts with specific populations, but also at the level of the individual.

In terms of strategy-based training, the Feuerstein and Das models have provided theoretically-based, but circumscribed cognitive interventions. Notwithstanding the criticisms that can be leveled at individual studies, information processing theory appears to be a substantive and viable foundation for assessment and training of problem solving. However, it has become clear that the solution to the problems of classroom interventions has not been found completely in any one approach that has been reported up to this time.

Central to existing approaches are the active involvement of students in the learning process, and the systematic application of a pedagogic sequence. These are certainly important features of an interactive teaching-learning model. However, the weaknesses of contemporary approaches lie in the failure to release both teacher and student from a relatively rigid instructional framework; one in which teaching of the strategy is a teacher responsibility, and learning the application of the strategy remains the student's role. There have been few attempts to re-orient classroom instruction in terms of how to teach, and how to learn. These are key issues that are discussed in the following chapter.

4

Issues in Cognitive Intervention

Three issues have emerged above others from the plethora of research dealing with cognitive interventions for students with learning or intellectual disabilities. These are: the role of metacognition in learning and problem solving; the achievement of transfer of learning to situations and conditions outside the training context; and, the application of laboratory procedures to the classroom. These topics have been accentuated by three facts. First, each represents a fundamental issue which has governed, and will continue to influence the development and direction of cognitive research as it applies to education. Second, each has been resistant to resolution over at least the past two decades. Third, each is intricately woven into the fabric of information processing literature.

In this chapter, we consider each topic in turn, considering the history, limitations, the positive results obtained by researchers and the relevance of the research to the development of instructional procedures suitable for application in special education.

METACOGNITION: MAGIC OR MYTH?

Research interest in executive processes developed from the realization that learners and problem solvers must be aware of their cognition to take advantage of it. This awareness encompasses how thinking occurs, how strategies are used, and the effectiveness of one's cognitive activities. While there has been some minor debate over the most appropriate definition, the distinction between cognition and metacognition may perhaps be best illustrated diagrammatically (see Figure 4.1).

Figure 4.1: An Illustration of the Relationship between Cognition and Metacognition

Metacognition came to prominence following research on metamemory in the early 1970s. Flavell and his colleagues gave meaning to the concept of metacognition by referring to the monitoring and regulating activities that typically occur during a problem solving activity. Flavell's research followed earlier discussion of the differences between knowing, knowing how to know, and knowing about knowing. In fact, some writers claimed that both the acquisition of memory strategies and the ability to monitor them were essential skills that must be mastered before a person could begin to deal with a complex environment (Brown, 1975). This position was by no means universally accepted although it provided an important early statement of the need for students to monitor their performance.

The Early Development of Metacognition

In one of the earliest studies, Flavell, Fredericks, and Hoyt (1970) interviewed children about memory span and their knowledge of how memory operates. They discovered that grade 4 students (the eldest in their study) had a greater understanding of memory devices and of the existence of memory than the nursery, kindergarten, or grade 2 students.

In a more substantive study, Kreutzer, Leonard, and Flavell (1975) interviewed children from grades K, 1, 3, and 5. They were concerned with identifying how children expressed the effects of metacognition on the quality of performance on a memory task. In other words, they wanted to know what the child might come to know, or know how to find out about memory as a result of maturation and learning experience. Kreutzer et al. asked children several questions related to:

* their memory in comparison to other children (for example, "Can you remember things better than your friends?");
* their knowledge about memory (for example, "If you wanted to phone your friend and someone told you the number, would it make a difference if you called straight away or after you got a drink of water?"); and,
* their ability to remember how to perform certain activities (for example, "Suppose you were going ice skating with your friend after school tomorrow and you

63

wanted to be sure to bring your skates. How could you be really certain that you didn't forget to take them to school in the morning?").

They found that children in grades 3 and 5 appeared to be far more planful and aware of their memory processes than their younger peers. The older children seemed to understand how memory worked and how people use their memories effectively. In contrast, the younger children knew about forgetting, but they appeared to be more dependent than the older children upon external resources (such as notes and other people) when confronted with memory problems. These results suggested a link between metamemory, decisions about the use of memory strategies, and performance.

As a consequence of such early investigations, researchers argued that metacognition appeared to be a control agent of cognition, affecting strategy use and subsequently, what we learn. Others implicated personality variables and cognitive style as additional factors to be considered when evaluating memory performance. These investigators have claimed that a person's beliefs, motivation, and emotional condition influence the way in which problems are approached. In other words, how students deal with problems is related to self-perception of ability, and to the belief (or otherwise) that while a problem may be difficult, it is solvable.

The relationship between personality and metacognitive factors in children with learning difficulties has opened a new research domain. Hagen, Barclay, and Newman (1982), for example, argued that knowledge of past experiences was a determinant of what is noticed, learned, remembered and inferred about oneself in the future. Many other studies have dealt with issues such as: children's and adults' recognition of their capabilities and limitations; personal control over school achievement; reasons for success or failure at certain tasks; and, expectations of future success. In the current literature related to metacognition, these personality factors have taken on new significance (Borkowski, Carr, & Pressley, 1987).

The Relationship between Metacognition and Achievement

Awareness of thought processes and memory activities has been used as an explanation of a wide range of behaviors, from young children's ability to maintain attention (Loper & Hallahan, 1982) to their tadpole drawings of people (Taylor & Bacharach, 1981). Metacognition research also has encompassed various educational fields, from social and clinical applications, to computer education, mathematics, study skills, and teacher education (see for examples, Cohen, 1983; Garofalo & Lester, Jr, 1985; Harris, Graham, & Freeman, in press; Hartman, 1983; Kirby & Ashman, 1984; Linn & Dalbey, 1985; Lovelace, 1984; Spring, 1985).

From the mid 1970s and into the 1980s, researchers turned their attention to the metacognition of children with learning difficulties and intellectual disabilities. The view that many of the learning problems that children experience are related to metacognitive deficits had appeal, especially in the light of research suggesting that metacognition can be improved through instruction and experience. Two of the most commonly researched areas have been reading and mathematics. The examination of these two curriculum areas has provided some insights into the relationships between metacognition, achievement, and training.

Reading

There appears to be a strong link between reading ability and metacognition. Metacognition provides an awareness of how strategies are used to reduce reading demands, how we learn from text, and how effectively strategies are used. In other words, knowledge of metacognitive processes facilitates control over reading behavior according to the complexity and purpose of the task (Brown, Armbruster, & Baker, 1986).

Researchers who first became interested in knowledge about reading skills interviewed children using techniques similar to those reported in Kreutzer et al. (1975). Multi-item interview procedures were used to investigate students' knowledge of how content influences: comprehension; speed of reading as a function of task demands; the structure of text; and, the resolution of comprehension errors. Not surprisingly, the results of these studies not only indicated that age and ability affected children's awareness of motivation on reading performance, but also that there was need to vary strategies to suit the specific demands of the reading task (Moore, 1983; Myers & Paris, 1978).

In general, researchers have agreed about the importance of metacognitive skills in establishing task specific reading strategies.

The issues seem to fall into one of two categories: Awareness of the goals of reading, and awareness of the form of text.

In terms of reading goals, five points have been made:

1. Children must be aware of the purpose of reading;
2. Immature readers must understand that they can modify their reading strategies according to the purpose of the task, that is, to read slowly if they are reading to remember facts or determine issues;
3. Poor readers can learn to watch for cues that identify important information within the text;
4. Poor readers must learn to evaluate information being read in terms of their existing knowledge; and,
5. Poor readers must know about effective strategies to deal with comprehension problems.

In regard to awareness of the form of a text, three conclusions have been reached:

1. Young and low achieving children must become aware of the logical structure of text which is important for quick detection of information;
2. Poor readers must become sensitive to contextual constraints and linguistic cues that highlight semantic or syntactic errors; and,
3. Metacognitive skills assist in the evaluation of the consistency, completeness and clarity of information in a passage or a story. This involves the monitoring of cognition and the recognition that sufficient information has been collected to establish meaning.

Developing children's metacognition about reading has been the focus of many studies. Paris, Saarnio, and Cross (1986), for instance, compared children receiving regular reading instruction in grades 3 and 5 with a group of children who received periodic instruction about strategies such as skimming, locating main ideas in stories, making inferences while reading, and monitoring comprehension. The children who received the metacognitive program increased their awareness about reading and comprehension strategies while other children did not. However, Paris et al. argued that metacognition appears to be an intermediate goal in development and learning, being important when students are consciously directing their attention to remembering, comprehending, and monitoring their learning. It is less important for early learning, or later in the process when effective use of automated skills has been achieved. How awareness is stimulated appears to make little difference, whether this is achieved by discovery as children encounter difficulties, by discussion, or through teacher intervention.

Mathematics

The study of mathematics has also shown the importance of metacognition as a determining factor of academic success. In this regard, *knowing how* to solve a mathematical problem is different from *knowing that* one knows how to solve it. In other words, being able to do the calculation when faced with a particular problem is different to knowing what kind of mathematical operation is involved. This distinction was examined in a series of studies conducted by Bryant (1985).

Children aged 6-7 years were presented with two types of problems: one type involved the addition or subtraction of real objects, and the other with written addition and subtraction sums. Children were more successful on real object problems than on the mental computation problems. The typical strategy employed was counting once the required number of objects had been removed physically from the group. However, many of the children who used this physical subtraction method to solve the problem worked out the answer by mental subtraction when given the written version of the same problem. These findings suggest to Bryant that children can be disposed to use a skill in one situation, but not in another.

In a follow-up study, one group of children (who used mental subtraction in the written problems in the earlier study) was given real object problems and asked to use their knowledge of subtraction to determine the answers. They were then shown written versions of the same subtraction operation and asked for solutions.

Another group of children was given twice the number of object problems over two sessions. For half of the problems, the children used their knowledge of subtraction in written sums, but they were prevented from counting. In the second half, they were encouraged to count but discouraged from using their knowledge of counting. Children in both groups used subtraction more than in the first study, and Bryant argued that there was little point in teaching children how to carry out a particular calculation unless they are taught how to recognize when a calculation is needed and what relation it bears to other problems.

In another study dealing with mathematical problems, Slife, Weiss, and Bell (1985) worked with grade 1 to grade 5 mathematically disabled children. Each day, students examined a set of problems and predicted the number they would get correct. These predictions, then, were compared with the children's actual scores until they achieved 60 percent correct. When this target was reached, children were timed while they identified those problems thought to be correct or incorrect. Each of these children was matched with a nondisabled student who gained the same scores on a general mathematics achievement test and on the set of problems on which the disabled children reached criterion.

A comparison of group results showed that the disabled children were less accurate than their peers in their knowledge about their problem solving skills (metacognition) and less accurate about the number of problems they could solve correctly. Furthermore, the disabled group was less accurate than the other children in regard to their strategic behavior (the regulation of their cognition) in dealing with which problems were right or wrong.

While Slife et al. were more concerned with the methodological issue regarding the separability of metacognition and strategic behavior, their study shows that awareness of information processing competence is closely related to mathematics achievement, and by implication, may spread throughout all areas of intellectual and academic achievement. Moreover, the study demonstrates that there is a need to consider how children with learning disabilities can best be guided in the development of their cognitive skills.

The studies reported in this section are several among the many that have identified a positive relationship between metacognition and specific areas of academic achievement. It may appear from the exponential growth of metacognitive literature that knowledge of one's learning and problem solving competence is the key to success in learning. However, the conclusions reported by Paris et al. would suggest that this may not necessarily be so: There are many other writers who also have questioned the value of metacognition as a functional concept (see for example, Brown, 1984).

Metacognitive Confusion

Metacognition is not a difficult concept to understand. It is clear that sophisticated problem solvers know how they achieve success or resolve a particular problem. For instance, given a telephone number to remember, it is not difficult to explain how the numbers are kept active in memory, either by rehearsal or perhaps by visualizing the digits so they can be successfully recalled. However, there are situations when metacognitive knowledge seems to have little relationship to performance.

Linking awareness with performance

We may know how to solve some problem in the most efficient way, but when faced with the real-life situation, we choose an inefficient strategy even though more effective options are available. Consider this example.

Teachers often ask students to prepare essays. In talking to students, it is easy to elicit "the best way" to prepare and produce an assignment. Typically, students report that the first step is to choose the topic, then to collect, read and take notes from information or written material related to the topic. The next stage is the preparation of a general outline so that reading and note-taking is specific. This "skeleton" outline is "fleshed out" and refined further. All these steps are completed before the first draft is written. Generally, students will report that the best time to begin an assignment is immediately after it has been set so that a specific amount of time per week can be allocated to the task before the due date.

Most students would recognize that this is certainly one of the better plans for writing an assignment, but it is a rare student who actually follows it. More typical is the eventual realization that the assignment is due in four or five days. This often prompts a frenzied and incomplete library search, followed by distress when material is not readily available on the topic. While most students generally follow a path somewhere between these extremes, the point we are making must not be lost: Students know how to plan and organize their time and materials to get the best grades, but regardless of this awareness, there is a gulf between the metacognition and the performance. Similar results have been found by researchers studying metamemory in children and adolescents.

To date, the arguments in favor of the importance of metacognition in academic endeavors have been presented as if the matter has already been debated and resolved (see Palincsar, 1986). While the notion of such an executive mechanism has "intuitive" appeal, the literature has been equivocal. In the area of learning disabilities, some consistent successes have been recorded. The investigation of metacognition with intellectually disabled persons has produced evidence strongly in favor of the link (Barclay, 1981; Dixon, Hertzog, & Hultsch, 1986; Waters, 1982) and against it (Cavanaugh & Perlmutter, 1982; Kramer & Engle, 1981; Lawson, 1980; Kurtz & Borkowski, 1984; Turnure, 1987).

Metacognition and intellectual disability

In what was possibly the first major study of metamemory, Eyde and Altman (1978) explored the metacognitive knowledge of 5 to 16 year-olds with mild or moderate intellectual disabilities. Using a modified version of the Kreutzer et al. interview, they reported that memory performance seemed to be a function of chronological and mental age. Eyde and Altman argued that changes in memory behavior resulted from interactions with the environment even though the students did not demonstrate broad-ranging responses to the environment and its demands. Interactions were characterized by passivity, especially for those in the lower range of ability.

Other investigators have reported limited successes in metacognition training. Kendall, Borkowski, and Cavanaugh (1980), for example, reported a study in which children with mild intellectual disabilities were trained to use self-questioning (that is, interrogative) strategies in a task in which word pairs were to be learned. The interrogative strategy involved thinking about possible relationships between the two words in any pair, forming a "why" question about the relationship, describing what is known about the words, and providing a reason to explain the relationship.

The results of the study showed that scores on a metamemory task administered before training did not reliably predict recall or strategy use during training. However, the metamemory scores did predict the quality of the children's strategic behavior when they were required to generalize the strategy to other tasks. Students with high metamemory scores following training were able to recall more word pairs during training, and on the maintenance and generalization tasks, though strategy training did not appear to produce changes in metamemory.

The results of other studies aimed at demonstrating a causal relationship between metacognition and the use of memory strategies have not been encouraging. Kramer and Engle (1981), for example, developed three training programs for children with mild intellectual disabilities and a mental age-matched group without disabilities (MA = 8 years). One program taught the children to use rehearsal to recall information. A second program trained the children to be aware of how their memory worked and how their thinking activities affected memory (metacognition). The third group received training in rehearsal plus metacognition.

The results of the study showed that rehearsal training led to an improvement in recall but rehearsal, metacognition, or the combination of the two programs was unsuccessful in promoting generalization to related tasks. Kramer and Engle also interviewed the children following the intervention and found that memory awareness improved the children's ability to describe appropriate strategic behavior though this did not necessarily lead to actual use of the strategy or to improved performance.

Further evidence in support of the Kramer and Engle results was reported by Justice (1985). She suggested that intellectually disabled children do not show the same development in their ability to regulate memory as is found with non-disabled children. Studies designed to train regulatory skills have shown that only those children with mental ages above eight years seem to benefit from strategy training, and there is little transfer of learning to new tasks even for these children. Thus, it appears that knowing about memory, however basic or inaccurate, may precede the ability to regulate memory activities.

One last point can be made in regard to metacognition. Someone who recognizes that a previously learned strategy or plan is appropriate to a specific task is more likely to begin work on that task, than another person who sits passively for lack of a starting point.

Having begun the task, learning how to do it proceeds by trial-and-error, and through interaction with the environment. Providing rules may shorten the acquisition time, but rules will not supplant the learning-how process (Tharp & Gallimore, 1985). In other words, while intellectually disabled persons may know how their memories work, and how memory affects performance, they may not be able to apply this knowledge because they lack information about the relationship between objects, knowledge and events specific to the task. This knowledge is called knowing-that.

In summary, it seems that cognitive researchers have adopted the position that metacognition is not only important, but vital for success in complex cognitive tasks and the facilitator of strategic behavior and success. While this position may find strong support in studies with regular students, it would appear that strategy and metacognitive training has not shown the same promise with students of low ability (especially if the achievement of maintenance and generalization is the indicator of success).

MAINTENANCE AND GENERALIZATION

From a teaching viewpoint, it would be a waste of time if children were taught how to spell "cat" one morning, but were unable to keep this knowledge intact until the following day. It seems important that children integrate the newly acquired information into their knowledge bases (or schemata) where it can be retrieved as desired and applied when appropriate. The storage of knowledge for future use refers to maintenance.

Generalization (or transfer of learning) was introduced in Chapter 2 during our discussion of behaviorism. Behaviorists would claim that it is the *stimulus control* that generalizes, not the behavior. In other words, they argue that generalization does not refer to the simple occurrence of a response in a novel setting, but the control of that response by non-trained stimuli (Horner, Bellamy, & Cohen, 1984).

Generalization from the cognitive viewpoint does not involve the association between a response and the consequences of it. The cognitivist would refer to generalization as the transfer of learning from the training environment and/or the task to other tasks that are conceptually distant from those used in training.

The matter we wish to consider here, is not the issue of definition. Rather, we look for guidance from the strategy training research that has been directed toward achieving performance gains, maintaining these gains over time, and showing that training has led to increases in performance on other tasks including measures of academic achievement.

Promoting Transfer of Strategy Training

Many review articles and book chapters dealing with the use of memory strategies alone have shown that training in rehearsal, chunking and so on, has generally been successful in producing and maintaining learned behavior, though generalization has been elusive (for instance, in Brown et al., 1983, or Pressley & Levin, 1983). Optimism concerning generalization has come from research that has considered the role of the executive control mechanism. Several researchers have emphasized the importance for transfer of strategy-related information presented with, or following training.

One way of improving knowledge about strategic behavior is to tell students some of the many ways in which a task can be attempted, with some being more useful than others. Students can be cued or sensitized to the importance of training, and learn about the strategies in addition to their use. When sensitized in this way, they seem to be more successful in performing and generalizing their skills than other students who have not been sensitized. Elaborating upon the effectiveness of strategy-related information seems to have a similar effect. Gick and Holyoak (1983), for instance, used the cuing technique and reported that generalization was most likely to occur when children were given an explicit hint about the relationship between one problem and another, or when they explicitly compared the problems. In a later study, Gick (1985) found that unguided generalization was aided by including a diagram or cue in the target problem.

Kurtz and Borkowski (1984) considered that success and failure to generalize memory strategies depended upon both motivation and cognitive competence. They assigned children in grades 1 and 3 to one of three experimental conditions. Children received either:

1. specific strategy instructions appropriate for three memory problems;
2. general metacognitive information about subordinate (strategy use) and superordinate (executive) processing; or,
3. specific strategy and metastrategy training.

The results of their study indicated that children who were initially high in metamemory skills profited more (than those who were initially low) from training which provided metacognitive insights to aid the transfer of newly acquired strategies. More importantly, children who attributed their success to effort were both more strategic and metacognitive than others in the study and were more likely to generalize the skills they had learned. In other words, they found an interaction between motivation and cognitive processes that could be altered during training. The effect of this interaction is to provide children with the desire *and* the ability to act more strategically when generalization is required.

While the generalization literature concerning children without learning or intellectual disabilities has been promising, the same optimism has not been generated from studies dealing with students of low ability. Two studies that illustrate this point are reported briefly below.

The Tower of Hanoi, or the Tower of Brahma puzzle (as it is sometimes called) has been used in a variety of studies which have compared the problem solving competence of children with and without intellectual and learning difficulties (see Figure 4.2). The puzzle was invented by a French mathematician, sold as a toy in the late 1880s, and has been used in psychological research since the 1930s. The standard puzzle consists of three pegs that are arranged in either a triangular or straight-line configuration. One of the pegs holds a number of (usually) wooden disks of graduated diameter, with each having a hole in the center. The largest disk is generally on the bottom and the smallest is on the top forming a pyramid pattern. To solve the puzzle, the pyramid of disks must be transferred to an empty peg so that the end result is the same pyramid configuration as at the beginning. The disks are moved one at a time, but without placing a larger disk on a smaller one.

The standard Tower of Hanoi puzzle has been used in various studies of young adults with mild intellectual disabilities (Borys, Spitz, & Dorans, 1982; Byrnes & Spitz, 1977). Generalization tasks have also been included. For example, Minsky, Spitz, and Bessellieu (1985) used a set of clowns as a modification of the standard puzzle (small clowns could be stacked on top of larger one, but not the reverse). The study focused upon making the adults aware of the systematic step-by-step nature of solving the problem. They were able to show gains by some, but not all of the adults on the puzzle, plus long- and short-term maintenance of strategy use. However, virtually no generalization to the clown puzzle was achieved. In other words, some subjects could understand the steps (that is, small on large disks) using the standard puzzle, but could not extrapolate that to the solution of the clown puzzle.

Figure 4.2: The Tower of Hanoi puzzle

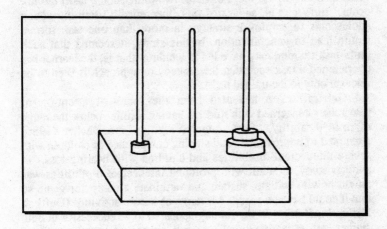

A replication study by Spitz, Minsky, & Bessellieu (1985) also produced limited gains following training. Consequently, Minsky et al. were pessimistic about the possibility of achieving generalization following training. They suggested that whatever was learned in the training program, was apparently quite narrow and specific to the standard Tower of Hanoi puzzle, as it appeared that the clown task was susceptible to decay of strategic behavior as a result of confusion in the task demands.

Traditional laboratory tasks, such as attribute identification, have also been employed in the study of generalization in students with mild intellectual disabilities. For instance, Burger, Blackman, and Clark (1981) showed line drawings of objects representing a single category (for example, bus, car, train) to children and young adolescents. Training included the identification of relevant attributes, self-management instruction, and modeling during which students watched others receiving self-instruction and attribute identification. The results of this study demonstrated generalization by each group to a verbal task very similar in nature to the training task (referred to as *near* generalization).

In a later study, Burger, Blackman, Clark, and Reis (1982) used tasks that involved identification of attributes in which one picture satisfied the demands of two categories (measuring *far* generalization) in addition to those similar to the 1981 study.

Maintenance and near generalization were reported but far generalization (to the more difficult two-dimensional task) did not occur. Burger et al. suggested that (theoretically) training young adolescents to employ a strategy in more than one task format would lead to generalization. In this study, it seemed that such multi-task training may have led to welding (that is, the learner has overlearned a task such that the strategy or approach is seen to be relevant only to the trained task).

Generalization has also been the focus of attention of researchers concerned with students having abilities below the range of mild disability. For example, Manion and Bucher (1986) attempted to improve the hand signing competence of children with severe intellectual disabilities and children with hearing loss. In another study, an adult with profound intellectual disabilities was taught how to initiate, sustain and terminate a computer game so that it could become part of her range of leisure activities (Duffy & Nietupski, 1985). While training appeared to be successful in both studies, generalization did not occur in either case to tasks having a similar format.

In spite of the difficulties confronted by cognitive instructional psychologists, optimism seems to be fairly common, especially when training for generalization. The studies we have examined, including those described above, have shown that generalization of information processing strategies remains an elusive consequence of training. Most researchers claiming generalization have reported transfer of learning to simple tasks that are very similar to those used in training, that is, they have discovered near generalization only. Transfer of learning to complex tasks, or those in which the relationship between training and testing is somewhat obscured, has remained elusive indeed. Some writers have suggested that success in achieving generalization is a function of the nature of training and the tests used to measure transfer, and of the context or setting in which training takes place. Others (such as Das, 1985), have argued that there may be an IQ threshold that limits the size of the inductive leap that is demanded by generalization.

Practical Gains from the Generalization Research

As can be seen from the discussion above, generalization appears to rely upon the development of both the representational system (for example, coding strategies such as matching, labeling, rehearsal, and elaboration) and the executive system (for example, planning, metacognition). Some writers have clarified the role of each system in the transfer of learning to tasks outside the training context. Butterfield (1983), for instance, proposed that *training for generalization* referred to the transfer of basic processes, whereas *teaching prerequisites for transfer* in future lessons required the development of executive processes. Therefore, generalization depends not only on the use of learned strategies outside the learning task, but also on the modification and combination of strategies to enable the solution of novel problems. In much of the information processing literature, this distinction is implied, though it is infrequently made quite so explicit.

Many writers and researchers have accepted the difficulties associated with generalization and have challenged the value of traditional strategy training approaches claiming that instruction for generalization must be exact, extensive and explicit. Indeed, some have suggested that such methods do not provide the optimum experience for students to master specific strategy content or self-regulatory skills. Gelzheiser, Shepherd, and Wozniak (1986), for example, argued that when children are required to attend to the performance of newly acquired skills, they are not able to devote sufficient attention to analysis of the task goal, planning how to attain the goal, or the evaluation of their plan. With attention directed only to the strategy, students have limited knowledge of when it is appropriate to use it and remain unprepared for generalization.

Gelzheiser et al. revised their initial training program by simplifying the strategy content, minimizing the language and conceptual demands, and removing some of the self-evaluation demands placed upon students. In the program, teachers assisted in the monitoring of strategy effectiveness, thereby providing some support to students. Support could be reduced as student independence increased (this concept was called *scaffolding* by Rogoff & Gardner, 1984). Gelzheiser et al. suggested that three features of strategy training induce generalization. These are shown in Table 4.1.

Gelzheiser et al. suggested that their program reduced the demands of strategy implementation and regulation, thereby ensuring that students have the resources available to attend to the task goals. Demands could be minimized by allowing students to master one skill before learning another, and by giving feedback to assist in the regulation of their behavior.

Table 4.1: A Strategy Training Program Devised by Gelzheiser et al.

---

1. *Teaching of specific skill content.* This entails (a) explicit skill training, providing sufficient practice for mastery and automaticity, (b) the introduction of training with easy materials, progressing to more difficult materials when students are proficient, and (c) the use of incentives to encourage proficiency (in their case they used monetary rewards);

2. *Teaching general, self-regulatory skills.* This involves minimizing task demands to enhance self-regulatory activity, explicitly teaching self-monitoring, providing support as students gauge the effect of the newly-acquired skills, and having students graph results; and,

3. *Teaching appropriate skill application.* This includes teaching the components of a task for which skill training may help, teaching students to identify and discriminate tasks where the skills will help, and using a variety of materials for practice.

Some Implications of Generalization Research

What do the generalization studies show? There are several points that can be made. First, the notion of degree of generalization has remained unclear. In other words, how do we distinguish between tasks that are "closely related" to the training task, and others that are "not-so-closely related"?

One way of making the distinction may be to define two extreme positions as near generalization (intra-domain transfer) at one end, and far generalization (inter-domain transfer) at the other and suggest that a continuum exists between the two points. Of course, confusion will still exist about the placement of the task on the continuum. Certainly, in several of the studies noted earlier in which generalization was reported, the relationship between the training and the transfer tasks was close. When the generalization task was more difficult, almost inevitably transfer of the newly acquired skill did not occur.

Second, there still remains the question in regard to the value of the generalization being sought. Certainly, strategic behavior is important within the broader context of information processing, but children in many of the laboratory studies might well have confused the relevance of the tasks they were performing, as a result of the information that was being given to them. This lack of perceived value may play a significant part in the achievement, or lack of achievement of generalization. When a child fails to see the relevance of training, it may well lead to what Shif, Burger and others have called welding. Indeed, Minsky et al. alluded to this difficulty by their admission of the narrow and specific nature of training in their study in which generalization was not achieved.

Are we asking too much of children to make the conceptual leap between training and generalization activities? Researchers appear to assume that their training is related directly to the task(s) they have chosen to represent generalization. However, we know far too little about the nature of the relationship between the demands of laboratory and academic tasks. In other words, the nature of one task may confuse the link with another regardless of the similarity perceived by teachers or researchers.

To obtain effective generalization, two alternatives might be considered. First, the learner might be encouraged to consider generalization before the task-specific aspects of learning are introduced, or at least consolidated ("How is this task similar to others?" or "Could this strategy be helpful in other tasks?"). Second, the conceptual distance between the training task and the transfer activities may be reduced. This implies overlap between training tasks so that a chain is formed between the training activity and the desired generalization task (as is depicted in Figure 4.3).

One last matter could be raised here. The notion of teacher and student responsibility in learning during the intervention process has been raised in several contexts. Ellis, Lenz, and Sabornie (1987) have referred to four levels of generalization that apply prior to, during, and following teacher intervention (Table 4.2)

Up to this point, we have drawn attention to several of the significant issues that have plagued cognitive researchers. Our final concern is one that is of specific interest to educators, namely the application of theory to practice, or perhaps more accurately, the interrelationship between theory and practice.

Figure 4.3: Overlap of Task Characteristics Leading to Generalization

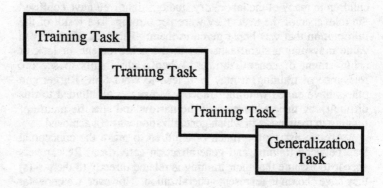

APPLYING COGNITIVE RESEARCH TO THE CLASSROOM

The integration of disabled students into regular classes has placed demands upon classroom teachers to adapt current teaching techniques to multidimensional student populations. For our part, this change has demanded consideration of the nature of the teaching and learning process that takes into account a range of students' skills and the context in which instruction should occur. The goal of learning, as suggested earlier, is the development of independent learning skills that will generalize to events and tasks outside the learning environment.

There have been numerous attempts to develop models and procedures to increase strategic behavior and the likelihood of generalization to other curriculum tasks and skills. Moreover, literature reviews often express optimism in regard to information processing techniques that purport to overcome the cognitive deficits associated with learning and intellectual disabilities (Wong, 1986). Whether training works in the narrow confines of the experiment is not the issue. The crucial issue is the continuing relevance and value of interventions within the school or classroom context.

Table 4.2: Four Levels of Generalization

---

1. *Antecedent level.* This involves engaging the student in certain activities before instruction in a specific learning strategy takes place (getting the student motivated and interested in learning) and this may lead to the changing of negative attitudes that may affect the transfer of learning. This level implies the active participation of students in the learning event.

2. *Concurrent generalization.* Here, the concern is with the application of generalization principles so that the student acquires the skill to a degree sufficient for it to be transferred. The student learns how a strategy works and how it can be used. The classroom teacher, a resource teacher, or the student's peers may play a role in the learning procedure.

3. *Subsequent generalization.* This involves the application of the skills to various contexts, tasks, and situations. The teacher and peers may also be involved in the instruction.

4. *Independent generalization.* This involves transition from teacher to student responsibility for generalization. It is a student-mediated activity which may well be a form of generalization in its own right.

There is one substantive question that we have not addressed up to this point: Has existing theory and research helped educators discover, develop or refine innovative classroom teaching strategies? We will deal with this question by referring to three issues: First, the nature of information processing theory; second, the focus of contemporary research; and, third, the context in which research has been undertaken. We will deal with each of these in turn.

Are Theories Too Theoretical?

A theory is a convention for keeping information in order. It is a device for stating the relationships between one event or fact and another, and for drawing together relevant assumptions that are systematically related to one another. In our present discussion, these assumptions relate to human behavior and learning. In essence, theory provides the structure that links our observation with beliefs or hypotheses about the nature of human behavior.

What is a good theory? A good theory has several characteristics. First, it is succinct; it describes behavior in the most efficient way. Second, it is explicit; it has precision by defining constructs in an understandable way that allows for checking their application in the real world. Third, it is comprehensive; it has an all-purpose utility and at least attempts to explain all. Finally, a theory must be capable of generating research; it must be testable or capable of being validated.

The study of information processing, from the early work on memory to the more recent studies of metacognition, has led to the development of models that represent the process of thinking. In Chapters 2 and 3, we described models that attempted to explain how complex cognition occurs (Figures 2.3 and 3.1). These models were derived from research to reflect systems of ideas or principles that explain facts or phenomena. In other words, they represent theories.

These theories of memory and complex human cognition and those of others, such as Sternberg's componential theory of intelligence (Sternberg, 1981), are far from complete. They may account for certain phenomena but efforts to train cognitive skills using memory models have not provided satisfactory results. Other approaches, such as the Information-Integration Model, likewise, have not shown sufficient application to typical classroom learning situations to substantiate teachers' commitment to the model in its present form. Moreover, Sternberg's model of intelligence remains at the conceptual level only, not having been tested empirically at the time of writing.

Given the mystery and complexity that is often associated with theory construction, it is perhaps again not surprising that little intervention research has been based on general information processing theories (Brickner, 1982). As researchers have not attempted to demystify theory and research, it is perhaps not surprising that educational innovation has remained firmly rooted in Piagetian and neo-Piagetian principles of development.

The question remains: Why have the theories been impractical? There appear to be two reasons. First, the research foci and goals have been narrowly defined, and second, data have been collected in laboratory environments that do not reflect real-life learning or problem solving situations. We will deal with each of these considerations in turn.

The Narrow Focus of Research

Perusal of the journals dealing with human cognition and special education will show that much of the information processing research undertaken over the past two decades has been fairly narrow in its focus, and largely atheoretical in nature. What do we mean by this?

Early investigations (and indeed, some contemporary studies) have focused upon specific problem areas. Their objectives have been the exploration, definition, and refinement of concepts and their relationship to performance on selected tasks. Good examples of this orientation can be found in work on visual perception and discrimination and the research dealing with the characteristics of memory (see Dempster, 1981). In a sense, such narrowly defined research may have provided insights into perplexing conceptual problems, but it is difficult to identify practical applications.

Of course, all contributions to the literature have not been "pure" or theoretical in character. This has been obvious from the major contributors of several teams working in the area of strategic behavior and generalization. Notable among these have been the exemplary efforts of teams headed by Belmont, Borkowski, Brown, Das, and Pressley. They have championed the cause of information processing training for students with learning and intellectual disabilities, and in more recent times, such efforts have shown the fruits of diversification and cross-pollination of ideas (see for example, Borkowski, Carr, Rellinger, & Pressley, in press).

Reconciling Laboratory Research

The literature reported in the previous chapter on strategy training provides many examples of studies undertaken in laboratory settings far removed from the classroom. While many of these investigations have demonstrated the influence of certain training approaches and techniques, they are inconsistent with common educational practice. As a consequence, we are concerned about the relevance of procedures that have been developed in controlled learning environments when application to quite different settings is required.

In the applied behavior analysis literature, the value of withdrawing children for intervention was questioned as far back as the mid-1960s. Such research neglects factors that aid integration of learning such as the regular, though perhaps unscheduled review and reinforcement of skills. Experience, trial-and-error learning, and feedback play major roles in classroom learning. Indeed, some writers have noted the importance of these mechanisms. Kurtz and Borkowski (1984), for example, suggested that reliable changes in information processing competence require multiple exposures to, and experience with strategies before they become readily accessible to the user. This implies the need for learners to automate the use of strategies and other memory aids over an extended period. The opportunity for such a review of skills is not provided during typical cognitive interventions, regardless of the recognition of the important differences between the laboratory and the classroom (E. C. Butterfield, personal communication, November 6, 1987).

In summary, laboratory studies are ideal for examining the relationship between variables, or for compiling and validating the rudiments of an intervention program. They have provided a window on the intellectual abilities and information processing competencies of children, adolescents, and adults with learning and intellectual disabilities. Moreover, such studies have led to the identification of information processing variables that contribute to successful performance on various academic and intellectual tasks.

However, we have become concerned with the continued study of information processing variables in the laboratory when there is no guarantee that the findings or the conclusions drawn from the studies are valid in terms of their application to the classroom. In other words, researchers may be traveling up the wrong path. The methodological problems faced when conducting classroom research are immense, but this must not act as a deterrent, but rather a challenge to the research teams working in the area of cognitive educational psychology. Difficulties also have to be faced in conducting cognitive research within the classroom, and we turn now to consider some of these.

Process Training in Large Groups

Conduct of cognitive training in classrooms has been addressed by relatively few cognitive researchers. Most, if not all of the studies in this area have used students attending regular mainstream classes, presumably excluding students with learning or intellectual disabilities. A review of the literature suggests that educational researchers have not come to terms fully with the idea of adapting the procedures of intensive one-to-one interventions to whole classrooms, despite of the need to do so (see Bloom, 1984).

In developing interventions appropriate for the classroom, it is difficult to satisfy all conditions demanded by rigorous experimental methodology. Vast individual differences are found in the classroom and it is difficult, if not impossible to choose or assign children randomly to specific groups. Moreover, teachers implementing innovative programs are often committed to the achievement of performance changes in their pupils, and typically they will know to which experimental group the children belong, perhaps leading to a systematic bias in the data. Finally, there is a real concern of producing changes that result from simply teaching to the test, especially when they are inappropriate. This was a major concern in the 1960s and early 1970s with the Illinois Test of Psycholinguistic Abilities (ITPA) and the Frostig programs. It has been raised recently in criticisms of Feuerstein's Instrumental Enrichment (Reynolds, 1986).

Several matters have been raised that might limit strategy training in the regular classroom. These include:

1. Unreasonable demands on students to learn and use strategies during lessons when the focus is upon curriculum content;

2. The diverse student proficiencies represented in any class which would limit the teacher's ability to provide individual prompts and assistance when necessary;

3. The likelihood that students would drop behind in class work if they experienced difficulty changing from their preferred strategy to one provided by the teacher;

4. The time allotted for a particular lesson and the amount of information being presented that may be insufficient for additional strategy training; and,

5. The need to allocate attention to basic processing requirements (such as the identification of task demands,

and maintaining attention and motivation) which would mitigate against strategy training presented in a laboratory form.

There are several indications that these five limitations can be overcome readily by flexible teachers and innovative researchers. In their review of classroom studies, Peterson and Swing (1983) suggested that the most practical and cost-effective way to introduce cognitive strategies into the classroom was via the teacher. However, they reported that class teachers have infrequently been given training on how to introduce strategies. As a result, in most reports strategy training is conducted by the experimenter or a member of the research team rather than the class teacher.

Evidence presented by Peterson and Swing showed that teachers who were trained in the intervention procedures were as effective as strangers in the classroom in implementing strategy training especially through the use of flexible teaching practices. Moreover, the demands of learning new processing skills during the early phases of strategy training can be reduced, and gradually increased as students learn how and when to apply their newly acquired skills. In other words, pacing instruction can maximize student performance.

Is there anything to be gained from the study of research on strategic behavior undertaken in regular classrooms and similar training in special education contexts? The answer is likely to be in the affirmative, but there are some major differences in the nature and characteristics of instruction in the two settings. We will consider these differences below.

Transferring Procedures to Special Education Classrooms

Translating tasks and procedures from one environment to another when there are marked differences creates practical and methodological problems. While there are many similarities between regular and special classrooms, there are notable differences, especially in terms of classroom dynamics. These dynamics vary as a function of the instructional approach adopted by the special education teacher, the curriculum content, the rate at which learning takes place, specific characteristics of the children attending the class, and the somewhat different approach by teachers toward classroom behavior of children with learning and intellectual disabilities.

Specifically, we might ask: Do children in special education settings respond to academic and non-academic situations in the same way as children attending regular classes? Several studies have examined this issue and the results of these investigations suggest that there are both behavioral and performance differences between students.

The relationship between classroom behavior and academic achievement has been examined in classes for children with an educational handicap (sometimes called slow learners) and for children having a mild intellectual disability. In one study, Forness, Silverstein, and Guthrie (1979) used a time sampling technique to collect data related to several categories of behavior. These included: positive verbal behavior (task-oriented verbal responses or gestures such as the student asks or answers a question or raises a hand); attending behavior (eye contact with teacher, task material, or a peer who is reciting); non-attending behavior (no eye contact with teacher, materials or peers); and disruptive behavior (behavior incompatible with on-task behavior, such as talking when not permitted, speaking out of turn, throwing objects or aggressive activity). They found that teachers responded more frequently to low-achieving children, and to the younger and more disabled children. The results did not show a strong relationship between behavioral and academic measures, which was in contrast to earlier findings for nondisabled children in regular classes.

Distractability has also been a distinguishing characteristic of students with learning and intellectual disabilities. Disabled and nondisabled students have been observed in classroom settings when they have been working individually on academic tasks (such as language arts or mathematics). Under such conditions, children were not to be out of seat or engaged in conversations with other children. Krupski (1979) found that children with intellectual disabilities spent less time on-task than children in regular classes, more time out of their seats, and more time apparently looking busy but not working. She suggested that children with intellectual disabilities behave differently in academic and nonacademic activities but their behavior was not inflexible as often thought.

In the light of studies such as those discussed above and others dealing with the classroom behavior of regular and special students, teachers may expect to encounter some difficulties in implementing strategy training as part of their regular teaching program. On the other hand, special educators may be in an advantageous position when it comes to developing and refining their teaching strategies. They often have considerably greater flexibility than their colleagues in regular classes in preparing innovative teaching materials, re-organizing their teaching program, and changing the focus of instruction to meet the specific needs of their students.

In summary, we have drawn attention to several dilemmas which have been confronted by cognitive researchers concerned with the development and refinement of teaching strategies for students with learning and intellectual disabilities. Although the deliberations and research have led to numerous theoretical and practical dead ends, they also have provided several potential leads that may result in practical teaching innovations.

From the classroom teacher's point of view, these positive indicators have been likely hidden within a body of scientific documents that has been accessible only to those with specialized knowledge. In the following chapters, it is our intention to consolidate this literature into a framework which will have clear implications for classroom practice.

5

A Conceptual Foundation for Instruction

In the absence of curricula or curriculum documents that specify a particular instructional approach, special educators may be left to their own devices to develop methods that, through use, will pass the "test of time". Fortunately, most school programs for students who have a learning or intellectual disability have been developed on sound pedagogical principles rather than on the notorious test-of-time. They have depended upon accurate task analyses and the systematic presentation of content. However, there is a growing sense of awareness that there is more to offer the teacher than simply a sequence of learning events.

Our review of information processing instruction (in Chapters 3 and 4) was designed to provide a cognitive foundation for instruction using contemporary theory and research (see for example, Brown & Campione, 1982; Derry & Murphy, 1986; Sternberg, 1983). It is our general goal in this chapter to provide a conceptual framework from which meaningful and useful teaching strategies may be derived.

There are four sections in this chapter. First, we overview the area of problem solving. We deal with the nature of problem solving and how problem solving skills may be developed. In the second section, we discuss the nature of planning and the relationship between planning and problem solving. In the third section, we examine several matters that would appear to facilitate the integration of problem solving procedures into classroom teaching practice.

In the final section, we consider how teachers can use their time in the most effective way while dealing with children who have diverse abilities and skills. Student-mediated learning systems, such as peer tutoring have become incorporated in instructional procedures within the cognitive literature. These are rapidly expanding research areas, and the evidence for their success in generating independent learning skills is sufficient to justify their general use in classroom-based teaching programs.

DEALING WITH PROBLEMS

Throughout our lives we are constantly confronted by problems. We may need to buy a Christmas gift for an aging uncle who "has everything", decide on a dinner party menu, complete a cryptic crossword puzzle, or find the time and a quiet place to read the Sunday paper. Each of these situations represents a problem that will require both a plan, and an action to change the existing undesirable state into the ideal (McDermott, 1978). As living creatures, we are continually required to solve problems. Acquiring knowledge, satisfying curiosity, and trying to understand the unknown are also problems (Bransford, Sherwood, Vye, & Rieser, 1986; Maslow, 1954).

For the learner and the teacher alike, the primary mission of education is the development of students' problem solving skills which will generalize across curriculum tasks and learning situations. This objective applies equally well to preschool and kindergarten children who are grappling with the manipulation of play-dough, to the senior graduate student who may be studying quantum physics, and to the student with a learning disability who may be mastering consonant blends.

Educational psychologists have examined various factors that seem to be necessary prerequisites for successful problem solving by young children. These have included:

* the isolation of relevant variables (Siegler, 1976);
* the importance of experience (Cantor & Spiker, 1978; Smith & Dutton, 1979; Spiker & Cantor, 1979);
* the accurate interpretation of task demands (Boehm, 1967; Sternberg, 1980); and,
* the correct identification of goals (Borys et al., 1982; Spitz et al., 1985).

They have also studied difficulties experienced by developmentally young and learning disabled students in problem solving activities. These include:

* insufficient motivation or attention;
* inability to disregard irrelevant information presented in the problem (Englert, Culatta, & Horn, 1987);
* inability to comprehend the requirements of the problem;
* the use of random, trial-and-error methods rather than planned approaches (Harth, Johns, Cloud, & Campbell, 1981);
* inadequate organization and place-keeping operations;
* lack of problem solving strategies;
* the use of low-level strategies (Borys et al., 1982; Byrnes and Spitz, 1977; Spitz, Webster, & Borys, 1982);
* difficulty in retaining information about the problem;
* inability to shift attention to relevant problem details;
* lack of feedback concerning problem solving success; and,
* frustration leading to perseveration and inefficient use of strategies (Parrill-Burnstein, 1978).

It appears that students with learning and intellectual disabilities are likely to be thwarted at nearly every stage of problem solving. When we find such a list of potential blockages, it is clear to see that the narrowly defined research on strategy training is completely inadequate to deal with classroom learning. It seems appropriate, then, to focus upon the nature of problem solving and appropriate teaching strategies.

THE NATURE OF PROBLEM SOLVING

The successful and efficient resolution of problems, from the most basic to the most complex, requires the use of essentially the same information processing skills regardless of whether the problems are social, political, or arithmetic (Simon, 1978). Each of these activities requires an interplay between a knowledge base, the organization of incoming information, the use of information processing strategies, and the enactment of appropriate goal-oriented activities (Anderson, Greeno, Kline, & Neves, 1981).

For most of us, effective problem solving behavior is generated from an informal, long-term learning process that results in the establishment of a large, easily accessible and highly integrated knowledge base. As we have indicated earlier, the knowledge base includes discrete information and strategies and both general and specific plans built up over many hours and even years of practice during which patterns of integrated strategies are developed (Chase & Chi, 1980). It is the quality of our knowledge base that determines our level of performance, that is, our expertise.

Well-structured and ill-structured problems

Problems confronted can be termed well-structured or ill-structured (Simon, 1973). Problems that are *well-structured* are clearly presented and contain all the information and strategies necessary to guarantee a correct solution. For instance, the area of a triangle is represented by the formula: Area = 1/2 bh. Knowing the values of the various elements (b = length of the base of the triangle, h = height of the triangle) leads directly to the solution. Instruction in academic areas, such as mathematics and the physical sciences tends to contain well-structured problems. That is, there is a specific knowledge base to be acquired and various formulae or well-documented practices to be followed.

Conversely, *ill-structured* problems are those in which information is not totally available. There may be no clear strategy, or there may be no single answer that can be shown to be clearly correct. Furthermore, we may not be certain about the adequacy of our knowledge base for the task at hand. Many of the real-life problems we confront in the course of our daily activities are ill-structured. For instance, what is the best car to buy? Which political party will best represent our views? Issues within the social sciences involve the comprehension and consideration of social, moral, and political issues. Problems in these fields, by their nature, are ill-structured.

New and novel problems are generally ill-structured. Determining the solution may be a tedious process involving persistence, frequent review of the propositions and available knowledge, and a search for relevant rules and information. With experience and practice, the features of the problem become apparent, as does the the manner of dealing with it using existing strategies and plans. The problem then becomes well-structured with definable procedures, practices and available algorithms. Teachers might well recall their first experience teaching a concept in reading or arithmetic. How to teach the concept may have been an ill-structured problem at the outset of the teaching career. With more experience (knowledge) and practice, established patterns and strategies have simplified the task and hence, a lesson may then become a well-structured problem.

For students who experience few learning difficulties, making the transition from well-structured to ill-structured problems does not constitute a major transition. They learn quickly to generalize across tasks and across curriculum areas. General problem solving procedures become established and applied. In contrast, students with learning and intellectual disabilities confront a different situation. For many of these students, even academic tasks that appear simple for regular students may have the characteristics of ill-structured problems. For these individuals, education traditionally involves the presentation of well-structured problems and procedures to ensure that the basic skills required across the range of tasks can be established and become automatic.

The heuristic (discovery) approach to idea seeking may be most appropriate for ill-structured problems. Such methods might include looking for analogies and other procedures that demand flexibility and creativity (Fredericksen, 1984). Providing practice together with clear and precise feedback will aid students' discrimination of successful and unsuccessful procedures and help to establish a substantive knowledge base that can be organized effectively for retrieval. Furthermore, teachers must not overlook the need for students to learn how to monitor and assess problem solving behavior.

Problems with Knowledge and Organization

In Chapter 2, we referred to the interdependency of knowledge, motivation and organization. The practical application of the Venn diagram (Figure 2.2) to problem solving can be exemplified in the puzzle in Figure 5.1 below (it is similar to one given by Fixx, 1979).

If you don't know who the various people are in the grid or in the options, your chances of solving the puzzle are considerably reduced (but not necessarily to zero). You become a novice learner in this problem situation, and for you, the problem is ill-structured. Your understanding of the role played by a suitable knowledge-base will be obvious if you have ever sat for an examination without adequate preparation, or if you've played Scrabble or Trivial Pursuit with "experts".

Figure 5.1: An Example of a Problem Requiring a Specialized and Organized Knowledge Base

Fill in the blank space by selecting either *Option 1, Option 2, Option 3 or Option 4* below so that the lettered spaces in the grid correctly correspond to the names given beside the letters (A-D) in the chosen option.

Richard Dreyfuss	Ingrid Bergman	Ingmar Bergman	A	Igor Stravinsky
Sarah Miles	B	Jackson Pollock	Charles Ives	Anthony Hopkins
Luis Bunuel	Pablo Picasso	Sergei Prokofiev	C	D

Option 1: A - Paul Klee; B - Joan Miro; C - Hayley Mills; D - Rudolph Nureyev
Option 2: A - Georges Braque; B- Federico Fellini; C - Robert Redford; D - Helen Hayes
Option 3: A - Jon Voigt; B - Marcel Pagnol; C - Leontyne Price; D - Richard Tucker
Option 4: A - Aaron Copland; B - Paul Cezanne; C - Marilyn Monroe; D - George Burns

Comparing the performance of experts and novices in a variety of tasks has demonstrated the importance of knowledge. It is not simply the presence or absence of a knowledge-base that matters, but rather the nature of the information, and how the base is organized. For instance, you may sense that you know who the people listed in Figure 5.1 are. That is, you may have heard others talk of them, or you may have read the names somewhere (for

94

instance, Leontyne Price). However, if the information is not organized in any useful way (for instance, what career Price followed), you might as well not have any knowledge at all. Studies in area such as engineering, computer programming, physics, medical diagnosis and mathematics have shown that problem solving depends heavily upon the organization or the knowledge available to individuals (Bransford et al., 1986).

Cognitive Mechanisms Involved in Problem Solving

How does problem solving occur? It almost goes without saying that problem solving involves the operation of the various representational and executive mechanisms to which we referred in Chapter 3. Gagné (1980) provided a description of the cognitive activities that appear to be involved in problem solving. These included intellectual skills, verbal knowledge, and cognitive strategies. It is important to identify the role of each of these factors if teaching procedures are to be based upon problem solving.

Intellectual skills

Intellectual skills are those capabilities that develop as a result of cognitive growth. In Piagetian terms, this growth leads to the transition from pre-operational thought, to concrete operations, to abstract operations. It is the ability of the individual to generalize basic skills such as number concepts, and to understand and use rules when confronted by novel problems, that demonstrates the importance of intellectual skills in problem solving.

Intellectual skills are assumed if we can solve problems. For instance, if the answer to the puzzle in Figure 5.1 can be obtained without much thought, then we assume that the necessary conceptual knowledge is available to solve reasoning tasks of that type. This conceptual knowledge enables us to perform mental operations that make direct and specific reference to aspects of the environment, for example, combining elements to form a "whole" such as in a jigsaw puzzle, or adding numbers together to get a solution.

95

Verbal knowledge

This second capability refers to the meaningful organization of general and specific knowledge. This is called *declarative knowledge*. In its simple form, declarative knowledge involves the naming of objects or events; in its complex form, it involves the organization of large bodies of information. As our knowledge base expands and as we gain the competence to talk about what we know, the more successful should be our problem solving confidence.

Cognitive strategies

Humans have capabilities that enable them to exercise control over learning and thinking. As we have described earlier, cognitive strategies modify attention, perception, the input and storage of information, and the retrieval of knowledge from memory. In the context of problem solving, strategies are tools that enable us to select and operate upon intellectual skills.

In summary, to solve a specific problem, several proficiencies are required. Learners need skills that enable them to comprehend symbol systems and rules governing the relationship between objects and events. They need to demonstrate their knowledge of symbols and rules by expressing them, and they need competence in manipulating and integrating information - being received, or already available - that is relevant to the problem. Problem solving is, therefore, the embodiment of cognitive theory. How then, are problems actually solved?

How Problems Are Represented

When a problem is confronted, we need to know what it is about. Conceptually, we form a picture in our minds about the nature of the task. This is called *problem representation* and it refers to the way in which we take, and develop the picture. There are two dimensions to problem representation. First, we need to know what facts are presented and how they relate to one another within the problem. This is called the task environment. In Figure 5.1, the task environment is represented by the names, information about the people, and the structure of the matrix which forms the problem. Second, we must know where to look in our knowledge base to find information about the task. This is called the problem space. Even

96

for very simple tasks, the problem space we explore is very large. More importantly, the way we search the problem space leads us to seek solutions that are nonrandom, that is, we move in more, rather than less promising directions (Simon & Newell, 1971). Problems that are poorly presented or ill-structured may be very difficult, if not impossible to solve (for example, in Figure 5.1, replace Picasso with Bugs Bunny).

Problem solving is concerned with finding patterns in the information presented to us. *Pattern recognition* is one feature that distinguishes experts from novices. Experts recognize patterns more quickly than novices because they look at the whole, rather than at individual pieces of information. Seeing "typical" patterns in a problem will reduce solution time. This is how chess experts can compete against many novices at the same time, and how experienced physicians can diagnose diseases quickly by observing the pattern of symptoms (syndrome).

Successful problem solvers are deliberate. They have a repertoire of problem solving procedures available for use that enables them to establish goals, and to monitor and evaluate progress by comparing the present status of the solution with the goal. Thus, problem solving is not a random activity but involves the use of the totality of our information processing talents. As a systematic process, there are several stages that can be identified.

The Stages of Problem Solving

Successful problem solving is a systematic procedure. It involves the examination of all information and the methods available to help us solve a problem. The process of problem solving can be divided into three phases which are listed in Table 5.1.

Whether the goal of problem solving is the solution of a puzzle or learning how to do mathematical calculations, the ideal procedure would follow the same sequence of events. For instance, people who are interested in cryptic crossword puzzles begin problem solving with the declarative phase, then move to the knowledge collection, and finally streamline their methods through procedural learning. Some crossword fanatics can solve the most difficult puzzle before the novice has deciphered the first clue.

Table 5.1: Three Phases of Problem Solving

---

1. *Declaration.* The person receives and interprets the instructions, and generates a procedure to deal with the problem. Knowledge about novel tasks always begins in declarative form. If the problem type is known, this stage may proceed quickly.

2. *Knowledge collection.* The learner generates procedures (activities or productions) for a given task. Efficiency is achieved by building procedures to perform specific tasks (such as reason-giving in geometry). For instance, activity sequences can be abbreviated into a single sequence to speed up the problem solving process. In addition, productions that no longer require the retrieval of domain-specific information are treated as procedures containing all essential facts and strategies. In other words, this phase converts knowledge into a set of procedures that require no interpretation.

3. *Procedural learning.* Procedural learning occurs after a skill has been compiled. For example, a person can improve the problem solving method being employed as a result of a search of different paths that may lead to a solution. Experts are more judicious in their choice of paths and may alter their search methods as a result of learning achieved during problem solving.

   Three mechanisms facilitate the search activity. *Generalization* involves the comparison of rules and the extraction of elements which may apply to a range of tasks and problems. Thus, it involves additional learning over and above the development of the initial rules. *Discrimination* limits the application of rules only to situations in which they apply. A testing operation occurs to check whether the path is suitable for a current problem. *Strengthening* reinforces successful or efficient rules and weakens the less-efficient or troublesome rules.

Similarly, the child learning the process of long division learns about the task (the declarative phase) from the teacher, then the procedures (knowledge collection), and finally learns how and when to apply the operations efficiently (procedural learning).

Teaching Problem Solving Skills

There are two matters to be considered here; what to teach, and how to teach (Burns & Lash, 1986). On the surface, the process appears to be quite simple. Teaching problem solving focuses upon how to derive maximum information from the problem as presented, how to formulate a suitable strategy for its solution, enact the strategy, and monitor performance until the goal is achieved. However, this can be said much more easily than it can be achieved. Let us examine the *what* and *how* components of problem solving.

What problem solving skills to teach

A synthesis of the problem solving literature provides a list of skills necessary to enhance the problem solving abilities of children and adults. There has been some debate about whether there is a single set (or small number) of problem solving elements that can be applied to a large number of tasks, or whether problem solving simply means having very specific knowledge that is relevant to a particular problem. We would tend toward the first option and have summarized the general competencies that appear to be involved in the problem solving process and which need to be taught (Table 5.2).

It is by no means clear to what extent it is necessary to teach each aspect of problem solving listed in Table 5.2. In some cases, students can be given explicit instruction on what must be done to solve a particular task, while in other cases, general directions may be all that is required to initiate the process. Doyle (1983), for instance, distinguished between direct and indirect instruction for problem solving. The former provides systematic and explicit problem solving directions with attention being given to the sequence of events and the development of cognitive skills. Direct instruction seems to be more suitable for novice learners and students with intellectual disabilities.

Indirect instruction involves the teaching of higher level cognitive processes with students being left to discover appropriate problem solving procedures and their application to other tasks. Doyle suggested that indirect instruction appears more appropriate for older students who have established basic skills and suitable knowledge bases.

Table 5.2: Problem Solving Competencies: What to Teach

---

* Teach cognitive processes (strategies and executive mechanisms underlying successful performance in any specific task)
* Teach how to deal with the structure of problems (for example, using appropriate strategies or plans to deal with ambiguities in the instructions)
* Teach the recognition of patterns within the problem (looking for relationships and rules based upon experience and practice)
* Teach problem solving procedures (systematically applying steps to search, scan, organize, set goals, plan, and monitor)
* Teach the knowledge base (forming the information networks required to complete the task)
* Teach development of knowledge structures (how information is organized to ensure that success generalizes to other situations)
* Provide practice with feedback (reinforcing performance and the development of insight)
* Use models of instruction (using approaches that systematically address problems)

How to teach problem solving skills

There have been several proposals relating to how problem solving skills should be developed. Most researchers have concentrated on detailing procedures which relate to a limited range of well-defined problems. For example, Derry, Hawkes, and Tsai (1987) outlined a set of procedures for remediating arithmetic skills using a problem solving orientation which included many of the theoretical elements outlined above. However, concern with generalizable problem solving procedures has led to approaches that may be applied to a range of cognitive activities.

In Fredericksen's (1984) review of cognitive theory and problem solving, he listed details of how a general class of problems might be addressed. These included several points that prompt the learner to structure the problem solving activity, including the following:

1. Get the complete picture without being concerned about the small details;
2. Withhold judgment until all relevant information has been gathered;
3. Simplify the problem using words, diagrams, symbols or equations;
4. Try changing the way the problem is presented;
5. State questions and vary the form of the question;
6. Remain flexible in approach and challenge the assumption being made;
7. Try working backward;
8. Work toward sub-goals that are part solutions;
9. Use analogies and metaphors; and,
10. Verbalize the problem.

A simple problem solving sequence was suggested by Bransford et al. (1986) in the form of an easily learned mnemonic. IDEAL is the mnemonic for **I**dentify, **D**efine, **E**xplore, **A**ct, **L**ook.

Identification suggests that the first stage of problem solving is the recognition that a problem exists. Although this may appear trite, novices and low ability learners are less likely than others to recognize that a problem exists. For instance, novice chess players may not recognize that they are one move away from being in "checkmate". Students with a reading disability may not recognize that a passage of text contains incomplete or inconsistent information or that irrelevant information has been included. As a consequence, low ability students fail to deal with the inconsistency and it becomes a blockage to task solution (Englert et al., 1987).

Once there is a recognition that a problem exists, students must have the ability to analyze what the problem is, that is, to define the source of the problem. Some ineffective problem solvers do not take the time necessary to consider the root of the problem and as a consequence, they are unable to identify a suitable strategy.

Exploration refers to the student's collection of information about the problem and its sources. This is the strategy selection phase of problem solving when various options might be considered depending upon the type and nature of the task.

Once the problem has been identified, defined and considered, the student uses the resources available to maintain a watch on the success of the strategy. This monitoring procedure is used by successful problem solvers to amend their activity when they encounter stumbling blocks. In contrast, intellectually disabled students tend not to adapt their activity to suit the new demands of the task. For instance, Byrnes and Spitz (1977) reported that low ability students working on the Tower of Hanoi puzzle tended to repeat their errors when unable to complete the problem. They reported that the youngest children in their study committed many rule violations following wrong initial moves. Instead of profiting from their mistakes, and in spite of the need to obey the rules to succeed, they repeatedly made errors and rule violations. Similar inflexibility has been noted in the strategic and problem solving behavior of learning disabled children (Gerber, 1983).

Our discussion of the nature and character of problem solving has introduced a practical component to cognitive theory, one for which the potential exists for the establishment of close links with classroom practice. Another important and related concept is that of planning.

PLANNING AND PROBLEM SOLVING

Planning and problem solving are considered generally to be two closely related notions. However, there are significant differences at both conceptual and theoretical levels. Planning can be conceived as a neurological activity that is virtually continuous.

Planning differs from problem solving in several ways. Planning involves mental processes that integrate information passing between various areas of the brain; it relates specifically to future events; and, it is activity or performance oriented. In contrast, problem solving may take many forms; may relate to themes that have nothing to do with future action; and, may focus on issues other than the manner of performance, for instance, the causes or results of hypothetical events. Problem solving is a consequence of planning when an automatic response (or reflex) is not sufficient.

Planning and problem solving are of importance within the classroom context because of the need to organize both the content and the methods used in teaching and in learning. To teach effectively, an instructor must present information in a systematic and organized fashion. To learn, the student must deal with the incoming information in an organized and systematic way. Problem solving provides a method for presenting and accepting information, but we are also concerned with the use of methods that are consistent with the way in which information is processed within the brain. In this section, we examine evidence of human goal-oriented activity recorded in medical and neuropsychology literature, and then how cognitive psychologists have operationalized the planning process.

Medical Observations of Planning

The study of the neurophysiological sciences over the past 100 years has provided an understanding of information processing activities that take place within the brain. Of course, there is much that is still unknown. We have an incomplete understanding of the physiology of memory, and only the most basic comprehension of the manner in which the brain is able to integrate and retrieve knowledge. However, the neuropsychological literature provides an explanation of coding and planning functions, and of their interdependence in both simple and complex thought (see for example, Luria, 1973, 1980).

Planning is not a new concept in the medical or psychological literature. Possibly the first "scientific" report of planning arose from a description of an accident that occurred in Cavendish, Vermont (USA) in September, 1848.

Phineas Gage, the foreman of a construction gang undertaking work on the Rutland and Burlington Railroad, was preparing a gunpowder charge in a hole drilled in a huge rock in preparation for blasting. Gage was sitting on a rock shelf above the hole compressing the gunpowder slightly with a tamping iron before pouring in sand. His attention was drawn from the charge to the activity of his men who were loading rock from a pit onto a platform car a few meters behind him. As he turned his head away from his task, the tamping iron sparked on the rock. The powder exploded, driving the one-meter long, six kilogram iron through Gage's head and high into the air. It fell to the ground some distance away smeared with blood and brain.

103

The rod had entered through Gage's cheekbone just under the left eye and made its exit through the top of the skull almost along a central line. In the words of the physician who attended him:

> I am informed that the patient was thrown upon his back, and gave a few convulsive motions of the extremities, but spoke in a few minutes. His men ... took him in their arms and carried him to the road, only a few rods distant, and sat him into an ox cart, in which he rode, sitting erect, full three quarters of a mile, to the hotel.

(Harlow, 1848, pp. 389-390)

Gage climbed a long flight of stairs and waited for more than an hour before Harlow returned to town. Two physicians dressed the wound and he was treated using the most contemporary of remedies: calomel, rhubarb, and castor oil.

Remarkably, Gage survived and lived for another twelve and half years. Further events in his life were recounted some 20 years after the accident, again by Harlow (1868) who reported that both cognitive and personality changes had overcome Gage. Before the accident, Gage had been an even-tempered and patient man with a well-balanced mind; he was respected by those who knew him as a shrewd business man. He was energetic and persistent in executing all his duties. After the accident, he had became quarrelsome and aggressive. He made many plans but, no sooner arranged, they were abandoned. Given the substantial damage to both left and right frontal lobes of Gage's brain, changes in cognition and emotion might have been anticipated.

Since Harlow's accounts, there have been many examinations of frontal lobe trauma, notably following the two world wars. Generally, the conclusions have shown that frontal lobe trauma affects volition and affect (for a discussion of affective and intellectual brain function, see LeDoux, 1984). Studies typically have reported a loss of initiative and lack of capacity for planned administration, the destruction of the cognitive capacity to synthesize intellectual operations, and the loss of the patients' ability to project into the future. The many accounts of frontal lobe surgery have provided additional evidence of changes to planning capabilities following medical intervention (see for example, Klebanoff, 1945; Milner, 1964; Stuss & Benson, 1984).

Planning as a Psychological Construct

In the realm of psychology, planning has appeared in various domains. Planning generally has not referred to neurological activity specifically, but to the development of a scheme of action, or to the scheme itself (that is, a plan). Tests of foresight and planning ability were included in the US Military Printed Classification Tests which were used in the 1940s as screening devices for air crew recruits. The various planning tests involved preparing a series of maneuvers or activities, and to foresee and avoid difficulties that could arise in their execution. Mazes were used in tests of pathway planning and map planning. Wiring circuit problems involved deciding which of several switches in a puzzle closed an electrical circuit, while another task involved planning the shortest route through a town (Berger, Guilford, & Christensen, 1957; Guilford & Lacey, 1947).

Plans and strategies entered the field of information processing following the release of *Plans and The Structure of Behavior* (Miller, Galanter, & Pribram, 1960). The authors provided a description of an organizational system that included Plans (which we would now probably call strategies) and metaplans which were strategies for generating plans. In dealing with new or known situations, the individual draws upon metaplans which are stored in memory and provide the mechanism for generating new plans. While there were a number of criticisms of the Miller et al. approach, the ideas are still quite comprehensible in terms of contemporary views of planning and problem solving (Belmont & Mitchell, 1987).

There have been many other views of the nature of planning and several approaches have attempted to describe the process. Some writers have dealt with planning as a conceptual entity and have described it as an opportunistic activity having five dimensions:

* The first identifies the intended action;
* The second identifies suitable sequences of events or procedures;
* The third deals with observations and data relevant to the planning process;
* The fourth allocates cognitive resources to the plan; and,
* The fifth identifies decisions about the enactment of the plan (Hayes-Roth & Hayes-Roth, 1979).

Others have examined the use of plans in the course of our daily lives. For example, Byrne and his colleagues studied the planful activity of expert adults in several everyday situations such as organizing dinner parties and interior decorating. Byrne analyzed spoken records of subjects "thinking aloud" while they worked through the problem of deciding upon menus and ingredients for specific recipes, or colors and furnishings for a house. He argued that planning involved the search of a complex and structured body of information which consisted of several interrelated parts. In his study of mental cookery, he suggested that cooking procedures were imagined during the preparation of the menus. By mentally executing plans in this way, we construct, test, and refine actions when real-world trials might be inappropriate (Byrne, 1979, 1981).

In quite a different context, Dixon (1987) developed a framework for understanding how people construct mental plans for carrying out written directions. He proposed that directions are used to construct mental plans within a hierarchical structure. The top level of a plan hierarchy is a general, high level description of the action to be performed (for example, "Go to bed!") and the lower levels of the hierarchy specify the component actions in detail ("Turn off the TV, clean your teeth, put on your pyjamas ..." and so on). Each element in the hierarchy may be represented by schema that describes a standard way of carrying out a given step.

Plans are constructed in parallel with other reading processes. As soon as the information needed for the plan becomes available, it is incorporated into the emerging plan. Dixon argued that for efficient planning, information relevant to the top level of the plan hierarchy should be given at the beginning of the directions (for example, at the beginning of a sentence or passage) and that information relevant to the lower levels of planning can be provided as required (as in the example above).

Finally, the motivation and availability of skills necessary for the implementation of planning has taken the study of planning into the realm of personality theory. One interesting facet of this research has been the identification of planning styles to account for the reasons different individuals may have for selecting alternative steps in the planning process.

Planning style refers not to ways in which plans are constructed, but to the significance of the content to the individual. For instance, Kreitler and Kreitler (1986) suggested that some cues may be recognized more readily than others when they have special importance to an individual. For example, people who are disposed toward emotional responses will notice affective cues faster, solve problems containing emotional information faster, and have a richer network or affective associations than others for whom another meaning dimension is preferred.

Problems and Plans

The overlap between planning and problem solving may seem somewhat overwhelming. Both concepts involve cognitive activities that deal with procedures and sequences. However, there are essential differences. Planning relates to the integration of existing knowledge with stimuli that may originate inside or outside of the individual and as such, it is an executive control mechanism. Planning is the activator and facilitator of problem solving. The product of planning may be a "generic" plan if the information is non-specific, or a task-specific plan if it relates only to a particular knowledge base.

For example, many adults have a general plan for car trouble which may have been generated as a result of experience. A typical initial reaction would be to identify the nature of the trouble. If it is solvable, a specific action may be employed to get the car moving again. Another general plan may be to find the first available phone and call for help. These plans are general across time, place, or type of vehicle involved. They will even work when you are controlling an aircraft (Ashman, 1986).

General plans are also used for academic tasks, for instance, in the mental arithmetic problem: $(a+b-c) \times d = ?$ The plan would involve engaging arithmetic skills relating to addition and subtraction, followed by multiplication.

Once a particular situation has been prescribed, problem solving begins. In the first example above, there is no solution until we specify that the vehicle engine stopped while traveling along a straight, flat stretch of road. In the second example, there is no solution (other than, of course, the algebraic solution $da + db - dc$) until we insert values for a, b, c, and d: $(9+14-7) \times 23$.

While the distinction between problem solving and planning may seem to be of academic interest only, recognizing their different roles will lead to the development of more refined structures for classroom practice than currently exist (see Table 5.3). The recognition of the value of general plans, and the application of problem solving methods will provide a flexibility and freedom for teachers and students alike to organize and control their learning and problem solving activities.

While we recognize that there have been many attempts to teach problem solving skills and to develop planful behavior in students with learning and intellectual disabilities, instruction over the last two decades has focused on "pure" procedures and obscure concepts such as creativity. There seems to be a more efficient way to generate independence within the problem solving domain through the integration of two factors. The first component of the instruction equation is the development of a teaching sequence or approach. The second component involves the interpersonal and

Table 5.3: Differences Between Planning and Problem Solving

Planning is:	Problem Solving is:
a brain function mediated by the frontal lobes	a learning system (or heuristic approach)
an executive control mechanism	based upon learned rules and symbol systems
the activator of problem solving behavior	the enactment of cognitive processes
action and performance oriented	content and knowledge oriented
related to future action	related to present events
generated by generic plans	the use of plans for specific purposes
prompted by systematic presentation of information	a procedure that can be taught

environmental factors that facilitate, or restrain the process of learning. We have referred to these several times in this book.

PROMOTING INDEPENDENCE IN LEARNING

One goal of education is the development of students' problem solving skills to the point where they are self-generating and may be engaged automatically when the appropriate conditions exist. This implies not only the obvious and unprompted use of memory strategies, but also the use of control mechanisms that monitor and modify strategic behavior (Borkowski et al., 1987).

To achieve flexibility in the use in problem solving, students with learning and intellectual disabilities must attain a level of competence that enables them to become independent in their goal-oriented behavior. That is, they must be able to analyze the situation and enact the most effective problem solving strategy. We have outlined the various cognitive elements that humans have in their repertoire of information processing strategies and how these are involved in problem solving. How can these abilities best be activated and reinforced in the classroom? To answer this question, we must move partly into the domain of social psychology to consider how the dynamics of the learning environment can assist in the development of intellectual skills.

Self-regulated Learning

Self-regulation refers to flexible problem solving which includes the development, selection, connection, and monitoring of effective strategies to maximize learning. Self-regulation of thoughts and behavior stands out as a long-term goal (or higher level aim) of educators and researchers (Paris & Oka, 1986). In other words, students must be prepared to make their own decisions, express their thoughts and wishes, set and accomplish goals, learn independently, and accept responsibility for errors. Many special education programs, particularly at the junior high school level, do not emphasize independence training. Instead, many teachers reinforce dependency by classroom practices that provide answers, rather than asking questions which demanded exploration or discovery (Schumaker, Deshler, & Ellis, 1986).

109

Numerous studies have shown that students with learning and intellectual disabilities can learn to control their learning behavior and experiences. There is no value in cataloguing studies exhaustively here, however, the following list will indicate that self-regulated learning is well within the capabilities of many students with special needs.

* Self-monitoring has been shown to increase on-task behavior, though only limited gains have been obtained in academic skills (Snider, 1987).

* Independence training has been included within structured curricula such as the *Learning Strategies Curriculum* (Schumaker, Denton, & Deshler, 1984; Lenz, Schumaker, Deshler, & Beals, 1984; Schumaker & Sheldon, 1985).

* Students with learning difficulties have been taught to control their own learning, and are as effective in their learning activities as those who are teacher-controlled (Graham & Freeman, 1985).

* Children with intellectual disabilities have learned to apply self-monitoring strategies independently and have been as effective as other students who have been taught academic skills using traditional didactic formats (Borkowski & Varnhagen, 1984).

* Young children have learned to evaluate their performance on memory tasks and to self-regulate when prompted (Jones, Ridgway & Bremner, 1983).

* Children with a moderate intellectual handicap have been able to set standards and regulate their behavior independently (Litrownik, Cleary, Lecklitner, & Franzini, 1978).

These and other studies have demonstrated that once trained in specific areas, students with learning and intellectual disabilities are able to control their own learning independently of others. This is an important finding that indicates that self-instruction and self-control procedures have an important part to play in classroom instruction. Indeed, such self-regulatory activities can be achieved through one-to-one or small group learning situations, as is evidenced by the literature relating to cooperative teaching and peer tutoring. We deal with these concepts in the next two sub-sections.

Cooperative Teaching and Learning

Teachers in mainstream and special classes are confronted with students who represent a huge range in intellectual abilities, learning potentials, and domain-specific knowledge. Teachers may call for assistance from special services to provide effective instruction across curriculum areas. In some situations, assistance may come from resource teachers, a teaching aide, other teachers in cooperative teaching ventures, or from parents. However, many forget the most readily available resource, namely, students.

The term, cooperative teaching, has been defined in several ways. It refers to the development of classroom practices and attitudes which enhance students' social and group participation skills with the aim of promoting learning in one another (Johnson, Johnson, & Johnson-Houlubec, 1984; Smith, 1987). Brainstorming, feedback, and sharing sessions in large or small groups are among the activities used by teachers employing cooperative teaching approaches. There are also formal procedures such as peer tutoring and reciprocal teaching.

Child-to-child interaction and learning have been studied since the 1970s. Several studies have evaluated children's performances after watching others perform specified tasks. The success of such programs is dependent upon the developmental level of the children. For example, some studies have led to the suggestion that some pre-operational children (in Piagetian terms) can perform tasks requiring concrete operational thought simply by watching others perform them successfully. However, developmentally younger children typically have not been able to explain or transfer the apparent newly acquired skills.

In the area of social learning, peer interactions have been used to mediate problem solving. Complex tasks such as the Tower of Hanoi puzzle and the parlor game, "Mastermind", were used to demonstrate that children could solve problems more efficiently working together in pairs than individually (Butterworth & Light, 1982; Light & Glachan, 1985). The educational application of cooperative problem solving has not escaped the attention of researchers and practitioners who have recognized the value of developing student-to-student interactions as a means of maximizing teachers' efficient use of time during classroom activities. But this is not the only benefit. It is interesting that much of the impetus for peer tutoring has come from the social and intellectual gains

111

reported to accrue to the young tutor, rather than from the intellectual gains of the child who is being taught.

At this point, we overview two common approaches, peer tutoring and reciprocal teaching. The latter was introduced over two decades ago.

Peer Tutoring

Peer tutoring refers to one student acting as a teacher or tutor of a peer. It may involve students of the same or different abilities. There are a number of studies that have dealt with children as teachers. Researchers have reported gains in text-learning following cooperative learning projects. For example, in one study, a dramatic improvement in children's ability to learn text material was reported by Larson et al. (1985). Children in each dyad read information to each other while one listened and attempted to recall and summarize the information. One at a time, the children then corrected errors and facilitated the organization and learning of the material.

Several studies have also examined the effects of using both nondisabled and disabled children to teach handicapped peers. Lancioni (1982), for instance, trained nondisabled 3rd and 4th graders to teach 9 to 13 year old peers with mild intellectual disabilities to solve addition, subtraction, multiplication, and division problems. The tutors (working in pairs with one pupil) used structured problem solving procedures that involved the transfer of numerals into spatial arrangements. The young tutors were highly reliable in conducting the training and in using probes to evaluate the performance of their tutees.

While several studies that have shown improvement following peer tutoring studies using high ability tutors and lower ability pupils, only a small number of studies have examined the effects of peer tutoring with low ability tutors. In one study, two adolescents (one moderately and one severely intellectually disabled) each taught three severely disabled peers to perform a complex packaging and assembly task. The trainers were taught how to demonstrate the desired behavior and how to correct their students' performance if it was incorrect. Following the training, tutors monitored their pupils' performances as they worked independently. In this study, Wacker and Berg (1985) reported that no extra intervention was required by supervisory staff.

The outcomes of peer tutoring programs have not all been successful. For example, Foot, Shute, and Morgan (1987, August) reported a study in which they predicted that tutoring would promote efficiency in using memory principles, though not necessarily memory for specific information. Using children both matched and mis-matched for age, Foot et al. reported that peer interactions had general benefits though there did not appear to be any differences in students' performances in regard to memory for specific information and the application of principles.

Reciprocal Teaching

Reciprocal Teaching has been growing in prominence as a successful method of reading instruction. In pairs or trios, students learn to ask questions about their reading activity and the content of the passage being studied. At the beginning of instruction, the teacher provides a model for students but gradually passes over responsibility for the teaching process as students become competent "instructors" in a peer tutoring environment.

Probably one of the first references to reciprocal teaching came from Manzo (1968). His *ReQuest* reading program encouraged students to formulate questions about the material they were studying. In summary, Manzo's program involved six steps:

1. Preparation of material;
2. Development of readiness for the reading strategy;
3. Development of student questioning behaviors;
4. Development of student predictive behaviors;
5. Silent reading by students; and,
6. Follow-up activities.

The development of this interrogative behavior (reciprocal questioning) encouraged students to adopt an inquiring attitude toward reading, and to improve their independent reading comprehension skills. Manzo claimed that it was important for students' to learn to ask questions and to set their own goal for reading, thereby enhancing the tendencies toward generalizing problem solving skills from one reading context to another.

The early 1980s witnessed the introduction of another reading program, developed at the Center for the Study of Reading at the University of Illinois. Reciprocal Teaching closely resembles

Manzo's *ReQuest* Reading scheme, involving small groups of children (usually in pairs) learning how to ask each other questions that might appear on a test or be posed by a teacher.

Reciprocal teaching has two main conceptual bases, scaffolding, and self-questioning. As mentioned in Chapter 4, scaffolding refers to the provision of a temporary, adjustable support provided by the teacher to assists students to develop and extend their skills in the early phases of instruction. The teacher models the desired behavior, and makes explicit to the children what behavior is required of them as learners. As questioning and other learning skills develop and begin to facilitate learning, the scaffold (teacher support) is gradually removed. This withdrawal of direction enables the gradual transfer of responsibility for the instructional input from the teacher to the students (Rogoff & Gardner, 1984).

Self-questioning derives from three perspectives, namely, metacognitive theory, schema theory, and active processing theory. A student using the metacognition base would generate questions dealing with self-monitoring of strategic behavior (for example, "What am I trying to do right now?"). Students instructed using the schema approach would ask questions related to the relevant, existing knowledge that could enhance understanding of the material being read (for example, "What do I know that will help me understand this material?"). A teacher using the active processing perspective would focus on instructing students to generate higher order questions (for example, "What questions could I ask myself about the information being given here?").

The instruction phase of reciprocal teaching involves several steps (Table 5.4) and is highly interactive. Such an approach provides the context for guided learning and for the giving and receiving of useful feedback between the students.

Reciprocal teaching has been enthusiastically promoted and studied. Advocates have claimed that students improve their ability to generate questions, to clarify and summarize information they have read. As they develop these skills, children move from being passive observers of learning to active teachers, able to lead discussions independently, and in some cases, to become involved in learning experiences as peer tutors. For instance, Brown and Campione (1986) reported that students who had been involved in a reciprocal teaching program have shown reliable improvements on classroom measure of comprehension, and that gains of up to two years were shown on standardized comprehension tests. In addition, there have been changes in generalization activities such as writing summaries, predicting test questions, and detecting text anomalies. In contrast, comparable students who received direct instruction over the same period showed small gains in independent competence which did not persist over time and contexts.

Table 5.4: Stages in Reciprocal Teaching

---

1. Students read a segment of text silently.
2. The teacher summarizes the content and asks a question about the passage, raising issues that may cause difficulties for comprehension and predicts what might happen in a subsequent section of the text.
3. The teacher assigns responsibility to one of the students for summarizing, questioning, predicting, and clarifying aspects of the passage.
4. The next section is read by the teacher and students.
5. The children change roles, and the second child acts as a teacher while the instructor models strategic ways of dealing with various issues that arise.

In spite of its success, reciprocal teaching has not been without criticism. Reciprocal teaching does not necessarily lead to the same gains by all children, and students with a mild intellectual disability appear to benefit less than their non-disabled peers. Similarly, students who are poor decoders may not benefit from reciprocal teaching as their basic processing competence may limit the skills being addressed by the teaching method.

When improved student performance has not been achieved, deficient methodologies such as insufficient training prior to the administration of post-testing, a lack of specificity in regard to the generation of questions, and insufficient processing time available for students to read passages and generate appropriate questions have been noted (Wong, 1986a).

Regardless of these limitations, advocates have suggested that reciprocal teaching may be adapted easily to academic skill areas in addition to reading. Brown and Campione (1986), for instance, indicated that focusing instruction on the development of conceptual understanding of the skill is a more effective and efficient teaching strategy than identifying errors or concentrating on drills. Understanding is more likely to occur when students are required to explain, elaborate, or defend their positions and the burden of explanation may lead students to evaluate, integrate, and elaborate knowledge in new ways.

Summarizing Theoretical Issues

Two main points are made in the review presented in this chapter. First, learning difficulties and intellectual disabilities are not the consequence of one, or a small number of specific information processing deficits. These difficulties range across a variety of cognitive skills and across individuals. Consequently, strategy training programs that focus on one strategy (such as rehearsal) are unlikely to ameliorate that disability.

Second, the goal of training programs must be the development of independent learning skills through the use of content and material that are relevant to both teacher and students. In other words, programs must have ecological validity. Students must perceive that the strategies being taught are of value and that they can be applied across a broad range of tasks.

Finally problem solving and planning are concepts that refer to general information processing procedures. They provide a suitable basis for the development of a teaching program that can accommodate both the diversity of intellectual skills found in special education settings, and satisfy the demand for ecological validity. Both problem solving and planning rely on two essential features: the student must perceive that a problem exists; and, must recognize that there is a need to solve the problem. Both are fundamental to independent information processing activity.

In the next chapter, we continue our discussion of the integration of cognitive theory with educational practice. Attention will focus on the development of a classroom-based intervention for students with mild intellectual disabilities.

6

A Research Foundation for Instruction

Special education is an expensive business. Consider the number of hours spent in training before a teacher qualifies to teach a special class. Think of the hours of instruction devoted to students in special classes and to those who are integrated into regular classes, together with the hours spent by teachers planning lessons and preparing teaching aids. Consider also the consultation sessions between classroom and resource teachers, counselors, school psychologists, administrators and specialist consultants. All things considered, the human, monetary, and physical resources expended in special education are enormous.

With such an investment in special education, it is surprising that few substantive changes have been made to teaching practice over the past three decades. Researchers and practitioners have been engaged continuously in developing and refining intervention procedures, yet the reality is that much of the research and development has been directed toward specific strategies and laboratory settings, rather than toward curricula and classrooms.

In searching for guidelines and direction during program development, it is essential to be mindful of the passing parade of educational innovations that have been prepared, tried, and rejected. Remember the ITPA and the Ayres psychomotor programs? These were two among the many initiatives that were received by teachers with considerable enthusiasm only to be discarded when it became clear that "results could not match expectations". There were many explanations given for the dismissal of these teaching approaches, but the major causes often could be reduced to one of two; either they were inconsistent with sound educational practices, or they were methodologically or theoretically invalid.

117

The development of new educational procedures, such as those linking cognitive theory with curriculum content, must satisfy both practical and methodological demands. This chapter is directed toward consideration of these prerequisites during the formative period of the *Process-Based Instruction*. model. In the first section of this chapter, we consider methodological issues relevant to the development of educational interventions. In the second, we report the early development of *Process-Based Instruction*, together with three studies that provided evidence of the success of a prototype in a resource room setting. In the third, we review the intervention literature that has linked information processing concepts with academic achievement.

DEVELOPING A COGNITIVE INTERVENTION

Researchers and teachers can generate considerable enthusiasm for programs they have conceived, developed and implemented. However, the actual value of any teaching program depends upon many factors, such as the relevance of the program in terms of the context in which it is to operate, the clientele served, and through scrutiny of its impact by empirical examination. For programs that operate within the school, evaluation is judged by the relevance of the content, and by students' improvement on tests and quizzes that relate specifically to the curriculum. In most cases, little additional validation is needed.

Interventions that claim to enhance current school programs or provide innovations must be subject to comparison with traditional programs, but in addition, they also must satisfy the conditions which apply to the discipline in which they originated. In terms of our present discussion, the requirement is validation within the field of cognitive psychology.

Some Methodological Considerations

There are a number of issues which apply to the development of cognitive interventions. From the researcher's point of view, linking program development with theory has been an important consideration (see for example, Garrison & MacMillan, 1987; Kavale, 1987; Torgesen, 1987). If improvement in information processing is desired, then the theory and the practice must focus on what the student can or cannot do. From our point of view, there are few recognized, comprehensive cognitive theories which offer a suitable foundation for classroom instruction. Perhaps the most satisfactory at present is Luria's neurological organization of the brain with its concomitant cognitive processes. This view of human cognition is consistent with contemporary views of information processing and of the relationship between information processing and performance on intellectual tasks. Support for the theoretical constructs is to be found in the psychometric literature (Kaufman, 1984), and the information processing studies of Das et al. (1979) and Ashman (1984). These studies have examined cognition and the development of information processing competence of students with learning or intellectual disabilities and nondisabled students.

From a practical viewpoint, any new intervention must cater for individual differences in both the cognitive and affective domains. This implies first, the consideration and management of cognitive strengths and weaknesses of students. Second, it has become increasingly apparent that motivation and attributions of success and failure are important training considerations (Borkowski et al., in press). Indeed, some researchers have argued that it is necessary to show how learning disabled children's and adolescents' self-efficacy changes as a function of successful intervention and how this affective change is maintained (Wong, 1987). One way of resolving these demands would be through the use of on-going assessment and adaptation of the intervention program consistent with the needs of individual students whether in small groups or in class-size groups.

A major concern of researchers and educators alike is the *transfer* and *durability* of training. As we have indicated earlier in this book, the lack of transfer of newly acquired skills and strategies emphasizes the need for training which is related to real-world situations and events (ecological validity). Isolated training gives students little opportunity to perceive the application of their learning efforts. Durability refers to the replication of intervention results across training contexts. In learning disability studies, the issue is compounded by such factors as failure to use proper control procedures in treatment studies, failure of researchers to report the characteristics of their samples, unknown biases in sample selection, and the lack of awareness of the hetereogeneity of learning difficulties (Torgesen, 1987).

119

Problems of transfer and durability of training highlight the need for longitudinal research which addresses the issues raised above. Often, in the learning disability literature, interventions have focused on a single investigation that compares the treatment group with another group of students who are not educationally delayed. Moreover, many programs have investigated a particular question at a single point in time. While these efforts have produced substantive bodies of information, many such studies have been less than adequate in providing an overview of learning processes in students with learning disabilities (Lyon, 1987; Swanson, 1987a).

Table 6.1 provides a summary of these and other criteria that could be used in the validation of a training program (Sternberg, 1983). This checklist might be considered as a benchmark against which emerging training methodologies can be compared.

Our review of the cognitive psychology literature and of teaching practice has given specific guidance for the development of Process-Based Instruction. The incorporation of theory and practice was attempted initially using a resource model approach. This is discussed in the following section.

EARLY DEVELOPMENT OF PROCESS-BASED INSTRUCTION

In the development stages of Process-Based Instruction, strategic behavior was considered to be the most important feature. The theoretical and practical foundation came from the Luria/Das synthesis of cognition. The Information-Integration Model (Das et al., 1979) provided the initial orientation, both in terms of the interdependency of coding and planning processes, and as a starting point for intervention research (Das & Heemsbergen, 1983; Das et al., 1979; Kaufman & Kaufman, 1983). Various research teams have identified two coding processes using terms such as:

> simultaneous and successive,
> synthetic-appositional and analytic-propositional;
> parallel-multiple and sequential-serial.

> (see Kaufman, 1984)

Table 6.1: Sternberg's Criteria for Intellectual Skills Training

---

1. Training should be based upon a theory of intellectual performance. The theory should relate to information processing, be performance oriented, and experimentally verified outside the training context.
2. The theory of intellectual performance should be socio-culturally relevant to the individuals undertaking training.
3. The program should focus on strategy training (namely, Selective encoding; Selective combinations; Inference; Mapping; Application; Comparison; and, Justification) and training in executive control mechanisms (namely, Problem identification; Process selection; Strategy selection; Representation selection; Allocation of resources; Solution monitoring; Sensitivity to feedback; Translation of feedback into action; and, Implementation of action).
4. The program should be responsive to affective variables including motivation.
5. The program should be sensitive to individual differences.
6. The program should lead to generalization of skills to real-world events.
7. The program should be empirically validated in terms of the components of the program and the program as a whole.
8. Claims of success should be realistic.

The evidence amassed from the research in various cognitive domains provided support for the value of developing coding processes to enhance students' information processing activities (see Ashman & Schroeder, 1986).

The objective in the resource model approach to PBI was to train students to use and generalize simultaneous and sequential coding strategies. The most obvious feature of PBI from its inception was its movement away from models which focused upon the development of one or a small number of specific strategies, toward a model that might be called a generic approach able to be applied uniformly and consistently.

121

The practical foundation came from the problem solving literature (for example, Fredericksen, 1984). We have been mindful that many earlier strategy training interventions using students with intellectual disabilities have demonstrated the value of teacher, learner, and procedural variables (see particularly Borkowski and Cavanaugh, 1979). Together with other reviews and suggestions drawn from strategy training literature, it was possible to compile the following list of important program characteristics:

Teacher-Learner Variables

1. Meaningful analysis of content and tasks for the learner;
2. Active participation of the students;
3. Use of behavior management techniques to maintain motivation and maximize time on-task;
4. Fading of the teacher's input to encourage self-initiated learning;
5. Use of explicit feedback and verbal mediation of behavior.

Procedural Variables

6. Systematic introduction of strategies;
7. Use of multiple training sessions over several days each week for the duration of the program;
8. Emphasis on the value of the strategy being trained;
9. Extensive use of examples for strategy training and generalization; and,
10. Careful analysis and review of each stage of the training procedure to ensure a consistent and systematic intervention.

As will be evident, these ten points do not constitute an instructional sequence. They represent what could be considered to be the essence of *sound teaching practice*. The first five points govern the quality and quantity of interactions between the teacher and students. They relate to the manner in which students are engaged in the problem or learning task to ensure that they are active and able to perceive the relevance of the task. This represents the ideal condition in special education, or indeed, in any instructional setting (see for example, Ryan, Ledger, Short, & Weed, 1982; Wiens, 1983; Fotheringhame, 1986).

Procedural variables refer to *how* information is presented to students rather than *what* is taught. Whereas attention to the teacher-learner variables would assist students' reception of the information, the second five would assist in promoting the transfer of newly acquired skills to related activities. These 10 points were considered to be fundamental characteristics of PBI and they were translated into teacher-learner obligations.

These are not long lists of prescriptions and differ little from those that would exist in a traditional classroom. There are just three points in each.

The teacher is responsible for:

1. developing the students' problem solving skills through guided instruction ;
2. developing cooperation between the students; and,
3. developing an active teaching style (that is, forming and testing hypotheses about how students solve problems).

The student has responsibility to:

1. participate actively in the learning experience;
2. seek clarification when necessary; and,
3. support other students' learning activities when required.

The most important feature of PBI is the commitment by teachers and students alike to be active learners and instructors. For teachers, the challenge is to become learners about their students, that is, they become educational detectives that are not only dedicated to diagnosing students' difficulties, but also to learning how students solve problems.

We developed a PBI prototype to be used within an instructional setting in which one teacher worked with two students. The broad objective of this early phase of validation was to develop and maintain students' strategic behavior. The prototype is outlined below and its application is described in the subsequent section.

123

A Resource Room Instructional Cycle

Training, conducted with pairs of students, was divided into four phases: Task orientation and performance; Instruction; Intervention; and Generalization (Figure 6.1). These phases provided three opportunities for each student in the pair to manipulate the training material during their turn with any task (that is, they worked systematically from Task Orientation to Generalization) while the other student in the pair watched. The role of pupil and observer then changed as a second student worked with the material. Later in the program, as teachers became familiar with the process and the students became accustomed to the goals and the methods, the teaching-learning process was streamlined to ensure that the procedure remained relevant and engaging.

In the following four sub-sections, we discuss the PBI model in the sequence outlined in Figure 6.1. However, we will not dwell upon the procedures as a more extensive description can be found in Ashman (in press) and Conway and Ashman (1987).

Task Orientation and Performance

The teacher's goal in this phase was to introduce the exercise to be undertaken by the students and to ensure that they had the pre-requisite skills and knowledge base necessary to begin the training. Training would be ineffective if a pupil was asked to manipulate materials that were unfamiliar, to encode words or other sequences in which elements were unknown, or to apply rules or principles that were unnecessarily complex.

The first step was to provide an explicit statement of task demands to ensure that the words used, and concepts presented were understood by the pupil. The student then demonstrated comprehension by describing what was required. If confusion was found, the teacher clarified or asked the observer (the second student in the training pair) to help interpret the requirements and objectives.

The teacher then demonstrated and described (talked-through) the required learning behavior as both students watched. Verbalization of the procedure was important to emphasize that learning involved doing something "inside the head" to recall information being presented.

Figure 6.1: A Resource Room Model of Process-Based Instruction

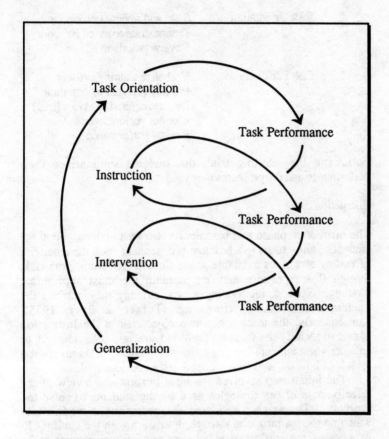

The teacher then identified task-relevant information so that the student recognized that specific information must be gathered. The student attempted the task and was encouraged to "talk through" the processing of the task.

Monitoring and regulating behavior occurred at various times to prompt performance or to encourage the use of a strategy. As training progressed and each student learned to self-manage behavior, either independently or through interaction with the other student this step was deleted. In summary, Task Orientation and Performance involved the following components:

*   Task Orientation   State and review task demands
     Demonstrate required behavior
     Review task demands

*   Task Performance   Verbalize training activity
     Identify relevant information
     Initiate required behavior (trial)
     Monitor performance
     Review performance

Following the learning trial, the students summarized their performance and the processes they used.

Instruction

The instruction phase was based upon two assumptions. First, the student's ability to solve a problem is dependent upon the repertoire of coding strategies available at the time of performing the task, though this repertoire may not contain the most appropriate strategy. Second, introducing a new strategy may confuse the student and reduce performance (Turner & Bray, 1985). Consequently, the teacher had two objectives in the Instruction phase: to identify the student's preferred strategic behavior; and, to enhance (or augment) existing strategic behavior. This involved a review of how the student performed in the previous trial.

The initial step involved the identification and review of the effectiveness of the strategies used by the students to solve the problem. The teacher validated the observations made while watching the learning trial through discussion with the student. In many cases, students' strategic behavior was fairly elementary at the beginning of training and the teacher and students discussed how strategic behavior could be enhanced. For instance, if a pupil used an inefficient strategy in a serial recall task (for example, naming only the elements), the teacher demonstrated how naming was part of a more effective strategy (such as rehearsal and/or chunking). If the student used an effective strategy, it was reinforced with an appropriate extension. For example, if the student rehearsed aloud, subvocal rehearsal was suggested to help reduce the processing demands of the task. The pupil then practiced the alternate strategy in a second trial using the same material. In brief, the Instruction phase involved the following:

*	Instruction	Identify and evaluate student's preferred strategy
		Reinforce and/or extend preferred strategy
*	Task Performance	As in the previous phase

Intervention

During this phase, the student attempted the task for a second time using the alternative strategies. The initial instructional steps were repeated to reinforce their importance. However, the focus of this phase was not simply on practice, but on the identification of blockages that were limiting performance. The teacher's responsibility was the evaluation of performance in order to derive suggestions that would enhance the effectiveness of the training. This component was important when students appeared to have reached a learning plateau. Extending students' performances beyond their plateaux became the key to success.

During this trial, the teacher interacted with the student to draw attention to blockages that were inhibiting the learning. The student was encouraged to suggest how the blockages might be overcome. These suggestions were discussed and evaluated. If the other student in the training pair had completed a training period, cooperative learning was promoted. That is, the teacher asked the student to help overcome the peer's problem. Once students had learned the task, asking them to explain how to instruct another student consolidated the skill. Effective strategies were reviewed and students began a third trial. In summary, Intervention involved the following:

*	Learning Analysis	Identify blockages to progress
		Recognize and evaluate blockages
		Initiate and reinforce cooperative behavior
		Review strategic behavior
*	Task Performance	As in previous phase

Generalization

The intent of instruction in general was to provide the opportunity for students to develop and use appropriate memory strategies and to learn how to go about solving a problem through the use of plans and cooperative teaching and learning. The involvement of both students tended to reinforce the importance of planful behavior. The Generalization cycle provided the opportunity for students together to consider activities for which the present strategies were appropriate. The teacher ensured that the students understood that strategies might be usefully employed in tasks and problem situations other than those in which they had been introduced.

After the review of the student's performance in the previous learning trial, the teacher asked both students to suggest a list of transfer activities and discussed how the strategy would help learning or problem solving. This exercise provided practice and feedback to the students about strategic behavior in multiple contexts and continued to promote dialogue between the students. Generalization involved the following:

*	Transfer Activities	Introduce transfer activities
		Evaluate strategy
		behavior for transfer tasks
*	Return to Task Orientation	

Evaluating PBI Procedures and Training Materials

The model described above was used in a resource room context with adolescent students who have mild intellectual disabilities. Three studies were undertaken to validate the procedures as a means of changing students' strategic behavior. It was expected that students would maintain the use of trained strategies beyond the end of the intervention.

In this section, it is not our intention to provide detailed descriptions of each of the studies as these are available in several sources (Ashman, in press; Conway & Ashman, 1987). Our purpose here is to summarize the studies and to draw attention to the results. In Table 6.2 is a summary of the studies and the training foci.

While each of the studies had a distinctly different focus, each aimed to validate the resource room PBI model using students having approximately equivalent age and ability characteristics. Students participating in the studies were attending regular high schools with special classes for adolescents with mild intellectual disabilities. The mean ages of the students across these studies fell between 13 years 6 months and 14 years 6 months; the range of mean IQs was 65 to 75.

Students were assigned to pairs by their regular class teachers on the basis of compatibility and then these pairs were assigned randomly to the training groups. In all cases, PBI was undertaken with the students in familiar, quiet rooms often in school libraries. In each study, the intervention involved two teachers, each working with a pair of students, for 2 sessions each week for eight weeks, totaling 12 contact hours. The teachers were involved in the development of the PBI materials extending over a period of six months prior to the beginning of the interventions and interacted with the first author, on a regular (sometimes daily) basis, during the preparation for, and execution of the studies.

The impact of PBI on students' cognitive competence was evaluated using a battery of information processing tests. As the training concentrated upon simultaneous and sequential processing, measures of these coding processes were collected from the Kaufman Assessment Battery for Children and from the pool of experimental tests used by Das and his colleagues. In addition, sub-tests of the Clinical Evaluation of Language Functions (CELF, Semel & Wiig, 1982) and from the Diagnostic and Attainment Tests (Schonell & Schonell, 1965) were included in Studies 1 and 3, and Studies 2 and 3 respectively. The achievement tests were included to assess transfer of learning to tasks considered to measure far generalization. The complete test battery was administered to all students prior to, and at the conclusion of the intervention, and 12 weeks after the end of PBI.

Study One

This study reported the development and assessment of the first version of PBI procedures and materials (Ashman, 1985; in press). In this study, training focused on the use of simultaneous and sequential coding strategies. The objective was to develop students' awareness of simultaneous processing by showing them how to integrate information in a quasi-spatial, holistic manner so that they could remember all the parts and readily construct patterns found within the training materials. Training also dealt with sequential processing, that is, assisting students to organize information in a temporal, sequence-dependent manner and be able to recall it as required.

Table 6.2: Three Studies using PBI within a Resource Room Model

Study 1	The initial PBI study examined the suitability of procedures and materials for the target group. As the generation of a repertoire of coding strategies appeared crucial for successful problem solving, the goal of training was the development of strategic behavior rather than school-related skills (such as reading or arithmetic).
Study 2	Attention was given to the development of two forms of training tasks: laboratory-type materials not related directly to activities inside or outside the classroom (called laboratory tasks); and, tasks using scenarios and materials analogous to situations encountered inside and outside the classroom (called general activity tasks).
Study 3	The study dealt with the integration of process training with academic skills and provided the first evidence for the appropriateness of PBI as a means of improving academic skills through training in strategic behavior.

The problem with earlier studies using the Information-Integration Model in strategy training studies was not so much that the materials used were inappropriate, but that the instructional methods did not unambiguously teach students how to use the coding strategies when attempting curriculum tasks. As a result, students in this study could not apply the strategies to tasks that depended upon one or the other process for success and consequently could not transfer training. In PBI studies, the primary focus was upon the method of teaching, rather than upon what content was taught.

The 17 pairs of adolescents were assigned to one of four groups (there being no significant difference between the groups in either mean age or intellectual ability):

* Group 1 received training in simultaneous processing only;
* Group 2 received sequential process training only;
* Group 3 received an intervention that dealt broadly with problem-solving, but without strategy training, using the PBI material or approach (called the stimulation control group); and,
* Group 4 received no intervention (called the control group).

Ten training tasks were developed for the study. They were adaptations of tasks previously used by Das or his colleagues. Four focused upon simultaneous processing strategies. For example in Kim's Game (a simultaneous processing task), students viewed a grid similar to a tic-tac-toe design that contained an array of objects. After a short viewing period, the array was disarranged and the students learned to replace items in their original location (for a complete description, see Drinkwater, 1976). Five sequential tasks emphasized information being received and processed in a serial fashion. For example, in Telephone Dialing (a sequential processing task), students learned to dial number sequences using push-button and dial-type telephones.

The activities undertaken with the stimulation control group focused upon problem solving in general. Most activities began with the implied question: "How would you ...?" Topics discussed included remembering the license plates on cars; unscrambling words; map reading; locating geographical features in the neighborhood; teaching games to a peer; and preparing favorite food or dinner menus.

PBI was used to teach the children *how and when to use coding strategies appropriately,* and to demonstrate in which situations, and to which tasks the strategies could usefully be transferred. Care was taken during the preparation of the training materials to ensure that their use did not constitute teaching to the battery of tests (the dependent measures), and no reference or implication was made during the generalization cycle to the dependent measures.

The analysis of data focused upon the successful application of the intervention model for developing competence in each of the two coding processes. The analysis showed that training assisted the students in the respective groups to improve and maintain their performance on the processing measures. That is, the simultaneous group improved on the simultaneous tasks but not on either of the sequential tasks. The sequential group improved on the sequential, but not on the simultaneous tasks. The two control groups did not show a significant improvement in their test performance following the intervention.

A secondary objective of the study was to examine transfer of learning to language processing and production. The results showed that the group receiving sequential training improved on language processing, but not on language production. No other significant gains were recorded for the other groups in the study. These data suggest some generalization of the process training, though given the short period of intervention, the gains reflected only minor educational advantages accruing to the group of students trained in the use of sequential strategies.

Study Two

In this study, the 30 student pairs involved were assigned to one of six experimental groups (no student had taken part in Study 1). Following pre-testing, 60 students were divided into one of two conditions on the basis of their sequential processing performance: Group 1 comprised students who performed above the median of the total group on sequential processing tasks, while Group 2 students scored below the median. Students were assigned to pairs by their regular classroom teacher and then randomly to one of three experimental conditions:

1. Two groups (low and high sequential processors) received PBI using laboratory tasks;
2. Two groups received PBI using real-life tasks; and,
3. Two groups received no PBI.

In this study, PBI concentrated on sequential processing only and 14 tasks were developed or adapted from previously used material. Each focused upon the development of the skills and strategies necessary for the recall of information presented in a sequential fashion. The training tasks used similar techniques and procedures; the difference between tasks was largely a function of the materials and/or the contexts in which learning took place.

132

Each task was designed so that exercises covered a range of difficulties from relatively easy trials (for instance, recalling 2 or 3 units of information) to tasks beyond students' initial performance level. This gradation of difficulty ensured that as students developed their processing competence, they remained challenged by the training. Furthermore, attention was given to the identification of appropriate strategic behavior and generalization activities consistent with the PBI model. Seven laboratory and seven general activity tasks were developed. The first experimental condition included tasks such as learning sets of geometric shapes and learning to recall a series of objects. In the second condition, tasks focused upon real-life activities such as remembering the license plates of passing vehicles, and reconstructing a carburetor that had been disassembled.

As was the case in the first investigation, PBI extended over 8 weeks with a 12 week follow-up period at which time testing was undertaken again. Both teachers worked with students in all the experimental groups. For the first half of the intervention, one teacher provided only training using laboratory material and the other worked with the general activity materials. At the mid-way point, the teachers changed groups. Training of the teachers extended over a four month period. One of the teachers involved in Study One assisted the first author in the training for approximately 4 weeks. Emphasis was given to the importance of limiting the intervention to the sets of materials specified for each group, as was the need to follow the PBI approach rigorously for the first two weeks of the intervention. Written records were kept for each student for each session, and audio taping was conducted according to a random schedule for review by the author and the teachers.

In this study, the primary interest was the effect of using materials of two different formats. Attention was not given to the improvement on individual test scores but to gains on processing composite scores. Once again, the data analyses demonstrated that training in sequential processing led to improvement on the sequential processing measures, but not on simultaneous measures. In this case, high and low sequential processors considered together demonstrated gains, though when studied separately, only the low processing group showed improvement. Others have reported similar results in regard to students' ability, suggesting that students of high ability may already have effective strategies and are reluctant to use the strategy being taught (Peterson & Swing, 1983). In the present study, it is more likely that a low level of motivation may have been a more plausible explanation for the minor changes in performance by the high ability group.

It is interesting that the groups using general activity tasks continued to show improvement on the processing tests during the follow-up period. This may indicate that the more broadly based training prompted the students to use their newly acquired skills beyond the training context, and thus, obtain experience that might promote the automatic use of sequential processing strategies. In contrast, the group using laboratory training tasks improved up to the posttest session and maintained this level at the follow-up session.

The effect of training on achievement test performance provided generalization results only for the Arithmetic sub-test of the Kaufman Assessment Battery for Children. This significant effect is of interest as it appears to show that the nature of training may have assisted students to deal with the Arithmetic items in a more systematic way, notably when the operations being tested are known skills (Ashman, 1987, August).

Study Three

The aim of this study was to compare the relative effectiveness of PBI with training that focused on coding processes only, with language skills only, and with an intervention that integrated skill and process training. Twenty-six pairs of adolescents were assigned randomly to one of four conditions (process training only, language skill training only, integrated language-process training, control). Due to student non-attendance at school and their consequent missing of training or testing sessions, the final sample used in the data analyses was 45 pupils. The training situation and personnel conditions were similar to those reported in the earlier studies.

The *Process Only* training tasks included materials that had been used in previous studies. The *Language* Training Program was based upon appropriate language activities for adolescents with mild intellectual disabilities: The primary goal of this program was improvement in the basic skills including vocabulary, word usage, comprehension, and aural discrimination.

The *Integrated Program* combined the Process and Language programs. It was a pilot intervention aimed at linking training of basic information processing strategies with specific curriculum skills for successful performance. The program aimed to teach students how to use both simultaneous and sequential strategies and then to provide examples of how these strategies could be used in laboratory tasks and in language tasks similar to those found within their usual in-class program. The primary objective of this intervention was to provide an obvious link between process and the skill areas, thereby reducing the transfer demands placed upon the students in typical cognitive interventions.

The integrated program was based on the premise that performance on dependent measures would be greater for this intervention than either the skill training alone, or process training alone. In training a skill (such as language or an arithmetic operation), students have been expected to learn regardless of the existence of the necessary information processing competence upon which success is dependent. In process training, students have been expected to experience the insight necessary to establish the link between their successful use of strategies in laboratory tasks (regardless of their nature) and school-related tasks that had similar processing demands.

Results of the study showed that the Language/Process and the Process only groups improved their performance on both simultaneous and sequential processing measures. The Language/Process group outperformed the Process group on simultaneous tests, while the reverse was true on sequential processing tests. These results are consistent with previous studies in the series. In addition, the Language/Process group made notable gains on the language processing measures but not on language production. The Language group outperformed others only on the Language Production tests.

Movement Toward the Classroom

The results of these studies have provided evidence of the benefit of a structured cognitive intervention for teaching information processing skills to students with mild intellectual disabilities. As each of the studies replicated the use of PBI procedures, it seems valid to suggest that the model would operate in other small group learning contexts. The true benefit of PBI rests not on its success in small group studies, but on the demonstration of success within a practical educational milieu using practices and techniques that are consistent with common classroom procedures. In the early studies there had been no opportunity for the reinforcement of skills and strategies outside the intervention (for example, by the students' regular teachers), or following the intervention. Such a situation mitigates against maintenance of performance gains and generalization to academic tasks, which, after all, is the goal of educational interventions. This consideration led to the decision not to proceed with further refinements of the PBI prototype, but to adapt this model to full class situations in which improvement in academic skills was the primary goal of teachers.

The key issue in implementing PBI in the regular classroom is eastablishing the relationship between information processing and academic instruction. In the following section, we will outline this relationship in order to identify curriculum content constraints on a classroom PBI model and to provide a basis for the incorporation of information within curriculum content.

INFORMATION PROCESSING AND ACADEMIC ACHIEVEMENT

The relationship between processing strategies and skills has cast a shadow over efforts to teach or remediate academic skills. For students with a mild intellectual disability, most processing skills are weak and teaching to a student's strength may lead to reduced academic progress. For students with learning difficulties who have poor processing strategies, the issue is whether to teach those weak strategies or focus upon alternate information processing strengths. Hence, in the case of learning difficulties, is it better to adopt an approach which strengthens abilities which were previously weak (*a skills deficit model*) or one that focuses upon existing strengths (*a compensatory model*)?

From a simultaneous-successive processing perspective, an argument in support of the skills deficit model would propose that both coding strategies are important in the development of academic skills. Failure to access each, or to select the appropriate strategy for a given task, will inhibit learning independence. Hence, teaching and remediation must focus on developing both processes.

The converse argument in support of the compensatory model would propose that a student will acquire academic skills only when instruction is matched to the student's preferred learning style. This argument is similar to the notion of aptitude-treatment-interactions discussed earlier in the book. Few training studies have adopted the compensatory model. Kaufman, Kaufman, and Goldsmith (1983) suggested that teaching approaches should be consistent with children's strengths in either simultaneous or sequential processing. Given the importance of both processing strategies, there is little to support the efficacy of that approach (Ayres & Cooley, 1986).

An important issue arising from training studies has been the reliance on strategy training in isolation from the classroom, and from tasks that have no direct relationship to the classroom. A "global" training program, in which the student is able to learn processing strategies free of the constraints of troublesome academic tasks, may well assist in the development of that strategy. However, the likelihood of its use by students in the classroom is diminished by the failure of the training program to clearly demonstrate the *application* of the strategy to those tasks. Moreover, elements of the training program generally are not incorporated into the repertoire of instructional techniques by classroom teachers, and no on-going support is given to the new strategy.

Following the failure of early strategy training models to promote transfer to academic tasks, researchers began to examine the relationship between academic tasks and processing strategies. With the clarification of the links between processes, strategies, and skills, investigators sought to validate the relationships through training studies. However, few investigators have sought to incorporate process training directly into academic exercises. Here, we consider a number of areas, specifically, reading, mathematics, and spelling as they form the foundation for most classroom-based instruction for students with learning and intellectual disabilities.

Reading

The cognitive processes involved in reading (also termed text processing) have been the subject of examination across the breadth of cognitive theories. Research by Das and his colleagues, for instance, dealt with the relationship between specific aspects of reading and the two coding processes of simultaneous and successive syntheses (Kirby & Robinson, 1987; Ryckman, 1981). Successive processing has been implicated in the development of elementary decoding skills, such as word recognition, and simultaneous processing has been linked to the development of fluent reading and comprehension skills (Cummins & Das, 1977; McRae, 1986). Studies by Leong (1974) on the differences in reading skills between average and disabled readers showed disabled readers to be weaker in both simultaneous and successive processing. More recently, Das, Snart and Mulcahy (1982) added planning to the catalog of deficiencies characteristic of low ability readers.

Studies based upon the Information-Integration Model (Das et al., 1979) have sought to remediate deficiencies in one process, or to develop competence in both for students attending elementary/primary schools. Process training in two studies led to students' improvement in successive processing and also in word recognition (Kaufman & Kaufman, 1979; Krywaniuk, 1974). In a third study by Brailsford (1981), training produced gains on both processing dimensions and on reading comprehension measures. In each of the three studies, process training deliberately excluded reading tasks in order to measure the degree of transfer from process training to the academic skills.

One way of integrating processing within a reading program is to teach reading tasks concurrently with the appropriate processing strategies. To do this, the teacher must be aware of both reading and information processing demands of the task. Robinson and Kirby (1987) suggested a hierarchy of reading tasks for simultaneous and successive processing. Simultaneous processing could be linked to the recognition of common sight vocabulary words, and the identification of meaning in words, phrases, and whole stories. Successive processing might focus upon decoding letter patterns to sound patterns, the identification of syntactic patterns within words, and the identification of plot or story sequences. Robinson and Kirby emphasized that training programs need to be hierarchical and systematic in their movement from lower to higher level skills.

Perhaps the greatest volume of research in the area of information processing and reading has come from the study of metacognition, reciprocal teaching (discussed in the previous chapter), and cognitive behavior modification strategies (Brown et al., 1986; Palincsar & Brown, 1984; Ryan et al., 1986). In the first area, metacognitive training, two approaches have been identified: those that commence training in a laboratory-type program which is transferred to the classroom; and, those that are based in the classroom using specially designed curriculum.

Palincsar and Brown (1982), for instance, taught comprehension-fostering and monitoring skills in a series of small group training studies that concentrated on four metacognitive strategies: self-directed summarizing; questioning; clarifying; and, predicting. The skills were trained using modeling, explicit instruction, repeated practice on concrete materials, and reciprocal teaching as teaching strategies. The investigators showed that students incorporated comprehension skills in their regular lessons both within comprehension exercises related to the training, and in alternate comprehension tasks. Brown et al. (1986) suggested that success in these studies was derived from the selection of training skills which were tailored to the needs of the students and which had relevance across learning situations.

Through the use of a special metacognitive curriculum, Paris, Newman, and McVey (1982) taught comprehension strategy training within a regular reading program. The reading sessions were structured so that they focused on a particular strategy during a week. These would be reflected in the bulletin board metaphor for the week, and in the goals and plans for each lesson. In addition, the lessons contained a reading trip in which road signs were used to assist the student to progress through the reading task. The success of the program was attributed to the concrete nature of the strategies and content, the value of which was clearly demonstrated in the maintenance of performance gains over a 6 month period.

The use of cognitive behavior management strategies in reading remediation has concentrated upon the use of self-instruction training, again largely in the area of reading comprehension in withdrawal settings (Ryan et al., 1986). Wong and Jones (1982), for example, taught learning disabled junior secondary students to use a five-step strategy (Table 6.3).

Table 6.3: Five Steps Toward Self-instruction in Reading

---

1.   State why the passage was being studied;
2.   Find the main idea;
3.   Think of a question about the main idea;
4.   Learn the answer to the question; and,
5.   Look back at questions and answers.

In another study of self-questioning in comprehension monitoring, Short and Ryan (1984) taught poor readers in grade four to aid recall by asking themselves "wh..." questions (such as "what" and "why") as they read. Students initially were prompted for rule usage and feedback although these prompts were withdrawn as the intervention progressed. The students who received training not only generalized the learned strategy to other single episode stories, but also to more complex double-episode flashback stories.

The results of the examination of the information processing literature in regard to reading can be summarized by a number of points:

1. In the area of coding strategies, the majority of studies appear to describe the relationship between skill and process (or strategy).

2. The majority of studies have concentrated on teaching content or strategic behavior under laboratory conditions without the direct involvement of the class teacher in the study or in applying the strategies to the classroom.

3. The majority of studies have focused on training processing strategies within the specific area of comprehension skills, and in some cases (for example, remediation using the Information-Integration model), students appear to be expected to perceive the relationship between the trained strategies and academic tasks unaided, and without specific cuing.

While some excellent programs focusing upon executive metacognitive skills involved in reading have provided a new optimism in information processing training, generalization still remains a problem. Ryan et al. (1986), for instance, summarized the use of self-instruction training in reading by arguing that although students may benefit from self-instruction training in reading, "the evidence for maintenance and generalization is still slight" (p. 527).

On the positive side, many of the studies have highlighted the possibility of an integrated process-content intervention model that would include: in-class, teacher-taught training models; instruction in the appropriate coding strategy for specific reading tasks; and, the use of cooperative teaching and learning. Based upon these ideas, investigators seem to be moving toward approaches that offer more benefits to the classroom teacher than in the past.

Mathematics

The move toward the integration of processing and academic skills has provided an additional dimension to the study of mathematical operations. While the process literature is not extensive, the emphasis on cognitive activities associated with mathematics has begun to develop as an important area of research.

Problem solving has been the main thrust of investigations dealing with information processing and mathematics. While several studies have dealt with the relationship between coding strategies and arithmetic, the results have generally been inconclusive (see for example, Conway, 1985; Cummins & Das, 1977; Johnson, 1986; Kaufman & Kaufman, 1983; Luria, 1980). In addition, few systematic studies have investigated the role of metacognition in mathematics. The results of these studies have shown typical developmental trends. Young students do not analyze problem information routinely, or monitor or evaluate progress and results, though it has been argued that awareness of the processing requirements of the mathematical task would facilitate effective problem solving behavior (Garofalo & Lester, 1985; Lester & Garofalo, 1982, March).

Given the nature of mathematical tasks, it is not surprising that problem solving has been a main concern. Students' understanding of the basic computational facts (declarative knowledge) and the procedures for solving a task (procedural knowledge) have been the foci of several investigations. However, the inclusion of managerial skills has provided the direct link with the study of problem solving behavior. These emphasize the need to: carry out a series of decision making tasks including comprehension of spoken or written language to understand the problem being posed; select the appropriate mathematical operation; and, execute that mathematical operation to produce a solution (Pellegrino & Goldman, 1987; Schoenfeld, 1981).

Spelling

In the shadow of reading and mathematics research, spelling has received little attention. However, there has been a small, but important body of literature that has emphasized the integration of processing and spelling skills (Gerber & Hall, 1987; Wong, 1986b). There has been a realization that spelling is a complex cognitive task requiring far more than rote memorization of word lists or the selection of an appropriate coding option from lexical (syntactic-semantic) and nonlexical (graphemic-phonemic) processing.

141

As in the case of reading, spelling acquisition progresses through a series of developmental stages that require the use of alternating processing strategies for optimal academic performance. Four stages have been identified. In the prephonetic stage, visual images are important and only initial or final sounds may be represented. In the phonetic stage, spelling is strongly phonetic and the grapheme-phoneme relationship is important though application of skills acquired in this stage will only succeed with words that are phonetically regular. In the transition stage, students become aware of spelling inconsistencies and the need to consider visual cues. Further development in the ability to recognize the correct spelling of a word leads to the final stage, correct spelling, in which the recognition and recall of the correct lexical representation is necessary. Throughout this developmental sequence, selection of the appropriate information processing strategy is important in order to maximize the learning of the academic skill (Gentry, 1978).

The necessity for training information processing skills in conjunction with spelling content has been proposed by several writers (Gerber, 1984; Wong, 1986b). Graham and Miller (1979), demonstrated the close relationship between information processing, plans, and academic (spelling) content in their description of a student's activity during a spelling exercise. In response to the need to spell, the student may have the word within the knowledge base, thus leading to immediate recall. If the spelling is uncertain or unknown, the learner may draw upon previously acquired strategies to help solve the problem. These might include strategies dealing with semantic, syntactic and morphemic information, direct phonemic spelling and a generate-and-test process. Alternatively, the learner can call upon extrinsic strategies including other people, and written aids such as dictionaries, books and charts.

The literature on information processing and spelling raises some important issues in relation to an integrated process-content intervention model:

1. the role of differing processing strategies at each stage of spelling development;
2. the need to teach the relationship between each processing strategy and academic content;
3. the value of a systematic plan for attacking unknown or uncertain spellings.

The relationship between cognitive skills and academic content demonstrated in the previous sections highlights the important need for a new approach to classroom intervention. However, translating laboratory techniques into classroom procedures requires adaptation rather than direct application.

Several warnings have been noted concerning the use of teaching methods developed in strategy training laboratories. Torgesen (1982), for example, warned that classroom and laboratory tasks which students find difficult may demand the use of quite different skills. Furthermore, Pressley, Levin, and Bryant (1983) suggested that the interpersonal dynamics in the classroom and laboratory are quite different. Students appear to be far less compliant and persevering in the classroom than they are when instructed and tested individually in an experimental setting. While these ideas may not constitute the same order of revelation for teachers and researchers, they emphasize the necessity of considering environmental variables before introducing strategy training into the classroom.

In the following chapter, we describe PBI as a classroom model. The approach incorporates curriculum content and information processing. The model was derived from the prototype and does not diminish the importance of both teacher and student responsibilities. In fact, if any changes have been made, the importance of the interdependency of teacher and student has been enhanced.

7

Process-Based Instruction:
A Classroom Integrated Model

The preparatory studies undertaken using the PBI procedures in a resource model context outlined in the previous chapter demonstrated that information processing skills can be learned and applied by students with mild intellectual disabilities. In all three investigations, the teenagers learned how to use simultaneous and sequential coding processes and to maintain this competence over a follow-up period. The success of these interventions supported much of the earlier strategy training research, indicating that students' cognitive abilities can be improved and that, given appropriate learning conditions, newly acquired skills will transfer to closely related academic tasks.

Perhaps more important than the gains in the students' processing competence were the benefits derived by the students in learning how to attack problems, and how to work cooperatively with others to solve them. In general, students responded favorably to situations in which they were given responsibility for their own learning.

The limitations of the three studies stem mainly from the somewhat artificial nature of the interventions. Simply, the PBI procedure was neither designed for whole class instruction, nor did it explicitly relate the learning process to the range of curriculum content areas typically considered by the classroom teachers. It was our specific objective to trial aspects of PBI prior to its translation into a form that would work successfully within the classroom context.

145

TRANSLATING PBI INTO A CLASSROOM INSTRUCTION MODEL

In a small group setting, it is relatively easy to match strategy training with individual differences. We referred to this earlier in this book as aptitude-treatment interactions (Chapter 3). In the seclusion of the laboratory or the resource room, teachers can evaluate the quality of the strategies being used by students, monitor their application carefully, and provide clarification and instruction to ensure that they have made the strategic behavior personally meaningful. This was certainly the case in the resource room PBI interventions as teachers guided and monitored students' problem solving behavior and intervened in the learning process when appropriate. In other words, the design of the learning environment and the style of presentation ensured that the opportunities to learn were maximized throughout each investigation.

In contrast, it is more difficult to maintain motivation and on-task behavior in the students' regular classrooms. In that context, interpersonal interactions and classroom dynamics may result in disruption of the teaching and learning process (Pressley et al., 1983).

Links between Small Group and Large Group Procedures

In translating PBI into a classroom model, we evaluated the small group methods to identify components that would have direct application to the classroom. Several essential components emerged.

First, regardless of the teaching material and the presentation of content, the outstanding feature of PBI was the structure that it imposed upon the content. As we have indicated earlier, problem solving and planning were the bases of the instructional process, so it appeared essential to translate this systematic approach into a classroom teaching strategy. The term *plan* became the core of classroom-based PBI.

Second, satisfactory use of a plan alone would not necessarily lead to success in either information processing or academic achievement. How students organize information into meaningful units, and how competent they are in doing so is important. This meant that some emphasis needed to be given to information

146

processing strategies. From this point on, we call these *coding strategies* to clearly define the importance of organizing (that is, coding) information during any complex cognitive activity.

Third, the interactive nature of PBI appeared to have a significant and positive impact upon students' attitudes toward learning. The teachers were involved with the students, and similarly, each student was involved in a partner's learning efficiency. We have used the term, *cooperative teaching and learning*, to emphasize the important role of communication and interpersonal skills in generating and maintaining the students' incentive to attend and to be full participants in the teaching-learning experience.

While little attention was been given to the role of curriculum content in the small group investigations, learning skills and content still remain the primary objectives of classroom activities. Hence, a focus upon the curriculum topics was needed, and in instructional terms, the development of students' knowledge bases. Thus, these four elements became the pedagogical pillars of PBI.

An Overview of the PBI Components

It is a premise of Process-based Instruction that these elements (plans, coding strategies, cooperative teaching and learning, and knowledge bases) are interdependent and of equal status. One must not be subordinated to another.

The problem solving orientation of PBI is derived from the use of plans and coding strategies. Plans provide a structured sequence that will lead to successful completion of the curriculum task if the student possesses the essential information and skills in the existing knowledge base. In carrying out that plan, the student employs coding strategies to organize and process task information. The teacher's role is to ensure that students are oriented to the use of plans and coding strategies and that they use both plans and strategies efficiently in a range of curriculum tasks.

Role of plans

In our adaptation of PBI to the classroom, it became necessary to use terms that have a common meaning. In the last chapter, we drew the distinction between planning and problem solving on the basis of a neurological and behavioral division. For students, this division would have little import and consequently we have adopted a definition of planning and plans that is more familiar to the student. The influence of problem solving theory will be clear in the description below.

Plans are general action sequences. They provide the means for students to work systematically toward the solution of academic tasks. Hence, planning became the activity undertaken in devising such action sequences. It is important to recognize that a plan is not the same as task analysis. Task analysis is the process of breaking complex behavior into a sequence of components and links (the what-to-teach). In effect, these components were the teaching objectives and they had to be sufficiently well-defined so that the task could be achieved by the student. The top section of Table 7.1 provides an example of a task analysis that relates to word attack skills. This task analysis is only one of many that could be developed to teach word attack skills. Each of the levels could be further divided into specific sub-skills.

Table 7.1: An Example of a Task Analysis and Plan for Word Attack Skills.

Task analysis for the decoding approach to word attack skills

Level 1	Individual letter sounds
Level 2	Three letter words in a consonant-vowel-consonant (CVC) pattern
Level 3	Initial and final consonant blends
Level 4	Digraphs
Level 5	Syllabication

Plan for students attempting word attack skills at levels 3 or 4

Step 1	Look at the word
Step 2	Find the sound-chunk
Step 3	Pronounce the sound-chunk
Step 4	Say the word

In contrast to task analysis, the plan in the bottom section of Table 7.1 provides a systematic method of achieving a particular teaching objective. The plan, therefore, relates to the how-to-do, or how-to-learn part of instruction.

It is important to recognize that the plan in Table 7.1 is a general example of a plan for a specific task-analyzed step and that it may look somewhat naive. The actual plan used in a classroom would need to be tailored to the needs of the students in that class. Additionally, it is possible to use the same plan for a number of steps within a task analysis when the steps toward task solution are common.

For novice learners, plans must be specific and detailed until the teaching and learning procedures are well known and can be retrieved and used automatically. The number of steps required within a plan might then be reduced without losing the inherent structure. As a consequence, proficient learners may not need a plan to carry out a familiar task, or may require only a general plan to cue essential steps. In other words, elaborate plans may be foreshortened for proficient learners without loss of meaning.

During the introduction to the use of plans and for new curriculum content, plans would be developed by the teacher. The lack of essential curriculum knowledge or the development of plans will restrict the students' direct involvement in plan construction. Care must be taken when using teacher generated plans as these may be inappropriate for students. Ellis et al. (1987), for example, referred to a plan in the form of the mnemonic EASY. EASY refers to:

E   Elicit questions to identify important information
A   Ask self which information is the least troublesome
S   Study the easy parts first, hard parts last
πY   "Yes" to self-reinforcement following each batch

It is obvious that the ability level of students for whom such a mnemonic is appropriate far exceeds that of students with mild intellectual disabilities. The point we need to make here is that students must be involved in the development of plans as early as possible. Once the concept of a plan is understood for one topic, students must be encouraged to develop their own plans. Plans that are personally relevant are more likely to be used across problem solving and learning situations, rather than being applied only to targeted curriculum tasks. Once the concept of plans has been established, plans can be tailored to meet the needs of each student both in terms of the number of steps and in the language in which they are expressed.

Role of coding

Coding refers to the input, storage and retrieval of information. It is the individual's method of deriving meaning from the information being presented. As we indicated earlier, coding can occur in either a concurrent or serial manner (see Table 7.2 for alternate terms). Each of these coding strategies is involved in solving curriculum tasks. If the information presented in a task is surveyable in total (as a whole), the coding strategy used by the student would be concurrent. If the information is surveyable only in parts, the coding strategy would be serial.

Table 7.2: Terminology for Concurrent and Serial Coding

Terms used for concurrent coding

Simultaneous
Holistic
As a Whole Thing

Terms used for serial coding

Successive
Sequential
In Steps

It is not important which terms are used to identify the two strategies. The main consideration is that students can identify with, and comprehend the terminology. Teachers working with young adolescents with mild intellectual disabilities have reported that the terms *As a Whole* and *In Steps* were easily understood.

In some cases, success in a task can occur from the use of one coding strategy. For example, serial coding would assist a student to blend sound chunks when reading words aloud. In other activities, competence with both concurrent and serial coding may be required for success. For instance, concurrent and serial coding are involved in completing a mental arithmetic calculation; serial coding will help students keep the information "active" in their minds while concurrent coding enables them to seek the relationship between the elements of the problem and the elements in the number knowledge base.

It is important that the teacher emphasizes the need for students to select the appropriate strategies at the time of presentation of the academic task especially if the task relies more heavily on one form than the other, as inappropriate coding may lead to difficulty in solving the task. The teacher can assist the student to select the appropriate strategy by clearly providing the information in a concurrent or serial manner, or by making clear the format in which the solution to the task is required. Both input and output coding requirements affect the final coding selection of the student. For instance, stimuli may be presented as a whole visual unit (concurrent coding) or verbally (serial coding). The output required may be a spoken sentence (serial) or a drawing (concurrent).

A student's preferred learning method may influence the approach a teacher may use with that student. We all have favorite ways of doing things. Parents will be familiar with children's cries of "We don't do it that way" when the adult tries to help the young student with mathematics homework. When the adult insists on "helping" the child using methods of the past, the typical result is a very confused child. In the classroom, the same principle applies. While it is the teacher's role to introduce new techniques for dealing with problems and academic exercises, it is important to realize that even young students have preferred coding and problem solving methods and it is important initially to provide a match between the teaching method, the requirement of the task or problem, and the students' learning styles.

The effect of the match-mismatch was exemplified in a series of studies by Pask and Scott (1972). In their investigations, students were identified as either serialists (who processed information in a step-by-step fashion) or holists (global learners who tested hypotheses about complex relationships). Two instruction programs based on a taxonomy of fictitious Martian animals were devised to match the two learning strategies, and the subjects in the serialist and holist categories were matched and mismatched with the programs. The results of the study were dramatic. All students for whom the program was matched with their preferred learning style (that is, serialists taught using the serial program, and holist taught using the holist program) performed exceptionally well, while students mismatched with the programs performed very poorly (Daniel, 1977).

The Pask and Scott studies are important because they serve to remind us of the impact of matching learner and teaching variables on students' recall. However, it must be remembered that these investigations dealt with competent students and relatively complex content. In addition, Pask and Scott concentrated on teaching *one* strategy relevant to *one* specific task. They were not concerned with the provision of information processing strategies to students with either limited strategies or those who lacked the ability to apply them appropriately. Furthermore, some care must be taken in generalizing from specific laboratory conditions and tasks to curriculum content in which both concurrent and serial strategies are necessary for maximum learning efficiency. It is the responsibility of the PBI teacher to ensure that both coding strategies are taught and employed by students.

Cooperative teaching and learning

In any classroom, the teacher is responsible for the selection of the academic content, the teaching sequence, and the organization of the daily and weekly schedule. In Process-Based Instruction, these responsibilities are extended to include the ability to develop plans and identify appropriate coding strategies for curriculum tasks. The teacher initially must develop plans so that they can be introduced as effective models for the students. Care must be taken to ensure that teacher plans are comprehensible to the students and hence, able to be learned by them.

Teacher plans also provide an initial assessment of the student's ability to implement a plan by requiring the student to implement the plan orally. Indeed, PBI establishes a close link between instruction and performance through on-going evaluation of the students' strategic behavior and performance. These assessment activities not only act as cues for the teacher in terms of the *what* and the *how* of instruction, but they permit the teacher to orient students to the *why* and the *when* of learning. In summary, the teacher's goal is the development of student responsibility for learning, rather than relying on imposed adult requirements to learn.

The responsibility for learning does not rest solely with the teacher. It is the shared responsibility of both teacher and students to evaluate the effectiveness of teaching and learning. In this way, students are full members of the teaching-learning process. In effect, the introduction of plans and coding strategies encourages students to become more involved. Students learn that it is their responsibility to apply plans and coding strategies correctly when attempting classroom exercises. They must work to interpret the demands of the task, establish what is needed to complete the task, and evaluate the extent of their knowledge base in terms of existing curriculum content, plans and coding strategies. Armed with this information, they must then apply the plans and strategies to obtain the task solution.

To assist in this activity, cooperative teaching and learning techniques similar to peer tutoring and reciprocal teaching are employed extensively to ensure that instruction is student-oriented. Student language and elaboration (that is, putting the plans and problem solving activities in students' own words) are the bases of integrating the new content and the new learning strategies. The learning process then becomes more meaningful to the student and more likely to be retained and generalized.

In effective Process-Based Instruction, there is little need for segregated teaching (that is, withdrawing students for individual/ group instruction) although the model can be integrated into the activities of a resource room or tutorial program (see Ashman, in press). In addition, PBI is particularly suited to team teaching situations in which a resource or consultant teacher provides additional assistance in the classroom to those students who are experiencing difficulty in planning or coding.

Curriculum content

There is no requirement for PBI to be taught as a separate curriculum area as is the case in other instructional approaches such as Instrumental Enrichment (Feuerstein et al., 1980). The model is not complementary or supplementary to the regular curriculum. It is an integral part of the curriculum and equally appropriate for academic and nonacademic tasks.

The difference between traditional task analyses and those undertaken by a PBI teacher is in the emphasis the PBI teacher places upon the identification of the coding requirements of the specific curriculum tasks. Not only are the component skills identified, but equal attention is given to the information processing demands of the skills. It is only through such analyses that coding strategies can be matched with the task, teaching materials, and the plans to be used by the students.

The curriculum content then includes plans and coding strategies as part of each lesson. The class teacher orients the instructional approach to the value of plans as an effective teaching framework and to the coding of information either concurrently (as a whole thing) or serially (in steps), depending on task content, its form of presentation and the required format of response.

THE PBI SEQUENCE

PBI involves five phases: Assessment; Orientation; Strategy Development; Intra-task Transfer; and, Consolidation and Generalization. The model is shown in Figure 7.1. It is important to note that although all students enter the Assessment phase, only those who require assistance in the solution of the academic task would proceed through the five phases of the model. In this section, it is our intention to describe the PBI sequence. A detailed account of how PBI can be introduced into the usual classroom teaching activities will follow in Chapter 8.

Each of the phases of the model will now be considered in detail.

Assessment

Assessment spans the teaching-learning process. However, in this phase of PBI, the meaning of Assessment is quite explicit. As in most academic programs, the assessment of entry skills is the initial phase of PBI. We are concerned not only to evaluate the student's curriculum knowledge about a particular task, but also their information processing competence, and the problem solving skills they possess which can be brought to bear on the specific task. We have avoided the approaches taken by many information processing researchers in administering a battery of cognitive or academic achievement tests. We are more interested in the skills as they relate to the curriculum task being confronted. PBI is not a means of evaluating intellectual ability.

Figure 7.1: The Process-Based Instruction Classroom Model

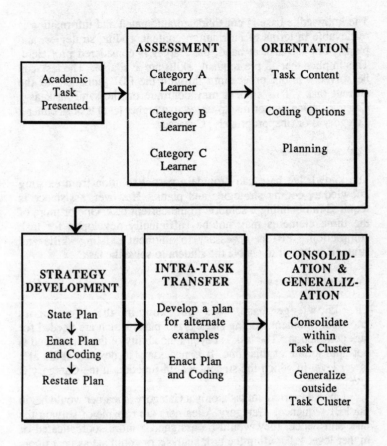

When a student confronts the task, the assessment focuses on each element: curriculum knowledge; coding competence; and ability to use a plan. The task presented to the students may be completed successfully, partially, or it may not be completed as a result of inadequate curriculum knowledge, inadequate coding competence, or the lack of an appropriate plan of attack. Three possible categories of learners emerge from the Assessment:

Category A learners

The knowledge base is consolidated/automated and information is retrievable in terms of curriculum content, coding strategies, and plans. For the task at hand, the learner is considered proficient. This implies that all pre-requisite skills are available. The task can be solved without proceeding through the PBI sequence for the current task. This student may continue on the same task as a Category A learner, or may proceed to a higher level task as either a Category B or (inappropriately) C learner.

Category B learners

The knowledge base can provide a partial solution from existing knowledge, coding strategies and plans. However, assistance is required in obtaining a solution to the current task. One or more of the three elements may not be sufficiently developed for task completion. PBI is necessary to augment existing skills and strategic behavior to enable the student to solve the task.

Category C learners

The knowledge base does not contain the prerequisite knowledge/content, coding strategy, or plans which are needed for task completion. The task is beyond the ability of the learner and is not appropriate at this time. It is necessary to develop skills at a lower level in which the student would function at the Category B level.

On that curriculum task, only a Category B learner would begin the PBI sequence. Category A learners are capable of solving the task and hence, they would be assigned a more sophisticated or higher level task within the task analysis or could act as peer tutors to Category B or C learners. As students become proficient in the use of coding strategies and plans, they will become Category A learners. In contrast, Category C learners have been confronted with an inappropriate task and the teacher must reconsider the selection of the task and commence the PBI sequence using a lower level task within the task analysis. Furthermore, it is useful to remember that at a particular level of skill, a student may be a Category C learner, whereas at a lower level in the same skill, the student may be Category A.

In any classroom, it is expected that there will be a range of Category A, B, and C learners (as in any mixed ability class). This means that teaching content and materials would be tailored to meet the curriculum and processing needs of each ability group. Table 7.3 reviews the assessment phase.

Table 7.3: A Summary of the Assessment Phase of PBI

PBI Learner Category	Learner's Processing Ability	Assessment Outcome
Category A Learner	Proficient Learner	PBI sequence not required. Exit
Category B Learner	Novice Learner	PBI sequence required. Move to Orientation
Category C Learner	Not able to be applied to task	Task is too difficult Apply PBI to prerequisite task

Orientation

The Orientation phase introduces (or, in later PBI sequences, it reviews) the three components of the model: plans; coding; and, curriculum content. The teacher's role during this phase is to focus attention on the value of developing effective plans as a means of working systematically towards solving the curriculum task. Plans are defined, described, and exemplified so that the students understand how they are used, why they are used, and where they can be used to help solve problems and to learn.

Students are introduced to coding, and emphasis is given to the importance of dealing with information either concurrently (as a whole thing) or serially (in steps). Once again, students learn how information is usually presented within that curriculum topic and how they can capitalize on existing coding competencies to help them process the new topic content. The involvement of students in referring to previous plans and coding activities is most important, as previous successes and failures provide valuable insights into the usefulness of plans and coding strategies in solving the present task.

Orientation to curriculum content follows the regular pattern practiced in the classroom for the introduction of new or existing content. The only difference is that curriculum orientation occurs in conjunction with orientation to plans and coding. In Table 7.4 we summarize the Orientation phase.

Table 7.4: A Summary of the Orientation Phase of PBI

	Action	Focus
1.	Orientation to Content	Understanding of the task requirements
2.	Orientation to Coding	The more appropriate coding option - in steps or as a whole thing
3.	Orientation to planning	The value of planning in moving systematically to task solution

Strategy Development

This is the main teaching phase of Process-Based Instruction. Here, it will be obvious that the focus of attention is planful behavior, rather than curriculum content. In adopting this approach, we are not minimizing or dismissing content. Rather, it is acknowledged that the teacher will have completed a task analysis that will ensure that the content presented is at the appropriate level. Our intention is to emphasize how the integration of content and teaching strategy is achieved.

The Strategy Development phase involves a three-step cycle: state the specific plan; enact that plan; restate the plan. The teacher continues the cycle until students are able to demonstrate their ability to use the plan and appropriate coding strategy on blackboard or worksheet examples. The teacher should determine the level of proficiency required to move to the next phase of instruction.

State the plan

The teacher or a student states the plan to be used, emphasizing the content requirements and coding options. The teacher remains conscious of the need to revise prerequisite skills if necessary. Wherever it is appropriate, the teacher refers to examples of plans and coding presently known to the students.

Enact the plan

The class/group works through a sample task using the plan and coding strategy. Students repeat the plan. They work through multiple examples using cooperative teaching and learning methods.

Restate the plan

To assist students to internalize the plan, they describe the plan in their own words, together with the coding strategy or strategies they might choose. That is, students generate a language format appropriate to their needs. Table 7.5 summarizes the major features of this phase.

Intra-task Transfer

In the information processing literature, transfer and generalization often are used interchangeably. Transfer and generalization refer to the use of acquired strategic behavior in tasks or problems other than those tasks used during training. However, we have separated the concepts and defined them in terms of the application of plans and strategies to *different aspects of the curriculum*.

Table 7.5: A Summary of the Strategy Development Phase of PBI

	Action	Focus
1.	State the Plan	All students have the opportunity to commence with a plan and coding strategy that will lead to a solution
2.	Enact the Plan	Practise to demonstrate the value of using a plan
3.	Restate the Plan	Student language to internalize plan

Transfer relates to the correct use of plans and coding strategies in tasks that are related in terms of specific skill application. For example, a plan for two column addition with carrying would be equally appropriate for other tasks involving multiple column addition with carrying. These activities are said to fall within the same task cluster.

In contrast, generalization refers to the application of plans and coding strategies to tasks that are outside the task cluster. For example, a plan for completing two column addition with carrying on paper might be used by a student when calculating how much money to tender for the purchase of three items at a local store. The point here is that written and mental arithmetic may be considered to be members of different task clusters as the student could be considered to be operating in a different curriculum area.

In order to ensure that students can apply plans and coding strategies beyond the demonstration plan and tasks, the teacher provides additional examples within the task cluster. Students are asked to develop a plan in their own words, and use that plan and the appropriate coding strategy to solve the task. This phase is designed to enhance the probability of obtaining transfer to alternate tasks within the same task cluster.

The importance of this phase lies in the deliberate move away from the original plan by requiring students to develop their own plans for similar tasks. Cooperative teaching and learning strategies are important in this phase as they highlight the roles of student language, and the elaboration of personal plans. A summary of the Intra-task Transfer phase is given in Table 7.6.

Table 7.6: A Summary of the Intra-Task Transfer Phase of PBI

	Action	Focus
1.	Develop a plan for alternate examples	Enables students to see the plan now expressed in their own language
2.	Enact the plan and coding	Students implement the plan expressed in their own language

Consolidation and Generalization

This phase has two important components: consolidation of the problem solving skill within the task cluster; and, generalization of plans and coding skills to tasks that are outside the task cluster.

Consolidation

Proficiency within the task cluster is obtained when students are able to reduce their reliance on working through all steps of the plan to solve the task. Merging of steps within the plan occurs as a result of practice, usage, experience and teacher guidance as measured by on-going assessment. As a result, an abbreviated plan may be developed by individual students, groups of students, or the whole class. The aim is to incorporate plans and coding strategies related to the focus curriculum task within the knowledge base so that the student(s) move to Category A status.

Generalization

This refers to the application of the plan taught in the preceding phases to tasks outside the task cluster. Students must be able to perceive the need to use a plan and the appropriate coding strategy in a situation where the knowledge base alone is insufficient for task solution. A summary of this phase is given in Table 7.7.

Table 7.7: A Summary of the Generalization Phase of PBI

	Action	Focus
1.	Consolidation	Reduction of steps required in the plan for that task cluster but retaining coding option
2.	Generalization	Ability to apply plans and coding options to tasks beyond task cluster

The knowledge of content, plans and coding gained during the current PBI sequence becomes part of the consolidated knowledge base and hence is able to be drawn upon in the assessment phase of the next PBI sequence.

A Summary of PBI Features

Process-Based Instruction has a number of important features that distinguish it from other strategy training models. These characteristics appear to facilitate constructive classroom interactions, and transfer and generalization of skills beyond the learning task.

Student orientation. PBI is designed to ensure that students focus on the task at hand and learn appropriate coding strategies and plans for successful problem solving. More important is the students' knowledge that success comes from their own efforts and motivation rather than from the energies and input of others, notably their teacher. It is this self-determination that is responsible for students' changes in attitude toward learning, school, and ultimately themselves.

Classroom based. Instruction is provided in the students' regular room by the regular class teacher. There is no requirement for resource or consultant teachers to be involved in PBI once it has become established within the classroom. In effect, PBI is self-generating.

Student involvement. While the teacher remains responsible for curriculum and information processing (especially in the early stages of PBI), the responsibility for applying and assessing the value of plans and strategic behavior becomes a shared responsibility. Students as individuals or as tutors of small groups provide an added dimension to the classroom activities, freeing the teacher to provide direct instruction to certain students or enabling the teacher to monitor progress.

Integration of strategic behavior and content. There is no requirement for PBI to be taught as a separate curriculum topic or area. The model is not complementary or supplementary to the regular curriculum, but is part of an integrated teaching method. The plans and coding strategies become part of each lesson and require no additional teaching materials. The fundamental character of PBI comes from the initiative and enthusiasm of the class teacher who orients teaching toward the importance of planful, strategic behavior in dealing with the subject content.

In conclusion, the instructional sequence described above has been designed to place responsibility on both the teacher and the students for the application of plans and incorporation of coding strategies. Following training in the use of plans and coding strategies, the teaching procedures emphasize the need for student practice of plans, the development of plans, and the evaluation of the success of plans in the task under consideration. As we have mentioned, PBI can be used in a variety of teaching contexts. It is easily adapted to the classroom in group and whole class lessons, and is designed to be an integral part of the regular classroom curriculum. In the following chapter, we describe the introduction of PBI in such classroom situations.

8

Application of the PBI Model Within the Classroom

Teachers have been concerned that researchers often fail to indicate how new procedures and methods can be adapted for use in their classrooms. From its initial conception, the goal of Process-Based Instruction was the adaptation and application of cognitive strategies within the curriculum taught by the classroom teacher. Consequently, our attention now turns to a discussion of how teachers can use this process within the classroom. To enable us to relate application to the various stages of instruction, we have divided this chapter into sections similar to those presented in Chapter 7.

ASSESSMENT

Teaching and assessment are essential in all areas of the curriculum. Assessment procedures allow teachers to determine what is to be taught, the ability or potential of the student to perform a particular task, and to measure gains in specific skills and curriculum knowledge during instruction. Thus, assessment occurs before, during, and at the conclusion of a teaching unit.

Traditional intelligence and achievement tests have concentrated on general ability and academic content and have limited utility either as a means of establishing the competence of students (Fuchs, Fuchs, Benowitz, & Barringer, 1987) or as a necessarily useful precursor to instruction (Newcomer, 1977). Measures more relevant to cognitive theory and practice have been developed over the past decade. These have focused upon the evaluation of coding and planning performance and we have referred to them in Chapters 3 and 6. With the integration of information processing and curriculum in Process-Based Instruction, assessment of strategic behavior and achievement are of equal importance. In the first section of this chapter, we outline several options for assessment prior to the introduction of PBI by the teacher.

Assessment Prior to Teaching

Assessment of strategic behavior may be made either in isolation from curriculum content, or during an actual problem solving activity. While we have argued for integrated process-content instruction, there is some merit in examining a student's processing characteristics on tasks remote from current academic content. Such assessment can:

* act as a measuring stick against which improvements in the student's application of coding and plans may be measured;
* provide useful information about the range of the student's skills within the class group, thereby aiding the teacher in the choice of content at the beginning level; and,
* give the teacher new insights into the student's performance in terms of problem solving strategies.

There are two ways of gathering information about students' information processing performance; by using published, standardized tests, or teacher-constructed testing materials.

Formal assessment

Three assessment devices using specific and reliable tests and techniques could be useful to PBI teachers: standardized tests; non-standardized tests; and, dynamic assessment. We will summarize these procedures briefly and direct the reader to references for further information.

Standardized tests. The Kaufman Assessment Battery for Children (K-ABC) is the only standardized test available that measures information processing competence (Kaufman & Kaufman, 1983). This test is administered to one student at a time and consists of

166

several subtests that assess either concurrent (termed simultaneous in the K-ABC) or serial (sequential) coding performance. The coding components of the test are given in Table 8.1.

Table 8.1: K-ABC Coding Subtests

Sequential (Serial) Processing Scale

Hand Movements. Involves repeating a series of hand movements in the same sequence as the examiner performed them.
Number Recall. Involves repeating a series of digits in the same sequence as given by the examiner.
Word Order. Requires touching a series of silhouettes of common objects in the same sequence as presented verbally by the examiner. More difficult items include an interference between the stimulus and the response.

Simultaneous (Concurrent) Processing Scale

Gestalt Closure. Involves naming an object or scene pictured in a partially completed "inkblot" drawing.
Triangles. Requires assembling several identical triangles into an abstract pattern to match a model.
Matrix Analogies. Involves selecting the meaningful picture or abstract pattern to match a model.
Spatial Memory. Requires recalling the placement of pictures on a page that was exposed briefly.
Photo Series. Requires placing photographs of an event in chronological order.

The K-ABC is the first of the "new wave" of evaluation tools which have lead clinicians away from the use of IQ as the definitive indicator of ability. Classroom teachers may benefit in several ways from its use. The battery is norm-referenced (for North American children) and provides standardized measures of both students' concurrent and serial coding ability as well as a composite mental processing ability score. The test is suitable for students aged from two and a half to twelve and a half years, and provides processing and academic achievement scores. For the PBI teacher, the K-ABC is a useful means of determining students' preferred coding strategy, provided that all subtests in the processing scales are administered. However, it must be remembered that both coding strategies are important and concentration on only the stronger or weaker strategy may not lead to a notable change in performance on complex tasks.

A large body of research literature has grown around the use of the K-ABC since 1983 demonstrating the psychometric characteristics of the test (especially reliability, validity, and use with special groups). Critique and criticism have also been extensive. A useful review of the battery can be found in the *Journal of Special Education* (Volume 18, number 3) published in 1984, and in numerous articles published in the *Journal of Psychoeducational Assessment*.

Non-standardized tests. Information processing competencies have been tested using a wide variety of "experimental" measures. Perhaps one of the most cohesive batteries which pre-dated the K-ABC was reported in Das et al. (1979). At that time, experimental tests of concurrent and serial processing had been used in numerous research projects. Planning measures were added to the standard Information-Integration battery by Ashman (1978). Many of these processing tests were administered individually though we have adapted many for use as group tests in our various research projects, thereby providing accessible and realistic tests for teacher use. Table 8.2 lists several of the tests that comprise the Information-Integration battery. Detailed descriptions can be found in Das et al. (1979).

Experimental tests have two major advantages. Copies of the tests generally are available from researchers and are easily adapted to suit the needs of individual teachers for use across age and ability levels. Alternatively, similar tests can be developed from descriptions given in research reports. Administration does not involve complex instructions or special equipment. Many of the subtests can be administered as group tests.

There are several drawbacks in the use of experimental tests. Perhaps the most serious is the use of a measure that has not been examined adequately in terms of its processing demands, or the use of a test for which the demands change across age or ability dimensions (such as the Hand Movements subtest in K-ABC).

Table 8.2: Tests Used by Das and Others as Measures of Successive and Simultaneous Processing and Planning

---

Successive (Serial) Processing

> *Auditory Serial Recall*. Requires the verbal recall of sets of words that are either acoustically similar or neutral.
> *Digit Span Forward*. Involves an orally presented list of numbers of increasing length, for recall by students.
> *Visual Short-term Memory*. Involves the presentation of geometric shapes to be recalled in their correct order.

Simultaneous (Concurrent) Processing

> *Raven's Coloured Progressive Matrices*. Involves presentation of geometric designs in which a part has been removed. Students choose the missing part from six alternatives.
> *Memory for Designs*. Involves the presentation of straight line drawings one at a time. The student draws each design from memory.
> *Figure Copying*. Requires the freehand copying of geometric shapes of increasing difficulty. This test is similar to the published test, Beery Test of Psychomotor Integration.

Planning

> *Visual Search*. Involves the location of one geometric shape from a visual field containing numerous similar geometric shapes.
> *Verbal Fluency*. Requires students to write down/say as many words as possible starting with a prescribed letter.
> *Trail-Making*. Requires connecting numbers, letters, or numbers and letters in ascending order. This task is similar to the join-the-dots parlor game.
> *Planned Essay*. Involves writing (or telling) a short story based upon the content of a picture. The essays or stories are assessed in terms of their planfulness.

Dynamic assessment. Dynamic assessment tests provide information on students' ability to transfer what has been learned. This is not easily discerned from static tests such as the K-ABC or the Das et al. battery as the nature of the data collected relates to the specific task at the time of testing only. Feuerstein's Learning Potential Assessment Device (LPAD, Feuerstein, 1979) is perhaps the most widely known form of dynamic assessment. It focuses upon the measurement of processes involved in learning, using a test-teach-test procedure which combines active teaching and testing while the student is engaged in the problem solving activity. The LPAD combines inferential questioning with task training to determine how readily the student learns a strategy, principle or rule for solving the task. Two important considerations for the tester are determining how much aid, or direction must be given before the student can deal with the task independently, and how effective the child is in retaining, applying, and generalizing what has been taught during the assessment session.

The LPAD consists of a three-phase process. Initially, a standardized version of the test battery is administered, followed by a training phase in which the examiner provides input (mediated learning experiences) to evaluate how much intervention is needed by the student to solve each problem. This is then followed by a second standardized testing phase to assess the student's retention and ability to generalize.

The LPAD may provide a practical assessment solution for the classroom teacher as it uses an interactive approach that is consistent with PBI methods. Research on dynamic assessment has demonstrated practical and theoretical advantages. Further discussion of dynamic assessment procedures can be found in Day (1983), Silverman (1985), Watts (1985) and Feuerstein et al. (1979).

Teacher-constructed measures of coding

The use of assessment procedures noted above will increase teachers' understanding of the cognitive characteristics of their students. However, being realistic, use of the K-ABC, LPAD or Information-Integration battery will require some degree of study and practice in order to become familiar with materials and to be consistent in test administration. As an alternative, classroom teachers may opt for the use of curriculum tasks which allow for direct observation of students' strategic behavior.

An understanding of the difference between concurrent and serial coding is essential before beginning informal evaluation of student skills. Equally important is the identification of the coding and planning demands of the chosen curriculum task.

One way to develop skill in identifying a task's coding demands is to attempt a series of trial examples through thoughtful consideration of how the task is attacked. For instance, think about how you pronounce the word "glebe". You may not know what the word means, but you could say it because you recognized a familiar word form. You most likely dealt with the word using a concurrent strategy; seeing the whole word rather than breaking it up into parts. Conversely, unless you are familiar with the next word as a result of a particular leisure activity, your pronunciation of the word "psittaceous" would have required a serial strategy.

The type of strategy used in complex academic tasks often is dependent upon the person's knowledge base. Generally speaking, concurrent coding strategies are used when the knowledge base is familiar. For instance, knowledge of the pronunciation of consonant digraph "ps" as "s" in psittaceous means that "ps" is concurrently coded. When the network of information is less well established, serial processing is used to combine elements before the meaning can be established. Students with an intellectual disability or a learning difficulty may not follow the practice described immediately above. Their ability to use concurrent or serial coding strategies effectively does not always lead to task success. For example, when pronouncing a word, these students will use concurrent coding strategies when a word is recognized without difficulty, but also when the word is unknown and the student is guessing. Serial coding is used only when the student is unsure of the word and is able (or prepared) to sound out the parts of the word first.

Figure 8.1 shows an example of an assessment sheet used by a teacher to record the coding strategy employed by a student in reading sight words. "C" (Concurrent) or "S" (Serial) would be entered in the column at the right. The teacher also has left some space to note the student's syllabication. In this case, students were asked individually to read each word in the list. The teacher watched the student's eyes and mouth closely to detect clues about whether a word was read as a whole word (concurrent), or broken into syllables and blended (serial).

171

Figure 8.1: A Sight Word Recording Sheet

How did I do that...?

Name:

Group:

PHONICS	Ser / Con.	SIGHT WORDS			Ser / Con
cat		MEN			
fit		XRAY			
chips		DOCTOR			
spend		NOT TO BE TAKEN			
morning		POSTCODE			
flutter		AMBULANCE			
bark		VACANT			
tripod		CHILDREN CROSSING			
brackish		WET PAINT			
increasing		FIRE EXTINGUISHER			
oil			PHONICS		SIGHT
toil			✓ X		✓ X
enjoin		Serial			
rejoice		Concurrent			
rejoinder		Total correct:			

Teacher-constructed measures of planning

Although no published tests are available to assess students' ability to develop and use plans in school-related exercises, teachers can use existing curriculum tasks to observe and evaluate the quality of students' planful behavior. Testing should encompass the ability of the student to develop a plan for a specific task, to use that student-generated plan, or to use a plan supplied by the teacher. Measuring the perimeter of a rectangle prior to teaching the concept of "perimeter" provides an example of how students' ability to generate and/or use a plan can be assessed. A possible scenario is shown below.

The teacher may show the student a rectangle and ask: "If this were a playing field, tell me how you would find out how far it would be around the outside"? The quality of the student's response would indicate how systematic the student would be. For example, the student might say: "I'd take a tape measure all around". This response demonstrates knowledge of the use of a tape measure, but does not indicate efficiency in measurement. The teacher may then provide a drawing of a rectangle and a ruler, and a plan for measuring the perimeter of any rectangle. Such a plan may look like this:

1. Measure the length of a longer side;
2. Measure the length of a shorter side;
3. Add the two measurements together;
4. Multiply by 2;
5. Write the units (such as cm, km, ft).

This would enable the teacher to assess the student's proficiency in applying the plan to a specific arithmetic task.

Following the introduction of plans, the teacher may wish to assess the ability of the student to generate a personalized plan before progressing to a new topic. This would be particularly appropriate within the consolidation and generalization phase described in the previous chapter. An example of providing a task and asking the student to develop a plan is shown below.

Following the teaching of 2 column subtraction requiring borrowing in the units column, the teacher may provide a 3 column example for the student, such as:

$$284-$$
$$\underline{138}$$

The student then would be asked to give a step-by-step plan to solve the task, and then use that plan to achieve the answer. The requirement for a student to develop a plan has a secondary purpose. It permits the teacher to gain insight into the personal language used by the student in developing the plan. This provides a guide to the plan format, and the language that may be expected in any cooperative teaching used in the PBI sequence.

Teachers can assess coding and planning skills through a variety of presentation formats. The same mathematical operation can be presented to the student as a word problem:

> If there were 284 students in the grade 4 and 138 of them were girls, how many would be boys?

In this case, the teacher can assess the student's ability to carry out the operation when the mathematical facts are embedded in prose.

In teacher-made tests of plan usage, a scoring code can be established to provide a pre-intervention baseline. This scoring code would emphasize the serial nature of a plan and the importance of providing sufficient steps to ensure that the solution is attained.

On-going and final assessment

Coding and planning assessments will be incorporated into the normal assessment process that occurs during, and at the end of a lesson sequence. Within each academic content area the two aspects of plans need to be assessed: using a plan; and developing and implementing a plan. In other words, at least one assessment item should contain a given plan which the student is required to implement, and another should ask the student to develop a plan and then implement it. The format could be similar to those outlined in the section above (that is, informal assessment of individual students) or it might involve a class exercise. The extract of a tape-recorded session below shows how the teacher can work with one student to evaluate the child's current performance.

The teacher is working with a 13 year old girl who is in a class for adolescent students with mild intellectual disabilities. There are 12 other students who are presently working in groups of three on word attack skills.

Teacher:	Julie, I want you read out the words on this sheet for me, starting at the top.
Julie:	Trap, little, mouse, egg, ... (Girl continues through known words) ... angel, ceiling, appeared, s-ora, g ..., g-nom, canry, attach, ... attached, engine, ...
Teacher:	OK, stop there for a minute. Do you have a plan for working out how to say a word?

174

Julie:	Yes.
Teacher:	What is it? (The girl thinks for ten seconds)
Julie:	Look at the word, say it if I know it, if not, look for parts I know starting at the front, join up the parts.
Teacher:	That's an excellent plan, Julie. Were you using it when you started to get into the words you didn't know?
Julie:	(Pause) Sometimes.
Teacher:	Can you say the plan for me again?
Julie:	Yes.
Teacher:	OK, say it for me.
Julie:	Look at the word, say it. If I can't, break it into parts starting at the beginning. Put them together and say the word.
Teacher:	That's good. Alright, let's look at a couple of the words, here (Pointing first to the word "saucer"). I want you to use your plan to work out what this word is.
Julie:	(Put her index finger under the word) S... au ... cer. Saucer.
Teacher:	Good girl. Saucer. What is that?
Julie:	It's the dish you put a cup on so that you don't spill your tea.
Teacher:	Yes that's right. See how easy it can be to work out the word using the plan? In your plan, work in steps to say out the word, one bit at a time. Let's look at one or two others.

This is only one way in which the teacher could have undertaken an informal assessment with this student. The teacher could have asked Julie to read aloud from an age and ability appropriate novel and elicited the plan in the same way.

In this case, the teacher chose not to prompt the use of the plan before the student attempted the words. It is clear that the student knows a word attack skill plan but she does not use it all the time. The teacher also has assessed the student's present sight word vocabulary level. It is possible that the teacher's individual attention may have prompted Julie to hurry through the words using a concurrent strategy.

Whenever possible, assessment activities are best undertaken on an individual basis so that the teacher can assess the student's use of coding strategies and plans more adequately. An example of the incorporation of plans within on-going assessment is shown in Figure 8.2, while an example of incorporating coding was shown in Figure 8.1.

ORIENTATION

Orientation relates to content, coding, and plans. Teachers are familiar with techniques with which to orient students to academic content and consequently that process will not be discussed here. However, orientation to coding and plans is perhaps less well understood and will be considered here in some detail.

Preparing for the orientation phase

In orienting students (and indeed teachers) to coding and plans it is important that two criteria are realized:

    * There is a recognition of the need to solve a problem.
    * There is a desire to solve the problem.

Until these criteria are met, purposeful coding and planning will be undertaken only when the teacher instructs the students to do so. Student recognition of a problem should trigger an automatic response to begin solving that problem in a systematic way (refer to student-teacher dialogue on p. 175) Hence, the orientation phase is crucial to the success of PBI.

Coding

As we have indicated in the Assessment Phase earlier in this chapter, it is important that the teacher be familiar with the meaning and the significance of coding strategies in curriculum tasks. One way to become more confident in selecting the appropriate strategy is to examine an area of academic content and look for tasks that clearly require concurrent or serial coding. For example, sight word recognition, recall of comprehension facts, or shape recognition will normally require concurrent coding. Recall of word lists or groups of objects in which each student in a group adds an additional item would normally require serial processing. By becoming familiar with coding options so that the appropriate selection becomes automatic, the class teacher will be better able to advise students.

Figure 8.2: An Assessment of Plans in a Mathematics Test

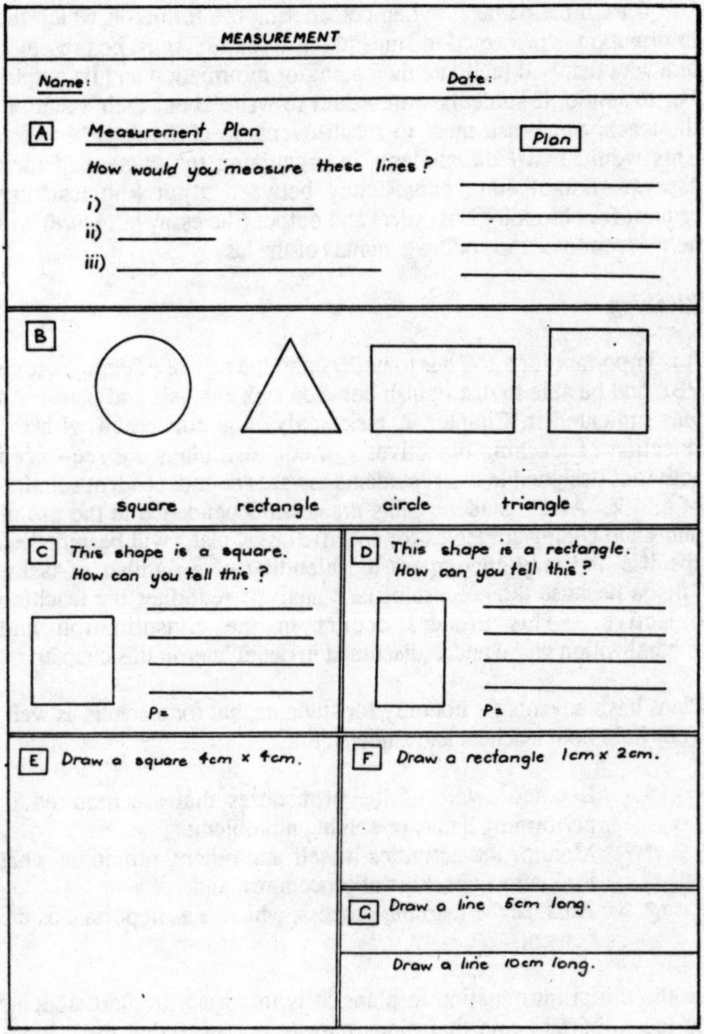

In introducing PBI to a class, it is advantageous to choose academic tasks that have a clearly defined coding option. This will reduce the degree of student confusion at a time when they also are learning about planning. Early coding success will motivate students to persist and increase the likelihood of coding becoming an automatic information processing activity.

Care must be taken when considering the format in which the information is presented to students. Information must be presented in a way that will facilitate the coding of information and its output. For example, if students were asked to write about their vacation, the teacher may ask them to recall events in chronological order. This would assist the students in organizing the content of their essays. Establishing consistency between input (the teacher's request for chronological order) and output (the essay structure) will help to reinforce the coding demands of the task.

Planning

It is important for a teacher to understand the role of planning within PBI, and be able to distinguish between task analysis and plans. As was indicated in Chapter 7, task analysis is concerned with the selection of teaching objectives. In contrast, plans are sequenced activities designed to assist students towards an independent solution of a task. As the student gains greater independence in the use of plans and coding strategies for specific tasks, plans will become less specific and may encompass the blending of a number of tasks. This is because the process of task analysis redefines the teaching objective. This process occurs in the consolidation and generalization phase and is discussed in detail later in this chapter.

Plans have advantages not only for students, but for teachers as well. They help both teachers and students to:

* Become aware of the procedures that are required in performing a task or solving a problem;
* Monitor the activities of self and others, providing what is akin to a checklist of procedures; and,
* Analyze the learning process, which is as important as the content.

In the initial introduction to plans, it is important to alert students to the important role that plans play in our everyday life. Plans may be consciously written (such as recipes or operating directions), or informal mental notes (such as setting priorities for routine daily jobs).

It is also important to discuss the differences between good and bad plans to emphasize the value of the systematic, sequential nature of developing and implementing a plan. Having examples of good and bad plans visible in the classroom reminds students of the importance of good plans and illustrates that PBI can bring a new approach to learning curriculum tasks. Figure 8.3. shows an example of good and bad plans from a classroom.

Figures 8.3: An example of a Good and Bad Plan

Which man had a plan? This one?

Or this one?

These plans were displayed above the classroom blackboard with the caption "Which man had a plan?" as a reminder of the value of plans. The use of humor, as in the cartoon in Figure 8.4 illustrates that PBI can be enjoyable.

It is not necessary for plans to be set out in written form. A plan can also be formalized using a pictorial or rebus format or may use other communication systems such as Makaton or signs for the deaf. An example of a rebus format plan is shown in Figure 8.5.

Figure 8.4: An example of a Humorous Bad Plan

Figure 8.5: An Example of a Plan Using Rebus

Plan for learning to

spell words

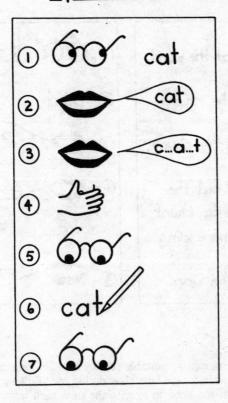

A plan can also encompass both a written and a rebus format so that both readers and nonreaders are able to use the same plan (Figure 8.6).

Figure 8.6: An Example of a Plan in Rebus and Prose Form

Plan for sounding words

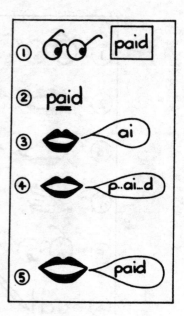

① Look at the word.

② Find the chunk.

③ Sound the chunk.

④ Sound out the beginning, chunk and the ending.

⑤ Say the word.

It is useful to make plans portable so they may be hung around the room and placed in front of the class during specific lessons. This not only avoids the need to rewrite the plan each lesson, it also saves preparation time.

As we have indicated earlier, PBI does not require the development of special teaching materials. However, coding and plan usage can be enhanced if the layout of teaching materials, particularly blackboards and worksheets, emphasize the role of coding and plans.

Designing teaching materials

The primary teaching resource in many classes is the blackboard. In these classrooms, the board is used to orient students toward the activities to be undertaken on any day, or for an entire week. The PBI teacher can use the blackboard to considerable advantage in emphasizing the use of plans and coding strategies. Figure 8.7 shows part of a blackboard layout for a lesson that introduces the use of plans in an academic area. Note that the plan is clearly set out for students to follow and that examples are prepared for the class to work through as a group when practicing the use of the plan.

Figure 8.7: A Lesson Plan on Percentages

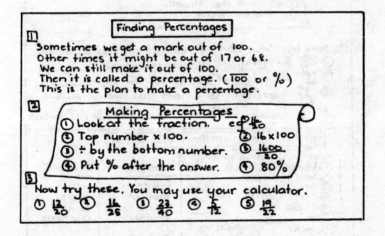

Figure 8.8 shows a general view of a blackboard layout for a series of lessons including the plan shown above. As can be seen there is no major difference in the content of the lessons from what would be seen in any other class for students at this level. The only difference is in the emphasis on plans and coding.

183

Figure 8.8: A Blackboard Layout of Lessons

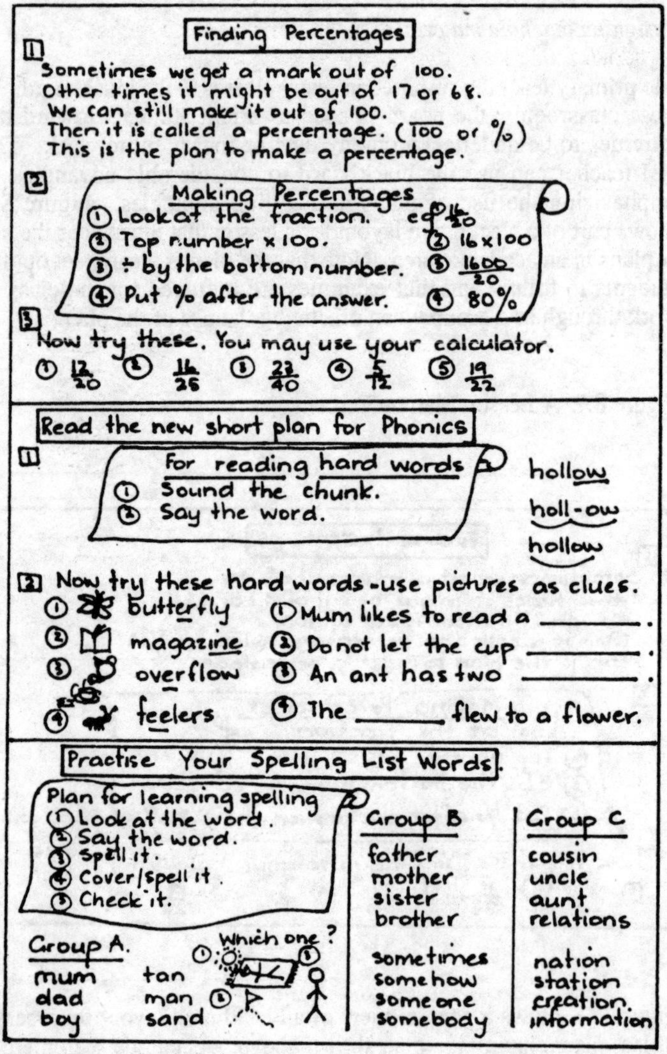

Finding Percentages

1. Sometimes we get a mark out of 100.
Other times it might be out of 17 or 68.
We can still make it out of 100.
Then it is called a percentage. ($\overline{100}$ or %)
This is the plan to make a percentage.

2.
Making Percentages
1. Look at the fraction. eg $\frac{4}{5}$
2. Top number x 100.   16 x 100
3. ÷ by the bottom number. $\frac{1600}{20}$
4. Put % after the answer.   80%

3. Now try these. You may use your calculator.
1. $\frac{12}{20}$ 2. $\frac{14}{25}$ 3. $\frac{23}{40}$ 4. $\frac{5}{12}$ 5. $\frac{19}{22}$

Read the new short plan for Phonics

1.
for reading hard words
1. Sound the chunk.
2. Say the word.

holl<u>ow</u>
holl-ow
holl<u>ow</u>

2. Now try these hard words - use pictures as clues.
1. but<u>ter</u>fly   1. Mum likes to read a _____.
2. maga<u>zine</u>   2. Do not let the cup _____.
3. over<u>flow</u>   3. An ant has two _____.
4. <u>feelers</u>   4. The _____ flew to a flower.

Practise Your Spelling List Words

Plan for learning spelling
1. Look at the word.
2. Say the word.
3. Spell it.
4. Cover/spell it.
5. Check it.

Group A		Which one?	Group B	Group C
mum	tan		sometimes	nation
dad	man		somehow	station
boy	sand		someone	creation
			somebody	information

Group B: father, mother, sister, brother
Group C: cousin, uncle, aunt, relations

Preparation of worksheets for individual lessons also requires no significant change in format. In the initial phases of teaching a plan, it is helpful to include a reminder of the plan on the worksheet to reinforce its value (see Figure 8.9). However, worksheets used in later lessons will look no different to those used prior to adopting a PBI approach. This means that existing resources do not have to be abandoned in order to introduce PBI into the classroom.

Figure 8.9: A Worksheet on Spending/Banking

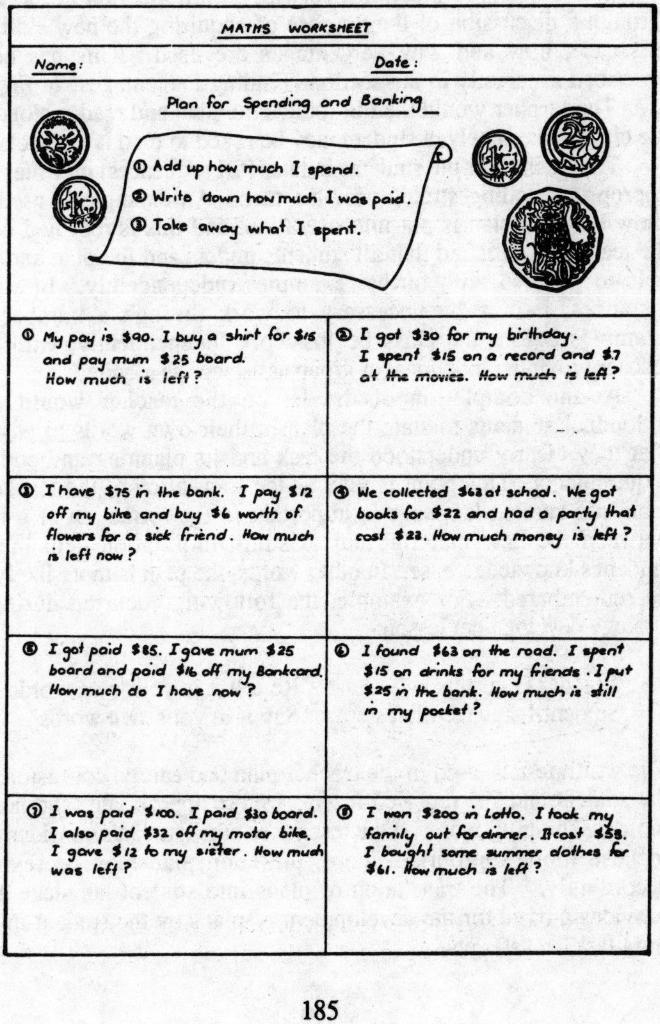

MATHS WORKSHEET

Name: Date:

Plan for Spending and Banking

① Add up how much I spend.
② Write down how much I was paid.
③ Take away what I spent.

① My pay is $90. I buy a shirt for $15 and pay mum $25 board. How much is left?

② I got $30 for my birthday. I spent $15 on a record and $7 at the movies. How much is left?

③ I have $75 in the bank. I pay $12 off my bike and buy $6 worth of flowers for a sick friend. How much is left now?

④ We collected $63 at school. We got books for $22 and had a party that cost $23. How much money is left?

⑤ I got paid $85. I gave mum $25 board and paid $16 off my Bankcard. How much do I have now?

⑥ I found $63 on the road. I spent $15 on drinks for my friends. I put $25 in the bank. How much is still in my pocket?

⑦ I was paid $100. I paid $30 board. I also paid $32 off my motor bike. I gave $12 to my sister. How much was left?

⑧ I won $200 in Lotto. I took my family out for dinner. It cost $58. I bought some summer clothes for $61. How much is left?

STRATEGY DEVELOPMENT

When introducing plans and coding strategies it is best to commence with a task that is familiar to students so that the amount of new learning will be minimized. Initial plans are best developed by the teacher to provide sound models. In this discussion, we use an example of a simple introductory plan (making percentages) which is shown in Figure 8.7.

The lesson would commence with an introduction to the task through a discussion of the purpose of acquiring the new skill, in this case, how and why percentages are used. This has been described succinctly in the section "Finding Percentages" in Figure 8.7. The teacher would then introduce the plan and read it aloud to the class. Alternately, a student may be asked to read it to the class.

The teacher (or the students in later PBI sequences) indicates the appropriate coding strategy for the task. An example is used to show how the plan is put into operation, and this is repeated until the teacher is satisfied that all students understand the plan and are able to proceed with further examples independently. In some instances, it may be necessary to work through a number of examples before the class begins work independently, with the teacher providing individual or group assistance as required.

At the completion of the lesson the teacher would ask individual students to state the plan in their own words to ensure that they clearly understood the task and its planning and coding requirements. This point is vital as the translation of the teacher's plan into student language is important in the formation of a link between the new material and existing information held in the student's knowledge base. In other words, the plan is more likely to be remembered. For example, the following occurred during a strategy development lesson:

Teacher Plan step: "Re-tell it in your own words"
Student-language Plan step: "Say it in your own words"

The word, re-tell, used in the teacher plan had caused confusion for the student and she replaced it with a more appropriate (and hence more meaningful) word. If the teacher or other students consider this to be a more appropriate word, the main plan may be revised accordingly. The translation of plans into student language also provides a basis for the development of plans by the student in the Intra-task Transfer phase.

INTRA-TASK TRANSFER

The Intra-task Transfer phase moves the responsibility for decisions about coding and plan construction from the teacher to the students. PBI aims to assist each student to become as independent in problem solving as possible. For the students to accept this responsibility they must satisfy the two criteria mentioned earlier, that is, recognize the need to solve a problem, and have the desire to do so.

Without an awareness of the need to problem solve there can be no independence in the application of plans or coding. This awareness can be achieved only through moving the locus of control from the teacher to the student to permit and encourage student generation of plans and student selection of the appropriate coding strategy. Hence, it is important to employ cooperative teaching and learning strategies.

Development of plans by students

The plans introduced by the teacher as part of the Strategy Development phase provide the framework for the development of pupils' plans in the Intra-task Transfer phase. The teacher provides an example within the same task cluster and asks the student(s) to develop a plan to solve that task. As discussed earlier, in the initial lessons, it may be more successful for the teacher to choose an example that has been used previously during the Strategy Development phase than to generate a new task. Using a familiar activity or problem will ensure that students have the necessary plan and coding strategies to deal with the task.

The plan for measuring the perimeter of a rectangle discussed in the Assessment phase will exemplify the Intra-task Transfer activities. This plan is now suitable for application to parallelograms with students providing a plan for each example prior to solving the task.

The use of cooperative teaching and learning strategies is ideal for this phase (see Chapter 5). Initially, the teacher introduces the academic task and provides a model of the application of a plan and coding. The class is then divided into small working groups and students have the opportunity to develop plans in their own language and have solutions tested by their peers. One student in the group becomes the teacher and is responsible for helping the group generate a plan that incorporates appropriate coding strategies and for leading the group discussion. The role of teacher is shared around the group so that all members have the opportunity to guide the learning. The class teacher is free to move around from group to group monitoring the accuracy of what is being taught and providing assistance when necessary.

The Intra-Task Transfer phase provides a valuable period for the reinforcement and overlearning of a specific skill or strategy.

CONSOLIDATION AND GENERALIZATION

The two aspects of this phase reflect the reduction of direct reliance on specific plans for each teaching objective. As students become proficient in the use of plans and coding strategies, plans become more general (more executive in the metacognitive sense), providing a set of prompts rather than a highly specific series of steps.

Consolidation

In consolidation two main activities may occur in relation to plans. The number of steps within a plan may be reduced, or a number of separate plans may be blended together to form a plan for a composite task.

Reducing the number of steps within a plan

Once a specific plan is well known and can be applied correctly by students, reliance on that plan is reduced by eliminating or combining some steps. Figure 8.10 provides an example of reduction in a plan for sounding words which included a vowel digraph, called a chunk in this teacher-developed plan.

The streamlining of plans becomes useful only when students have developed proficiency in a particular set of skills. Teachers must analyze their plans for specific or general needs. For example, the original plan in Figure 8.10 may be suitable for sounding words containing diphthongs (for instance, "shoulder" or "buy") but it may not apply to certain words, for example, "laugh" where the consonant digraph "gh" may be seen by the students as the chunk.

Once the range of skills has been developed by students, the short plan will be appropriate. Notice in Figure 8.8 that the teacher has used two words with quite different characteristics to exemplify use of the short plan. In this case, the number of steps was reduced from five to two as the result of class discussion. Note that the new plan is shown as a plan for "reading hard words" as it is not needed for words that can now be recognized as sight words. This means that for easier words, students are able to use a concurrent coding strategy (which is more efficient and draws upon existing knowledge) rather than having to use a plan which is now inefficient. Although the new plan contains fewer steps and is suited to the needs of most students, the original is still available for those students who may need to refer back to it should a word prove too difficult using the new plan.

Table 8.3: An Example of a Reduced and Generalized Plan

The original plan for vowel digraphs		A short plan for phonics	
1.	Look at the word "paid"	1.	Sound the chunk
2.	Find the chunk "p-ai-d"	2.	Say the word
3.	Sound the chunk "ai"		
4.	Sound out the beginning, the chunk, and ending "p-ai-d"		
5.	Say the word "paid"		

Blending of a number of existing plans

Where a series of plans have been learned as part of earlier teaching objectives, these plans may be incorporated in a new plan for a larger task. For example a plan may have been used to teach how to put on a sweater. This plan may be incorporated within a more general plan to teach students what to do if they feel cold. The teaching steps within the earlier plan for putting on a sweater would not be required, and may be replaced by a single step within the new plan ("put on sweater").

Teachers should use feedback from the students to decide when it is appropriate to blend or reduce plans. However, it is important to remember that failure to move towards consolidation will result in too many specific plans for known tasks.

Generalization

For many students with intellectual disabilities, generalization of learned strategies is difficult. Within PBI, the aim of this phase is to increase awareness of the importance of using plans and the appropriate coding strategy in tasks other than those directly taught. If confronted with an untrained task, students will have learned an important problem solving skill when they can say in their own words: "I'm not sure how to do this. What will my plan be? How should I look at the information?" It will indicate that they have:

* recognized that a problem exists;
* indicated a desire to solve the task;
* understood that a plan is a systematic method of working toward a solution;
* been aware that some form of organization of the information is required (that is, coding); and,
* recognized the importance of being a Category A or proficient learner.

As we have indicated earlier in this book, one of the constraints of laboratory research is the limited period during which instruction is undertaken. With little reinforcement of skills learned in the laboratory, it is not surprising that students fail to see the need for generalization. The teacher can promote generalization by making the concept of planning one that is familiar to students through consistent use. The PBI teacher will frequently draw students' attention to the application of plans and strategies beyond the current topic to other learning situations, thereby promoting transfer and generalization. For instance, the application of a plan for addition can be generalized to adding the cost of items when shopping, adding football scores, and adding measurements in building construction.

MAINTAINING THE PBI SEQUENCE

Once the sequence of Assessment, Orientation, Strategy Development, Intra-task Transfer, and Consolidation and Generalization have been clearly established, PBI will continue to play an important role in the integrated process-content curriculum of the classroom. Some points should be kept in mind as the teacher and students become more familiar with PBI.

Assessment phase

For all curriculum tasks, the teacher needs to assess which students will require the PBI sequence for that task. With practice, the teacher will recognize certain coding and planning patterns, and will recognize when a student possesses the necessary strategies but does not use them. This is sometimes called a production deficiency. The teacher will know from previous tasks which students are likely to experience difficulties, and which students will be able to act as teachers in a peer tutoring activity.

Orientation phase

As PBI becomes established as a teaching strategy, less emphasis will be needed in the Orientation phase as students will understand that some forms of information come to them in parts or as a totality requiring the use of either serial or concurrent coding strategies respectively. They will also automatically generate plans for new or novel tasks. The main emphasis in orientation will change from coding and planning to new curriculum content.

Strategy Development phase

This will remain an important phase in PBI as it provides the main teaching focus in terms of curriculum content and information processing competence. The cyclical nature of the phase means that the procedure of stating the plan, enacting the plan, and restating the plan in student language can occur as often as is needed for that task. As students become very familiar with the use of plans, they may suggest the format of the initial plan for the task, rather than relying on a teacher-generated plan. This provides incentive for the students and the opportunity for teachers to assess plan development skills for an unknown task.

Intra-task Transfer phase

The opportunity for students to develop plans for additional examples of the training task remains important as it provides the opportunity for cooperative teaching and learning. It also provides a time in which the class may be divided into small groups to allow for the differing needs of the Category A, Category B and Category C learners.

Consolidation and Generalization phase

The opportunities for consolidation and generalization increase as each student's knowledge base is enlarged. The development of a large number of plans, and the practice gained from their use, provides the opportunity for reducing the number of steps in specific plans, and for blending plans as more complex curriculum tasks are attempted.

The role of experience in consolidating the newly acquired skills can not be undervalued. It is through guided instruction and trial-and-error that students learn to discriminate between those situations in which a specific plan will, or will not work. Provided that failure does not lead to frustration, considerable learning will occur.

A TIME FRAMEWORK FOR IMPLEMENTING PBI

As the needs of each class are unique, the amount of time teachers will require to get PBI "up-and-running" will be a function of their specific situations. Up-and-running means that both teachers and students understand the concepts of plans and both concurrent and serial processing strategies, and are able to use these concepts fluently within the classroom. When PBI has been introduced in high school special education classes, the establishment period has been about a month. For higher functioning students, this period could be reduced.

In realistic terms, the establishment time will be a function of variables such as:

* The number of students in the class
* The age and range of student ability levels
* The appropriateness of students' existing coding strategies
* The rate at which the students are able to proceed through the instructional phases
* The level of teacher preparation
* The number of PBI lessons taught per day
* The level of personnel support available to the teacher

*   The commitment of the teacher and supervisor to the PBI method

Implementation will be easier if the teacher has had experience developing plans and establish coding strategies before commencing classroom implementation (as discussed in the section, *Preparing for the orientation phase*). Teachers who are able to take part in an inservice training course would be advantaged.

It is important that the introduction of PBI to students is taught thoroughly, and teachers should resist the temptation to rush through the phases of the model (that is, Assessment, Orientation, Strategy Development, Intra-task Transfer, Consolidation and Generalization).

SOME CONCLUDING REMARKS

We have attempted to show how a teacher can apply PBI in a classroom setting without the necessity to radically restructure teaching practices. Changes are required in the layout of lessons on the blackboard and in the format of worksheets in order to make plans clearly visible. These changes are not major and would quickly become a routine part of the teacher's lesson preparation.

There are a number of matters that teachers need to consider before introducing PBI. We have emphasized the importance of understanding the two coding processes, and the nature of planning. Also it is important for teachers to evaluate the curriculum content and topics, teaching strategies, and teaching materials that they have used in the past with a view toward compatibility with PBI. The age and ability level of the students, and the human and physical resources of the classroom and the school also require thought. The assistance of a teacher consultant, a teacher's aide, a resource room teacher, a parent-involvement program, or student teacher on practicum placement are several resources that can improve the impact of PBI.

The practical aspects involved in the introduction of PBI can be summarized thus:

*   Class teachers should practice the structuring of plans and selection of coding strategies on a variety of curriculum tasks to ensure that procedures are clear;

193

* Teachers should introduce PBI on one known task so that all students can become acquainted with the role of plans and coding, before applying the sequence in its normal format. This will also ensure that students become familiar with the cooperative teaching and learning activities used in PBI;

* Once introduced, PBI can be applied with all students regardless of their curriculum content competence, or their ability to use plans or coding strategies. Each student, whether they are Category A, B or C learners, will be encouraged to incorporate plans and coding in learning their current curriculum tasks.

In conclusion, the aim of PBI is to produce an integrated process-content curriculum to be employed by class teachers as part of their regular teaching for all students within the class. The use of traditional teaching structures such as individual, small group, and whole class lessons are compatible with a curriculum based on PBI. The change is in the presentation of content, not in what content is presented.

In the next chapter we will examine the extension of the PBI model of teaching beyond the single classroom to its incorporation in schools and school systems.

9

Cognitive Instruction Beyond
the Classroom

In this book, we have argued for the development of a teaching-learning process which is applicable to the total curriculum. For both teachers and students, the integrated process-content curriculum (*cognitive curriculum*) provides a consistent learning framework for both academic and nonacademic tasks. Its use in a class for students with learning or developmental disabilities will have obvious benefits in terms of improved student problem solving skills and learning independence. If students are to reap the benefits of a cognitive curriculum, their total school experience must be cognitively oriented. A single, short-term intervention in one class may not have lasting consequences and would be far from ideal.

In this chapter, we are concerned with the application of PBI methods across classrooms, schools, and ultimately school systems. We explore this broader environment in two main sections.

The first section deals with change at the classroom, school, and system level. In particular, it addresses the need for the inclusion of information processing skills training within all classroom programs together with some minor curriculum presentation changes. It also addresses the broader perspective of teacher training both at preservice and inservice levels. The second section deals with the partnership of research and practice in the application of information processing in the classroom.

CHANGE WITHIN THE EDUCATION SYSTEM

Sometimes change within education is considered to be anathema; disrupting the teaching process, causing vexation to teachers and administrators, and reducing the energy that might otherwise be directed toward instruction. Certainly, when change is introduced for the sake of change alone, there may be some reason for unsettling consequences. However, in most cases, programs that require change are aimed ultimately at improving the education offered to students and are directed at variations in teaching practice. This is certainly true in the case of Process-Based Instruction.

Some writers have suggested that change which is imposed on the classroom teacher inevitably leads to conflict and resistance (Blumberg, 1980). This may result simply as a reaction to the imposition of change, though others have suggested that resistance is a consequence of teachers being required to give up a highly over-learned pattern of teaching practices, and to reconceptualize these practices in a new form (Conway, 1986). In other words, the teacher must unlearn certain practices, and learn others (Sarason, 1971). The important implication of these findings is that educators need to ensure that change is not prescriptive, but rather is sought, and perceived by those involved to be a cooperative endeavor (Tarver, 1986).

Although some teachers may seek to introduce new methods into their classrooms, the ultimate value of those methods on a broader scale is determined by the support (or lack of support) given by other teachers and administrators. More importantly, interventions for students with learning and intellectual disabilities will prove valueless if they span only the duration of one teacher's contact: The cognitive curriculum must be an on-going and enduring teaching strategy. This means that the introduction of approaches such as Process-Based Instruction must extend across grades and teachers.

Change for Students and Teachers

Process-Based Instruction has been designed as an integral part of the on-going teaching and learning process within the classroom. As discussed in the previous chapter, integrating process and content does not require a complete readjustment of teaching strategies. It does not require unlearning in the sense that certain practices must

196

be discontinued. However, to introduce PBI does mean adding a new dimension to classroom practice, that is, the awareness and application of information processing concepts.

The student

The ultimate aim of any cognitive strategy training model is the demonstration of independent problem solving skills by the student. Unlike the behavioral approach in which emphasis is placed on the demonstration of a response, cognitive interventions focus on understanding how the response is obtained. In the same way as teachers need to change their approach to teaching to reflect a cognitive framework, students must be taught the method and value of approaching learning from a cognitive perspective.

Teaching students new cognitive strategies is somewhat like providing them with "new clothes" (Karoly, 1984). Many existing strategy training models have provided students with only one situation in which new clothes can be worn. Once teachers have provided the new apparel, they must reinforce its use in as many curriculum tasks as possible. The value for students of learning within a cognitive framework is illustrated clearly in the use of cooperative teaching and learning strategies. Teacher guidance of the new behavior to enhance students' awareness of the cognitive strategy is followed by student demonstration of the strategy through instruction of peers, accompanied by teacher and peer reinforcement.

As the student becomes more proficient in applying information processing strategies to initial curriculum tasks, more diverse tasks may be introduced in which coding and planning demands are not obvious, and in which greater energy on the student's part for solution is required. This transition from well- to ill-structured tasks and the students' successes in meeting the new demands signifies a movement from novice to proficient learner for that task.

The teacher

The prime change for the teacher is the need to approach instruction with a greater awareness of how students learn. Attention must be focused on the way in which students approach curriculum tasks, rather than what they learn in terms of rote memorization of academic facts.

Some restructuring of teaching style is needed to ensure that new content is presented in the framework of well-structured tasks which clearly demonstrate the application of information processing concepts. In other words, the teacher must make clear the cognitive requirements of the task in terms of plans and coding strategies. The teacher must ensure that these strategies are learned, applied and monitored, rather than expect that they will occur unassisted. Once the PBI framework has been established in a classroom, it replaces the existing approach and in turn becomes the on-going educational practice in the class.

To integrate a cognitive teaching focus successfully into the teacher's repertoire, change must occur across all teaching subjects, not only within one or two "critical" academic areas (such as reading or arithmetic). As this issue concerns all teachers taking the class, it will be discussed in detail in the following section. Moreover, changes to the educational environment within the classroom are relatively easy to achieve as they rely on the expertise and enthusiasm of the individual teacher and the cooperation of the students. Innovation at the classroom level often is effective only for learning within that class and on lessons taught by that teacher. In other words, there is only minimal generalization of new skills outside the specific learning context. For the benefits of an integrated process-content curriculum to last beyond the academic year or to be incorporated into lessons taught by other teachers, a much broader change needs to occur.

Changing the Educational Environment of the School

For cognitive strategy training to expand beyond the laboratory, beyond the isolated short-term classroom experiment, or even beyond the cognitive curriculum of a classroom teacher, a number of changes must occur. These changes must cross curriculum areas, and therefore require the support of the school administration, teaching staff, students and parents. The following section focuses upon various factors that support and contribute to change within the school environment.

A balance between general and specific strategies

Throughout our discussions of Process-Based Instruction, we have emphasized the need to teach cognitive skills that are "macroscopic" rather than "microscopic" (Rooney & Hallahan, 1985). Strategies must apply to a wide range of tasks rather than being applicable only to specific curriculum sub-skills. This implies a trade-off between general and specific strategies to ensure that students learn to recognize how strategic behavior applies to a variety of curriculum tasks (Conway, 1986). Within a specific school, the corporate body of teachers must decide how this trade-off may be achieved.

PBI provides a balance between the very general and the highly specific. For the full potential of PBI to be realized, coding strategies and plans must relate to the curriculum and to such noncurriculum issues as student motivation, attention, and attitudes to schooling. These aspects of the affective domain frequently are disassociated from the academic tasks upon which training has focused.

The legacy of the behavioral approach

The profound influence of the behavioral approach on both curriculum and instruction, particularly in special education, is well known to most teachers. The defining of behavioral objectives; teaching within a data-based instructional methodology with the accompanying probes; and the use of teaching strategies such as shaping, modeling, prompting and cuing are well-known features of the behavioral approach which continues to be recommended widely as the major teaching approach for special education classrooms. The major emphasis in the behavioral approach is on the teacher's ability to shape the performance of the student to achieve the mastery level set by the teacher, rather than the student working independently toward the task solution.

Curriculum methodology in special classes largely remains focused on highly task-analysed curriculum documents in which the instructional objectives, teaching strategies and mastery level required of the student are clearly set out. Many early direct teaching approaches (such as Distar) also regulated teacher behavior, requiring them to follow the instructional sequence without deviation. Although these curricula were valuable in providing teachers with clear instructional steps, they were often developmental rather than functional in focus, and frequently failed to acknowledge the processing needs of students. In addition to the teacher- or program-prescribed teaching sequence, behavioral assessment was directed toward the definition of appropriate curriculum skill areas and appropriate instructional objectives. Typically, assessment did not focus on students' understanding of their information processing capabilities necessary for achieving success.

It is important to emphasize that some behavioral teaching strategies are compatible with cognitive instructional approaches. Many cognitive approaches retain some behavioral techniques such as the use of reinforcement, initial teacher guidance, and the achievement of curriculum task competence. However, the difference between cognitive and behavioral approaches relates primarily to the goals of teaching. For those concerned with the application of the behavioral model, the instructional goal is the performance of the required curriculum behavior; for the cognitivist, it is the student's demonstration of understanding of the learning process (Tarver, 1986).

The employment of a cognitive curriculum

Cognitive strategy training models provide a new approach for teachers who are concerned with ensuring that students with learning and mild intellectual disabilities become more aware of their own cognitive skills. With learning disabled students in particular, the problem may not be simply a deficiency in one academic or cognitive skill area but in the ability to coordinate or integrate the information necessary to solve the task (Swanson, 1987b). For these students, the behavioral approach may not adequately address the issue of understanding the processing demands of a curriculum task.

Swanson argued that the strength of information processing lies in its broad application. It is important that teaching does not deteriorate into the training of highly specific cognitive strategies. Instead, it should build upon a broader framework of strategic behavior which include plans and coding strategies that apply across a range of tasks.

As discussed earlier, if there is a trap for those interested in developing teaching strategies, it is an over-emphasis on highly task-specific strategies with little general value. This criticism is particularly true of some cognitive behavior modification studies in which researchers appeared to be more concerned with the refinement

200

of specific techniques than with the educational welfare of the student (Rooney & Hallahan, 1985).

The adoption of the PBI model

Innovation can emanate from all levels within the school, from the classroom teacher, head teachers and subject coordinators, school administrators, and from the students themselves. The first essential characteristic is a commitment to introduce change. Let us first deal with the ideal situation, namely, the introduction of Process-Based Instruction at the school level.

Process-Based Instruction is a dynamic system, that is, it is a flexible teaching strategy that can be adapted by individual teachers to meet the specific demands of their students. During the development of PBI, we have been concerned not to prepare a "resource kit" that might give the impression of a complete, "teacher-proof" program. It is the model that generalizes, not the individual plans or techniques which might be developed by a teacher or consultant for a specific group of students. With this in mind, staff must agree to adopt the model and to develop unique applications to suit the needs of their class groups.

The implementation of PBI will depend largely upon the current teaching and administrative practices. Extra effort is required to produce change in traditional teaching practices particularly in the first year of PBI. However, the benefits of change, especially when it is introduced across grades, will be significant and obvious.

The role of the principal

A whole school program might seem to be a mammoth undertaking, but there are a number of steps and conditions which can expedite change. Generating broad interest in change is most effectively achieved by the senior administrative staff. There are numerous studies that have drawn attention to the important contribution of principals in effecting change in special education (Cline, 1981; Davis, 1980). Indeed, the active support of the school principal is vital to the successful implementation and continuation of change, especially in providing moral support to the staff and in creating a climate that provides legitimacy for the project.

The role of a project director or consultant

The most important issue in the introduction of PBI into the school setting is the acquisition by staff of new knowledge, skills, and attitudes. In the early introductory phase, a consultant (knowledgable in the theory and practice of PBI) can facilitate the easy transition from traditional teaching methods and techniques to those consistent with the PBI model. The project director or consultant may come from within the school, perhaps on part-time or full-time release, or from the employing education authority. The consultant's special skills and knowledge can be used to clarify project goals and operations, minimize daily difficulties encountered by classroom teachers, and provide relevant information and guidance.

The central role of the consultant is the integrate PBI into routine classroom activities. The ideal objective of consultants is to make themselves redundant. Once the classroom teacher has become familiar with cognitive instructional techniques, and has adapted these techniques to individual learning situations, the initial work of the consultant or project director is completed, and on-going monitoring should be sufficient to maintain the application of PBI across the school.

The value of community spirit

There is no joy in being the only teacher in a school who is implementing PBI, and for the students, there are limited benefits. The advantages that can accrue to students come from the continuation of specific teaching strategies as the students pass from one grade or level to the next, and from one teacher to the next. This is especially true when the students have a learning difficulty or a mild intellectual disability, as the continuity allows for the extension and reinforcement of information processing skills.

Teachers may gain moral support from others who are using Process-Based Instruction by forming a "critical mass" or core of teachers who can share problems and solutions and learn from each other (Berman & McLaughlin, 1980). In a sense, the group of teachers becomes the school-based agent of change. They act as the catalysts, helpers, solution givers and resource persons (Beare & Millikan, 1983). They could also become the "PBI advisors" to new staff entering the school or to supply teachers.

Implementation strategies

For each teacher, the implementation process consists of the development of methods and practices which are in accord with the age and ability level of students, and the curriculum topics that are presently addressed. Teachers need to gain a clear understanding of the philosophy of cognitive instruction, the use of specific coding strategies, the development and application of plans, and the actual process of combining strategic behavior and curriculum content. In reality, the staff needs familiarity and practice in the procedures which have been discussed in Chapters 7 and 8. In other words, they learn by doing.

In large schools, particularly high schools, coordination of change might involve the presentation of an initial overview presented to the entire staff, followed by each faculty working as a team. Berman and McLaughlin (1980) suggested several elements that should be incorporated in the introduction of models such as Process-Based Instruction, including introduction of the theory and practice via an in-service workshop, and individual consultations with teachers to develop specific introductory activities (Table 9.1).

The strategies suggested by Berman and McLaughlin do not incorporate consultations with students. However, in PBI, students become directly involved in the evaluation of the model. Together, students and teachers become instructional designers and problem solvers; teaching-learning teams who oversee the development of information processing competencies and academic skills in curriculum and extra-curricular activities.

The role of parents

Much has been written about the importance of ensuring that teachers and students are involved in the development of new instructional models. Parents also play a vital role in this process (Gallagher & Vietze, 1986; Turnbull & Turnbull, 1986). They can work effectively with teachers by reinforcing PBI principles when assisting their children with academic tasks at home or in the classroom. The benefits of such cooperation increases the possibility of students' generalizing planning and strategy use.

Parents can learn how to use PBI techniques by attending parent-teacher nights or mini inservice courses, by observing and participating in classroom activities, and by noting information bulletins prepared by school personnel. In this way they can become involved directly in the application of PBI and may include appropriate plans and coding strategies when assisting their children with homework or during home coaching.

Table 9.1: Implementation Considerations for School-based Change

---

* *Teacher training workshops.* Teachers will learn how to use PBI if they are given "hands on" training in translating the model into specific classroom activities. In a workshop setting, teachers may be introduced to the foundations and the principles of PBI, and perhaps even to strategy and plan generation. Within faculty meetings, the reality of the classroom and the specificity of curriculum topics can be addressed to facilitate the direct application of the model with specific student groups.

* *Classroom assistance using a resource or consultant teacher.* A resource teacher should be available within the school to provide relevant and practical advice. This teacher could provide on-the-spot assistance while not becoming involved in co-teaching activities, or could work in a team teaching role if asked by the teacher.

* *Observation of PBI in other classrooms.* Teachers can gain insights into the operation and success of PBI when they watch and discuss the use of PBI with other participating teachers. Videotaped sessions or segments of classroom activities, together with discussions may provide the most cost-effective in-servicing activity. Using this strategy, peers provide effective counseling, instruction, and encouragement.

* *Regular consultancies.* Regular meetings of participating teachers (and others who are being introduced to PBI) would focus on practical matters. Such sessions would provide a forum for feedback of the on-going monitoring, an opportunity to discuss new applications, and the chance to develop consistency in implementation (so important when students move from teacher to teacher and from grade to grade). Moreover, these consulting sessions could provide the stimulus for changes in curriculum foci and the planning and development of new curriculum content.

At a whole school level, meetings would provide individual teachers and adminstrative staff with the opportunity to overview the curriculum in terms of the whole school plan, thereby ensuring that all teachers were introducing the integrated process-content curriculum at the same pace, and throughout all lessons.

* *Project planning.* Teacher feedback can be an important means of analyzing the current use of PBI. It also provides the vehicle for modifying Process-Based Instruction for future implementation. Involvement of classroom teachers in these planning activities fosters cooperation and enthusiasm for the project.

* *Involvement of the principal.* The significant part played by school principals in supporting changes to teaching practice and curriculum, emphasizes their role in staff training. While principals may not require an intimate knowledge of PBI practices, it is important that they are well-informed of goals, directions, and matters which affect intra- and inter-departmental cooperation.

* *Information bulletins.* For new staff and supply teachers, the availability of an information bulletin on PBI teaching techniques would be valuable. It would ensure the continuity of PBI within the classroom and acceptance of the methodology by the new teachers. The bulletin ideally would be supplemented by assistance from the project director/consultant or existing staff members. Information bulletins are particularly important in school where there is a high staff absenteeism. In these cases, bulletins would need to be brief to permit easy reading and comprehension before a teacher takes a PBI class.

The challenge of a new approach

Resistance to change can occur at many levels and from many perspectives (Swanson, 1987a). School administrators may not be easily convinced to adopt a cognitive curriculum. The procession of ineffective "wonder" curricula of the past 20 years (for example, Ayres Perceptual Motor) has left teachers and administrators skeptical about new approaches. For many teachers, behavioral approaches have "stood the test of time" and both teachers and the systems which employ them are comfortable with existing approaches. For teachers seeking new instructional techniques, cognitive approaches must be considered in relation to other emerging approaches, such as holistic language approaches and discovery learning. If cognitive approaches such as PBI are unable to meet the two key teacher criteria - methodological rigor and sound educational practice - they too will be cast aside.

Incorporating Cognitive Strategies at a Systems Level

Education systems are open. They are not insulated from the environment, but are part of the social, cultural, and economic fabric of the community, state and nation. What schools are able to achieve in terms of the education of students with learning and intellectual disabilities will have a continuing impact beyond formal education.

The recognition that education is an open system is a constant reminder that change can come both from inside and outside the school system, whether this is a local school board, a regional or county authority, or a state or federal authority (Bernardo, 1980). In other words, change can result from governmental, employer and community interests, and from the initiatives of members within the educational system such as principals, teachers, or students (Harman, 1983). Policy makers are sensitive to major influences in the provision of services for students with special needs, and decisions often reflect these pressures. Two such influences have been mainstreaming and the provision of early intervention programs. We shall examine these in relation to cognitive learning strategies.

Mainstreaming

The increased emphasis on mainstreaming students with special needs has meant that students who were previously served in the special class must now cope with the demands of the regular classroom. The more individualized attention, different educational demands and often less stringent behavioral demands of the special class give way to a required compliance with the regular curriculum and conformity to the class standards.

The student who is able to understand the processing demands of curriculum tasks and who is able to structure a plan and to code information, has a much greater chance of success in the regular class. This student is able to function as a relatively independent learner, is able to understand the requirements of the task, and has the strategies to work progressively towards a task solution with minimal teacher supervision. The use of cooperative teaching and learning strategies prior to the mainstreaming of students with special needs enhances independence and the probability of successful integration.

The value of any information processing training would be lost if the regular class teachers did not reinforce the skills in the new setting. The cognitive "new clothes" would be left in the wardrobe. Hence, there is a need for education systems not only to encourage schools to develop a cognitive curriculum approach, but to involve teachers in special classes and units so that the process of transition from special to regular settings is enhanced.

Early intervention

Cognitive interventions have been conducted mainly with primary and secondary school-aged students with learning and intellectual disabilities. The early identification of young children with learning problems sufficiently serious to require special education services has produced an expanding body of literature with a major emphasis on Down's Syndrome (LaVeck & Brehm, 1978; Ludlow & Allen, 1979; Piper & Pless,1980). Findings have shown that negative emotional, behavioral, and educational consequence occur when service providers fail to address these areas before formal schooling begins.

Researchers have been concerned with the identification of cognitive and behavioral predictors of later school performance, and the suitability of assessment devices for use with preschool children (Aram & Nation, 1980; Horn & Packard, 1985; Schakel, 1986; Vietze & Coates, 1986). While there have been notable advances in performance prediction, less interest has been shown in the development of cognitive interventions for children below Grade 1. To some extent this is surprising given the recognition afforded to children's early learning experiences. For instance, nearly a decade ago, an early childhood conference entitled "Too late at eight" reflected the importance of the early childhood period as a vital stage in the reduction of disadvantageous educational experiences for children in need of special education (Atkinson, 1980).

Given the importance of the first few years of a child's cognitive development as the foundation of the knowledge base, it is interesting that early childhood educators have not moved more deliberately toward information processing theory. In the area of language development, some initiatives have been made in linking cognition with language skills to ensure that appropriate learning strategies are fostered. Whitman (1987), for example, argued that the extent to which young children benefit from an educational intervention is related to their linguistic ability and task knowledge. As young children develop sufficient receptive language skills and are able to follow adult directions, they are more likely to benefit from self-instruction than from external instruction.

Whitman's statements were made in relation to self-instruction models in which the teacher demonstrates the self-instruction statements prior to the young child using them as self-statements. These comments are even more appropriate in relation to other cognitive teaching models, such as PBI which rely on the student taking the initiative in attempting curriculum tasks while using their own language structures.

The importance of integrating language and cognitive strategy training within early intervention programs lies in the development of a knowledge base that includes not only curriculum content knowledge, but also cognitive strategy knowledge that is appropriate to a range of content tasks. Young children who possess a good knowledge base which includes relevant generalizable strategies will be more likely to apply those strategies when confronted with new tasks because of the likelihood of achieving success. Teaching appropriate strategies to young children at the earliest opportunity is more effective than replacing existing, inefficient behaviors at a later time. Hence, the value of process-content instruction would be intensified if introduced in early childhood, and maintained throughout school and tertiary education.

A general cognitive curriculum for young children has been developed at the John F. Kennedy Center at Vanderbilt University in Tennessee. The new curriculum was based on the premise that in spite of the proliferation of universally applicable curricula, too many children arrive in Grade 1 unprepared to commence scholastic activities because they have poorly developed thinking skills and processes that inhibit their ability to learn and problem solve (Burns, Haywood & Delclos, 1987). The Cognitive Education

Curriculum for Preschool Children addresses the cognitive processes that are needed to teach children how to think and learn effectively (Haywood, Brooks, & Burns, 1985).

The curriculum was based generally on the principles contained in Feuerstein Instrumental Enrichment (Chapter 3) and has the goal of increasing educability rather than imparting specific knowledge or skills. In other words, it aims to emphasize processes rather then simply to produce the correct answers, through the principle of mediated learning. Briefly, the program operates on a multi-dimensional approach using in-center teaching of concepts to the young, "at-risk" children; in-home application of these concepts by parents, parent training; and, home visits by the Center staff. The curriculum includes units that deal with:

* self-regulation and following rules to help children develop body regulation, to verbalize what they are doing, and to understand the meaning and utility of rules;
* cooperation, sharing, and thinking behavior to help children consider social behavior and its consequences;
* intrinsic motivation, matching, and classification to help children derive pleasure and challenge in learning to classify colors, shapes and sizes;
* summative behavior to teach children to relate past and future events to the present; and,
* comparison and planning behavior.

The cognitive intervention formed the core of an outreach project which began in 1984 to replicate the demonstration study at the Kennedy Center. Since that time, numerous preschools have introduced the cognitive curriculum, though at the time of writing, we are not aware of any published report reviewing the project or indicating the outcomes.

Curriculum Services and Support Documents

To permit teachers within a school, or a school district, to embrace process-based interventions as a general teaching approach, curriculum documents need to be examined with a view to incorporating strategy training components. Curriculum documents, either published or developed by educational authorities, are generally the most common way of disseminating new teaching content and they provide an ideal way of introducing a process-content model either in specific skill areas or in vertical curricula across the K-12 grade range.

In most cases, curriculum documents are prepared by specialists who have a detailed knowledge of content. To integrate process training within the curriculum, it would be necessary to involve not only these specialists, but also others who have knowledge of both the theory and practical application of process-based interventions. In most cases, these individuals would be practicing teachers and consultants who have used Process-Based Instruction within their classrooms. Through their input, the curriculum documents would become a functional framework for change within the school system.

A further method of inservicing the *concept* of PBI would be through the development of demonstration packages to show how cognitive instruction and curriculum content could be integrated across age, ability, and curriculum areas. These packages could contain examples of plans showing how they are developed, exemplify the coding options available in specified tasks, and provide sample lessons at several levels. They may contain such materials as video sequences, examples of worksheets, photographs of classroom layouts, and examples of students' work. The main consideration here is the demonstration of Process-Based Instruction across grade levels and curriculum areas (both academic and nonacademic).

It is important to stress that demonstration packages such as those mentioned above would not be intended as part of a teaching kit or as prescriptive curriculum documents for implementation. The important and unique feature of PBI is the involvement of both teachers and students in the development of plans and coding strategies to meet current curriculum needs.

Teacher Training

The successful establishment of a cognitive curriculum in the classroom, school or system is very much dependent upon the content of teacher training programs. The profound influence of the behavioral approach on teacher training, particularly in special education, is well known to most teachers. Within preservice training for regular education, less emphasis is placed on specific behavioral techniques, although classroom behavior management strategies are taught commonly as successful methods of class control. The major emphasis is not so much on the process of learning, as on the curriculum content to be taught. In training courses for high school teaching, lectures are even more heavily weighted toward content, with relatively little emphasis being given to students' understanding of the processes of learning.

Pre-service training

Hudson, Morsink, Branscum, and Boone (1987) examined the literature relating to areas of competency for teachers of students of learning disabilities. These competencies were synthesized from professional opinions, empirical research, descriptive studies and topical reviews. Competency statements were identified within five areas: general and special education; planning and evaluation; curriculum content; clinical teaching strategies; and behavior management. The majority of these related to cognitive interventions, and included the following:

* The implementation of programs which help students engage in self-monitoring behavior, predicting outcomes, and other deliberate attempts to study and learn;
* The selection of appropriate clinical strategies for individual students (for example, how a student can become a more efficient decoder in context or in isolation);
* The involvement of students as active respondents in learning tasks rather than as passive recipients of instruction; and,
* The reduction of impulsive behaviors, and increase of problem solving techniques.

These statements are generic rather than specific in nature as a reflection of the vast heterogeneity of students with learning difficulties. However, they do provide a guide for possible content in teacher training courses as well as a direction for applied research.

In a position paper on the preparation of professional personnel in the field of learning disabilities, the US National Joint Committee on Learning Disabilities (1987) defined seven areas of problems and issues in structuring training courses. Three are specifically related to the issues of broadening the understanding of the methodology and value of integrated cognitive interventions.

Firstly, the ability to effect changes in educational policy, curricula and practice has been impeded by the organizational complexity and rigidity of educational institutions. This problem is similar to that faced by schools and systems where the need to change teaching/learning approaches is confronted by strong pressures to persist with existing strategies. It would appear that the wealth of literature available to teacher educators on the value of cognitive interventions is infrequently translated into lecture content.

Secondly, the goals of professional education differ from those of accrediting, certifying, or licensing agencies, and this difference often has a negative effect on curriculum and training policy. The pressure to produce "employable" graduates is important in times of reduced enrolments and the temptation to teach to the employer's needs, rather than to innovative strategies is great.

Thirdly, many university faculties are distanced from the realities of educational systems and are resistant to modifications in professional education and training programs. In contrast to the previous problem area, many instructors in higher education institutions are either not in touch with innovative classroom strategies or fail to incorporate them in their teaching courses. Hence, they may not make students aware of the potential of innovative techniques. The position paper concluded that problem areas must be examined and solutions found either before or concurrently with bold changes in academic curricula and practical experience.

To the three areas of concern expressed in the position paper, a fourth can be added: The lack of convincing evidence from applied research to overcome curriculum and practice inertia. This remains a major stumbling block in the teaching of an integrated process-content curriculum. In the same way that teachers are reluctant to employ methods that remain untested, or which are based on very short-term studies, teacher educators also are sceptical of approaches that have gained little empirical support.

These problem areas and issues, together with others discussed in the position paper, highlight the need to produce professionals with knowledge of all relevant strategies so they may provide appropriate and effective service delivery. The National Joint Committee position paper recommended that training should allow for interdisciplinary input in such topics as Educational Theory and Practice in Learning Disabilities. Content would include areas such as "knowledge and appraisal of teaching/clinical methods, curriculum planning and sequences, systems of teaching content material, (and) systems for the development of adaptive, modified, or unique curriculum" (p. 230). The use of interdisciplinary teaching staff provides opportunities to experience innovative techniques in related fields and to examine issues from the perspectives of differing disciplines.

It would be misleading to suggest that there have been no attempts to introduce cognitive educational theory and techniques into teacher preparation programs. One such attempt was reported by Martin (1984) who introduced information processing content in a junior curriculum foundation course, a junior educational psychology course, and in a senior student teaching seminar.

Each alternate 45 minute lecture was set aside to allow input relating to strategy training. This included:

1. The introduction of a paper-and-pencil activity to emphasize a specified cognitive skill;
2. Class discussion relating to strategy use in problem solving;
3. Individual or small group work in problem solving;
4. Group discussion stimulating metacognition; and,
5. Consideration of the application of strategic behavior in teaching activities.

Martin's approach included many of the characteristics of effective strategy training programs that have been used with students in school. His initiative showed the ease of introducing a contemporary cognitive perspective in a teacher training program. Application can be readily achieved by:

1. Orienting tertiary instructors, practicum supervisors, and cooperating teachers to cognitive concepts;
2. Deciding upon generalizable skills that can be incorporated within teacher training courses;
3. Implementing strategy training in foundation subjects;
4. Requiring trainees to teach the cognitive skills to children;
5. Assessing trainees' strategic behavior in regard to their teaching practice;
6. Reinforcing the use of cognitive skills in practice teaching seminars; and,
7. Assessing the use of cognitive concepts by graduates.

While Martin emphasized concepts central to Feuerstein's Instrumental Enrichment Program, the application of his approach generally is consistent with the introduction of an integrated cognitive curriculum, such as Process-Based Instruction. Indeed, PBI concepts can be more readily applied across pre-service training, in foundation, and curriculum and instruction courses. The introduction of PBI within teacher preparation courses will constitute a reorientation in the classroom teaching practice of the future. However, at the same time energy must be directed toward in-service activities.

In-service training

Two forms of in-service training are available to teachers. The first involves the organization of workshops and short courses, typically organized by school systems. The workshop format provides the opportunity for demonstrations of how Process-Based Instruction would be translated into school and classroom practice. Teachers would need to become involved in an organized program which included activities such as the use of videotapes of actual class sessions, practical sessions in which participants would develop and refine plans, preparation of worksheets for specific curriculum content, and the preparation of assessment procedures and tests.

The second form of in-service training available to teachers is provided by tertiary education, particularly through higher degree studies. In some cases, postgraduate studies would provide the only opportunity for teachers to examine in depth the contribution of cognitive interventions to classroom teaching. It is of some concern that many higher education courses deal solely with theory and research and are often taught by staff distanced from the realities of the classroom (National Joint Committee, 1987). The apparent rationale for the empirical approach in postgraduate studies is that students have (somehow) reached a level of consciousness which enables them to translate statistics into effective classroom practices.

Let us make our commitment to research and theory quite clear. We support research-oriented courses, but we also believe that mediated learning is a key to effective instruction, especially in the area of cognitive educational psychology. For teachers to become more knowledgeable and involved in process-based interventions, the practical applications of cognitive instruction must be clear. The challenge for teacher educators is to examine the implications of teaching strategies and research in classroom models which integrate cognitive literature and curriculum content.

CHANGES IN RESEARCH APPROACHES

The role of researchers is critical in ensuring that any teaching/learning model is methodologically rigorous and educationally appropriate in the context in which it is to be applied. Existing research in cognitive strategy training has focused on the development and refinement of specific strategies such as self-monitoring for application within specific academic skills (Swanson, 1981; Wong, 1980). Specific strategies have been trialed most commonly with small groups of students in laboratory settings (Borkowski & Varnhagen, 1984; Kaufman & Kaufman, 1979). Studies of on-going classroom applications of an integrated process-content curriculum have not been reported.

In a review of learning disabilities research, Lyon (1987) argued that the field lacks scientific validity and clinical utility; in part, because it has failed to address the issues of definition, assessment and teaching practices. In particular, the use of the term strategy training has been widely misused. The failure of researchers to clearly define what they mean by strategy training has led to the obscurity of the precise understanding of the term (Gerber, 1983). This concealment is clearly illustrated in deBettencourt's (1987) review of three training approaches, each purporting to be a strategy training model, yet each having a different definition, methodology and measure of strategy attainment.

deBettencourt argued that research in specific strategy training models needs to state the training program more clearly, to be tied to an explicit theoretical framework, and be defined for a particular subgroup of students. The last point is particularly important as it reflects the reality that students with learning and intellectual disabilities do not represent a homogeneous group, but a group with varying degrees of skills in terms of receptive and expressive language, ability to use existing strategies, and curriculum knowledge.

As in the case of learning disabilities research, existing research in the area of cognitive instruction strategies for students with mild intellectual disabilities has also suffered from a tenuous relationship between theory and educational use (Whitman, 1987). In a review of self-instructional strategies, Whitman argued that theories have had more influence on the design of instructional strategies than on the guidelines directing the use of the strategies with specific students.

The impact of instructional strategies on the student is important and research must take into account the developmental status of the student. More attention must be focused on an examination of the interface between the individual student and the tasks being taught in the program. This, Whitman argued, must be considered at the time of formulating the program, not in retrospect.

The Future of Cognitive Research

In Chapter 6, we noted Sternberg's (1983) criteria for the validation of interventions designed to improve intellectual competence. There is one further condition that has special relevance to interventions that are related to school achievement, namely, the practical relevance of research. Some writers have tackled this issue by studying the statistical analyses used in educational research (Hanson, Abramson, & McNamara, 1986-87) though another alternative may be to study the educational practicality of interventions over an extended period of time. It will be necessary to develop longitudinal studies which will follow students' progress from their first introduction to the cognitive curriculum to well beyond their departure from school (Gaylord-Ross, 1979).

Longitudinal studies

Long-term studies of students requiring special education provisions are rare (McKinney & Feagans, 1984), as they require financial, logistic and professional commitment far beyond those of traditional one-shot studies (Lyon, 1987). Consequently, it is not surprising that many researchers are reluctant to undertake studies that have long gestation periods. Until researchers are able to look beyond these barriers, demonstration of the successful applications of strategy training will not occur, and teachers will remain unconvinced of their value, even in an integrated process-content curriculum.

An important issue for longitudinal classroom studies is the concern with monitoring changes in strategic behavior over time. Those studies which have focused upon highly specific strategic behaviors in laboratory settings have provided a wealth of information at a micro level. What is needed now is an equally rigorous examination of the effects of macro strategic behavior, that is, students' typical responses to a range of classroom activities. Evaluations of this kind will not be concerned with the control of internal and external experimental variables, such as maturation, selection and loss of subjects (Campbell & Stanley, 1963), but the adjustment of the teaching environment to meet the change.

Forgotten issues

It could be argued that the ultimate success of any research study is the adoption of a model by teachers and students and its persistent use in a variety of teaching settings. It is toward this goal that researchers must now focus cognitive research.

An important issue, not commonly considered in research studies, is ensuring that training continues until a performance criterion is achieved, rather than conducting training for a prescribed number of sessions. This would approximate the classroom situation more closely and would ensure that any failure to demonstrate the taught strategy was not the result of insufficient or ineffective training. Again, the use of a longitudinal study could overcome this problem.

Wong (1988) suggested that training must focus on both curriculum content *and* a specific cognitive strategy. However, many cognitive training studies have emphasized strategy use but have avoided their practical application to the curriculum areas in which the student is experiencing difficulty.

Wong also noted a number of neglected areas in cognitive strategy research that should be addressed in future studies. These included: the question of ownership of strategy; keeping clear the goal of strategy acquisition; and the strategy trainer's knowledge of their trainees. In regard to the first matter, many earlier (and current) studies have imposed adult-generated cognitive strategies upon students, often in the mistaken belief that students have no strategies of their own. Students with learning disabilities and mild intellectual disabilities do possess cognitive strategies though they may be inefficient or unable to be retrieved at the appropriate time. The ability to build upon existing strategies may increase the willingness of the student to use the new strategy. In PBI, student-developed plans and coding strategies ensure that the student is contributing throughout all phases of the learning cycle.

In order to keep the goals of the training program clear, Wong recommended that students be encouraged to see themselves as "co-researchers" and hence treated as equal partners. The concept of a co-researcher also has the benefits of enhancing the students' sense of commitment to the learning process, and the belief that their contribution is of value. Again, within PBI this is achieved through the use of cooperative teaching and learning practices. Student involvement enhances motivation during the training and increases the likelihood of continued use of the strategic behavior.

In many brief laboratory research projects, staff are not familiar with the students with whom they are working. They do not know the motivational background of the students and whether they are willing to participate in a new learning experience. Indeed, many research designs and experimental materials are not "user friendly", that is, they do not engender a sense of purpose or generate enthusiasm. In some cases, students simply appear to endure research. Any benefits that may have accrued from a "friendly" researcher are lost once the intervention program has been completed. However, longitudinal studies conducted in classrooms by the class teacher would provide more positive learning experience because of the extended nature of the training, and the familiarity of the teacher with student performance. Longitudinal studies also have the benefit that they allow the application of the learned strategy in a wide variety of learning situations both formally and informally, rather than being restricted to a short, segregated part of the day. They also provide the opportunity to involve parents in the training process.

Future cognitive intervention studies must move beyond the refinement of splinter procedures, towards strategies that are feasible for teachers to use as part of their on-going teaching. To satisfy this demand the strategies must:

* be taught within existing teaching programs;
* not require additional costly or time consuming teaching materials;
* be readily accessible and comprehensible to teachers as an instructional methodology; and,
* be relevant to current academic and nonacademic curriculum content.

Much current teaching is heavily teacher directed and places little emphasis on learner understanding of the cognitive processes

218

involved in attempting the task. Greater advances in cognitive skill and intelligent action will occur if teachers emphasize metacognitive understanding rather than providing specific knowledge and strategic information. Process-Based Instruction satisfies all of these criteria. As with other cognitive strategy training models, its final acceptance will be dependent on its ability to "stand the test of time" in teachers' classrooms, as well as satisfying the methodological rigor and sound educational practice requirements of the researcher.

SOME CONCLUSIONS

In this chapter, we have advocated a system-wide introduction of a cognitive curriculum. In doing so, we appreciate that other researchers have already initiated such changes. In the next five years, it is likely that curricula and curriculum documents will begin to appear which include strategy training as an essential component of the education process.

Our discussion in this chapter has identified where changes must start and how they can occur. We are aware that few education systems, school boards, or local education authorities will embrace a dramatic change in orientation toward process-based teaching strategies on request. Consequently, we believe that the start of a system-wide change must begin with individual classroom teachers and schools, and in the domain of pre-service training at the tertiary level.

In our final brief chapter, we take a rather different perspective to that which has dominated this book. We consider the impact of teaching and learning styles on students with special needs.

10

Looking Back: Looking Forward

In the winter of 1977, an educational consultant was working in a high school in a remote mining town in northern Canada. The school district had employed him to assess the intellectual ability of students who had been identified as learning disabled and to assist the classroom and resource teachers in designing individual programs. It was well below zero outside, and the climate in the small room where a 14-year-old sat with "the man from the city" was not much warmer. The grin that had started the session had disappeared quickly from the boy's face with the introduction of the intelligence and achievement test battery.

School records showed that the student had been through similar experiences several times before and yet his achievement (and classroom behavior) continued to show a gradual but obvious decline. Regardless of the good intentions of the psychologists and teachers, previous assessments and attempts at remediation had led to few educational gains.

The boy's educational history was not uncommon. Identification of students "at risk" had brought the resources of the school system into action. However, in this case, as with many others, the assessment techniques and remedial procedures that had been used by school personnel were inadequate to deal with the outcomes of years of missed opportunities and academic failure. As special education teachers know only too well, remediation often focuses on teaching students content and skills which are the source of continual failure. Few remediation programs have dealt with the student's understanding of how information is processed or the use of a systematic sequence to solve curriculum problems.

221

The foregoing chapters in this book have not reported educational conjury. They have dealt with the results of an evolution that has provided a rational instructional alternative for teachers in special and regular classrooms. The alternative is the integrated process-content curriculum, and in particular, Process-Based Instruction. In this short concluding chapter, we summarize the theory and practice of PBI and look toward benefits that may be derived from long-term changes in educational practice.

LOOKING BACK AT THEORY

Psychological theory has guided innovation in educational practice since the late 1700s. While certain periods in the recent history of education could be characterized by one approach (for instance, the dominance of the behavioral approach in the 1960s and 1970s), a more pragmatic view would assert the growth and decline of theoretical influences on education across nearly two centuries. This perspective would show the ascendancy of psychophysiology through the combination of sensory and motor coordination training (associationism) and its subsequent decline as instinct, psychoanalytic and personality theory became more prominent. These in turn waned with the emergence of theories related to perception and intelligence, and they too, gave way to behaviorism.

The study of memory was the first broad field cultivated within the domain of experimental psychology (Woodworth, 1938). While memory (or more accurately memorization) had been examined since the middle of the 1800s by noted researchers such as Ebbinghaus, and had been considered important in classroom learning, there had been a long period with few theoretical advances. Indeed, up until the late 1950s, the study of human memory had been restricted by simple association theory until it was thrust into the spotlight by the development of communication theory, linguistics, computing, and information processing theory (Estes, 1975). It was as a result of these developments that cognition began to exert its influence on the domain of education.

The student of information processing will be struck by two obvious characteristics of research on human cognition. First, the intensity of investigation into the minutiae of cognitive activity has led to a huge body of literature, in which the relationships between the many studies are not always apparent. This has resulted in the collation of fractional knowledge in which it is not easy to obtain the total perspective. Second, a bewildering collection of terminology has been generated. Terms and concepts have been created to account for subtle differences between concepts (for example, subordinate processes and coding processes), and even to label what seem to be the same concepts (sequential coding and successive coding).

The literature needs to be unified in order to explain how knowledge is gained and used, and also for an explanation of how information can be transmitted in the most effective way. From our point of view, the concepts of planning and problem solving provide the structure in which other information processing concepts (such as coding) can be satisfactorily incorporated. As a result, planning and problem solving relate directly to the efficient organization and presentation of information and thus, are fundamental to educational practice.

LOOKING FORWARD AT PRACTICE

The evolution of Process-Based Instruction has reflected the need to develop information processing competence in consort with the curriculum knowledge and skills being introduced and reinforced within the classroom. This approach encourages the establishment of a link and transition between the acquisition, knowledge, use, and application of strategic behavior by the students.

There appear to be several keys to the success of Process-Based Instruction. The first comes from the application of information processing theory and concepts to classroom activities and curriculum content. Using an integrated process-content curriculum, students are taught the necessary information processing skills to deal with specific tasks and problems. Gone is the obscurity of strategy training and the use of laboratory materials in isolation from a real-life context. Relevance and efficacy are two fundamental principles which apply equally to classes across the age and ability dimensions.

The second key to the success of PBI is the identification of students for whom instruction is appropriate for the specific academic task at hand (Category A, B, or C learners). Only when the academic tack is appropriate is it possible to effect change. This assessment procedure directs the teacher toward the selection of appropriate materials for individual students or for small groups.

The third key is the transfer of ownership of both plans and appropriate coding strategies from the teacher to the student. One of the important benefits of this transfer is the student's acceptance of responsibility for learning. Students will accept this responsibility only if they have a positive attributional belief system. In a study of metacognitive training with young children, Kurtz and Borkowski (1984) found that students with a prior disposition to attribute success to effort received a greater cognitive and motivational boost from the training than other students.

There are four principles that appear to apply to attributional retraining: it needs to be intensive to overcome students' entrenched negative beliefs; initial training should relate to task-specific beliefs and later focus upon program-specific beliefs; students must be able to compare their performances on tasks with and without the use of the appropriate strategies to encourage discrimination; and, training must link cognitive functioning to personality-motivational concepts (Borkowski, Weyhing, & Turner, 1986). These principles are prominent in Process-Based Instruction; success is attributed to effort rather than chance.

The fourth key to success is the explicit division between consolidation within the task cluster and generalization. Focusing attention on transfer of plans and strategies to very similar curriculum tasks within the intra-task transfer phase and later in the consolidation phase elaborates and establishes the value of strategies and plans for a specific cluster of tasks. In the consolidation and generalization phase, when plans are streamlined, students come to understand the concept of generalization beyond the task cluster.

While the terminology we have used in describing PBI may be "new", some may argue that PBI is neither novel nor necessarily innovative. To some extent, this is true. PBI is essentially appropriate student-oriented teaching practice, and as such, it is consistent with the methods used by many special and regular class teachers. However, PBI is more than just good practice. It combines logical and consistent teaching practice with procedures that have been derived from sound educational and psychological research.

The success of PBI comes from consistent application: Consistency in the augmentation of students' information processing skills, consistency in the application of these skills to new and known academic and nonacademic tasks, and consistency in use of process-content principles via the uninterrupted application of PBI experiences across the succession of grades.

224

In this book, we have expounded instructional principles that have found support in the special education and educational psychology literature. The future of PBI (or in fact, any process-content curriculum) will depend upon the belief of teachers in PBI's methods and practices together with a commitment to change and development. Teachers and students must also perceive obvious educational benefits accruing from the use of a process-content curriculum. At this point, we consider the long-term gains of cognitive curricula.

CHANGE IN THE POWER STRUCTURE

The history of special education is imbued with a spirit of succor. Students with special needs require protection and shelter from the world, and perhaps even from themselves. Remediation implies the provision of a cure or a healing. In short, the premise has been that these students need help.

Process-Based Instruction requires a change, if only a subtle one, from traditional philosophy toward an expression of support for the notion of equality of opportunity. Bayles (1985) argued that individuals with intellectual disabilities are entitled not only to the same rights as persons without intellectual disabilities, but they are also entitled to special considerations flowing from the duties and obligations of society toward them. In the case of PBI, equality of opportunity requires a change in the locus of decision making power, from one that is vested in the system, to one that rests with the individual. The special advantages (advocated by Bayles) are realized in PBI through the prescription of genuine educational outcomes for students with learning and intellectual disabilities.

In the first place, students are advantaged academically by the teacher's introduction of PBI. One teacher, using PBI for the first time, reported that she "fell behind" in the presentation of curriculum content to her 14 and 15-year-old students during the first part of the school year because she (and the students) "had to learn what PBI was all about". If this delay had continued, PBI would have been a failure. It didn't. By the end of the school year, the teacher had presented more material, and the students had learned more information and strategic behavior than would have been the case had she not used PBI.

Second, there must be a change in students' social-emotional development. Few cognitive training approaches have focused upon changes in attributional characteristics (Borkowski et al., 1986; Kurtz & Borkowski, 1984). Researchers have examined various social correlates of learning and intellectual disabilities, but the link between remediation and social skills has not been clearly enunciated (Ceci, 1986; Chapman et al., 1984; Corman & Gottlieb, 1978; Schloss & Schloss, 1985; Perlmutter, 1986).

PBI operates via social interactions and the use of cooperative teaching and learning procedures that hold considerable promise for improved classroom dynamics. In one class, there was a young teenager (Robert) who had very poor interpersonal skills and who was recognized by the other students as being the weakest scholastically. At the beginning of the program, Robert clearly was isolated socially by his peers. However, with the introduction of peer tutoring, Robert became an important member of the class. Students often stated explicitly that the plans being generated had to "work" for Robert otherwise the plans were of little value. Robert's status in the class changed and he was included in activities from which he would have previously been excluded. Perhaps more importantly, his interpersonal skills became more appropriate. PBI, therefore, had a secondary effect on classroom dynamics.

Third, students must develop learning and problem solving independence. There are three aspects here: the students' ability to organize learning within the classroom; their ability to perceive the relevance of their instruction for out-of-school activities; and, their ability to recognize their role in the teaching-learning process. During the year in which PBI has been implemented in a special education high school class for students with a mild intellectual disability, anecdotal records were kept of the interactions between students, and between students and the teachers. Below we have noted some typical examples which, among others, have provided insights into the way students viewed and incorporated PBI.

Many of the records relate to plans and their use as students' main problem solving strategy. However, more important were those instances in which it became clear that students had become responsible for at least part of their own education. In the long-term, PBI may gradually come to change the basis of student's "personal power" (Rogers, 1977).

Consider the difference between the common description of students with disabilities as passive learners and the very brief interactions below.

Teacher: Did you use the plan for doing that sum?
Sean: No.
Teacher: How did you do it then?
Sean: I never use your plans. They are other people's plans. I like to make up my own that works for me.
Teacher: Do you think you can explain to Karen how to do it?
Sean: Yes. I'll explain it to her. Kids can understand the words other kids use better than the teacher's.

In this case, the student had come to recognize that he had a role to play in his own education. Needless to say, the teacher played a significant part in guiding and encouraging the student to explore and discover his own abilities. Such an approach is fundamental to PBI, as it is future oriented.

We asserted the notion of genuine educational outcomes. For the student with special needs, the significant indicator of success has been embodied by the term generalization. Consider the following situation. In this case, the class was discussing the use of a subtraction plan and was diverted by the students into a general discussion.

Peter: You need to have a plan for racing go-carts too.
Teacher: Why?
Peter: Because you need a plan to drive around the corners.
Michael: Yes we need a plan for football too.
Teacher: What plan?
Michael: They are secret ones. They have names to confuse the opposition. Some teams video our game and copy our plans, so we have to change them all the time.
Teacher: That's life. We follow plans and then have to be ready to change our plans for better ones if things change.

These spontaneous comments by students indicate that the application of plans to nonteaching situations, particularly everyday life, is important. This may occur as a deliberate teaching event or it might occur spontaneously. Perhaps of more relevance were the unsolicited comments made by a teacher who had a class of students trained in PBI techniques for science. He commented that the students clearly understood the concept of plans and their application, and handled their science exercises much more effectively than they could have previously. When comparing these students with those of previous years, he believed that the current group was coping with the science curriculum content much more competently.

Perhaps the last comment we can make about PBI relates to its dynamic nature. PBI is a changing process that is very much influenced by the teacher's disposition, style, and enthusiasm. It will grow, develop and adapt as research explores both the theory and practice of process-content curricula. The success of PBI at a system level will depend upon ethnographic research techniques and longitudinal studies which provide a means of examining the development of interpersonal interactions, social behaviors, and the efficacy of planning and problem solving as classroom teaching methods.

In the final analysis, the success of Process-Based Instruction may not come from the examination of the students' school behavior, but from their ability to blend into the mainstream of society. After all, the aim of our formal education is to produce students who can adapt successfully to life's experiences.

References

Anderson, J. R. (1975). *Cognitive psychology and its implications.* San Francisco: Freeman & Co.

Anderson, J. R. (Ed.) (1981). *Cognitive skills and their acquisition.* Hillsdale, N.J: Erlbaum.

Anderson, J. R. (1982). Acquisition of cognitive skills. *Psychological Review, 89,* 369-406.

Anderson, J. R., Greeno, J. G., Kline, P. J., & Neves, D. M. (1981). Acquisition of problem-solving skills. In J. R. Anderson (Ed.), *Cognitive skills and their acquisition* (pp. 191-230). Hillsdale, N.J: Erlbaum.

Aram, D. M., & Nation, J. E. (1980). Preschool language disorders and subsequent language and academic difficulties. *Journal of Communication Disorders, 13,* 159-170.

Ashman, A. F. (1978). *The relationship between planning and simultaneous and successive synthesis.* Unpublished doctoral dissertation, University of Alberta, Edmonton, Canada.

Ashman, A. F. (1980). Changes in educational and residential care for the mentally retarded. In R. S. Laura (Ed.), *Problems of handicap* (pp. 8-16). Melbourne: Macmillan.

Ashman, A. F. (1982). Coding, strategic behavior, and language performance of institutionalized mentally retarded young adults. *American Journal of Mental Deficiency,* 86, 627-636.

Ashman, A. F. (1984). The role of planning and decision making in the training of retarded persons. *Human Learning, 3,* 19-32.

Ashman, A. F. (1985). Process-based interventions for retarded students. *Mental Retardation and Learning Disability Bulletin, 13,* 62-74.

Ashman, A. F. (1985, September). *Group and individual differences following process training.* Paper presented at the joint meeting of the Australian Group for the Scientific Study of Mental Deficiency, AAMR, and the Australian Association of Special Educators, Brisbane, Queensland.

Ashman, A. F. (1986). Aeronautical decision making. *SAFE, 3,* 1-8.

REFERENCES

Ashman, A. F. (1987, August). *Improving the cognitive competence of intellectually disabled adolescents.* Paper presented at the 2nd Conference on the Practical Aspects of Memory, University College, Swansea, Wales.

Ashman, A. F. (in press). Process-based instruction: Integrating assessment and instruction. In H. C. Haywood & D. Tzuriel (Eds.), *Dynamic assessment and instruction..* Hillsdale, NJ: Erlbaum.

Ashman, A. F., & Schroeder, S. R. (1986). Hyperactivity, methylphenidate, and complex human cognition. In K. D. Gadow (Ed.), *Advances in learning and behavioral disabilities* (Vol. 5) (pp. 295-316). Greenwich, CN: JAI Press.

Atkinson, J. K. (Ed.) (1980). *Too late at eight: Prevention and intervention.* St. Lucia, Qld: Schonell Education Research Centre, University of Queensland.

Atkinson, R. C., & Shiffrin, R. M. (1968). Human memory: A proposed system and its control processes. In K. W. Spence & J. T. Spence (Eds.), *The psychology of learning and motivation: Advances in research and theory* (Vol. 2) (pp. 89-195). New York: Academic Press.

Ayres, R. R., & Cooley, E. J. (1986). Sequential versus simultaneous processing on the K-ABC: Validity in predicting learning success. *Journal of Psychoeducational Assessment, 4,* 211-220.

Baker, L. (1982). An evaluation of the role of metacognitive deficits in learning disabilities. *Topic in Learning and Learning Disabilities, 2,* 27-35.

Barclay, C. R. (1981). On the relations between memory and metamemory. *Psychological Record, 31,* 153-156.

Bayles, M. D. (1985). Equal human rights and employment for mentally retarded persons. In R. S. Laura & A. F. Ashman (Eds.), *Moral issues in mental retardation* (pp. 11-27). London: Croom Helm.

Beare, H., & Millikan, R. (1983). Change strategies: A framework for systematic discussion and planning. In G. S. Harman, (Ed.), *Managing structural change in education in Asia and the Pacific: A blueprint for action.* (pp. 5-19). Canberra, ACT: Australian Government Publishing Service.

Belmont, J. M., & Butterfield, E. C. (1971). Learning strategies as determinants of memory deficiencies. *Cognitive Psychology, 2,* 411-420.

Belmont, J. M., Ferretti, R. P., & Mitchell, D. W. (1982). Memorizing: A task of untrained mildly mentally retarded children's problem solving. *American Journal of Mental Deficiency, 87,* 197-210.

Belmont, J. M., & Mitchell, D. W. (1987). The general strategies hypothesis as applied to cognitive theory in mental retardation. *Intelligence, 11,* 91-105.

230

REFERENCES

Berger, R. M., Guilford, J. P., & Christensen, P. R. (1957). A factor-analytic study of planning abilities. *Psychological Monographs, 71*, Whole No. 435.

Berman, P., & McLaughlin, M. W. (1980). Factors affecting the process of change. In M. M. Milstein (Ed.), *Schools, conflict, and change* (pp. 57-71). New York: Teachers College Press.

Bernardo, C. M. (1980). The management of instructional and administrative changes in large school districts. In M. M. Milstein (Ed.), *Schools, conflict, and change* (pp. 168-178). New York: Teachers College Press.

Blackman, S., & Goldstein, K. M. (1982). Cognitive styles and learning disabilities. *Journal of Learning Disabilities, 15*, 106-115.

Bloom, B. S. (1984). The 2 sigma problem: The search for methods of group instruction as effective as one-to-one tutoring. *Educational Researcher, 13*(6), 4-16.

Blumberg, A. (1980). School organizations: A case of generic resistance to change. In M. M. Milstein (Ed.), *Schools, conflict, and change* (pp. 16-29). New York: Teachers College Press.

Boehm, A. E. (1967). *Test of basic concepts*. New York: The Psychological Corporation.

Borkowski, J. G. (1987, August). *Understanding inefficient learning: Attributional beliefs and the training of memory and comprehension strategies*. Paper presented at the 2nd Practical Aspects of Memory conference, University College, Swansea, Wales.

Borkowski, J. G., & Buchel, F. P. (1983). Learning and memory strategies in the mentally retarded. In M. Pressley & J. R. Levin (Eds.), *Cognitive strategy research: Psychological foundations* (pp. 103-128). New York: Springer-Verlag.

Borkowski, J. G., Carr, M., & Pressley, M. (1987). "Spontaneous" strategy use: Perspectives from metacognitive theory. *Intelligence, 11*, 61-75.

Borkowski, J. G., Carr, M., Rellinger, E., & Pressley, M. (in press). Self-regulated cognition: Interdependence of metacognition, attributions, and self-esteem. In B. Jones (Ed.), *Dimensions of thinking*. Hillsdale, NJ: Erlbaum.

Borkowski, J. G., & Cavanaugh, J. C. (1979). Maintenance and generalization of skills and strategies by the retarded. In N. R. Ellis (Ed.), *Handbook of mental deficiency, psychological theory and research* (2nd ed.) (pp. 569-617). Hillsdale, NJ: Erlbaum.

Borkowski, J. G., & Varnhagen, C. K. (1984). Transfer of learning strategies: Contrast of self-instructional and traditional training formats with EMR children. *American Journal of Mental Deficiency, 88*, 369-379.

231

REFERENCES

Borkowski, J. G., Weyhing, R. S., & Turner, L. A. (1986). Attributional retraining and the teaching of strategies. *Exceptional Children, 53*, 130-137.

Borys, S. V., Spitz, H. H., & Dorans, B. A. (1982). Tower of Hanoi performance of retarded young adults and nonretarded children as a function of solution length and goal state. *Journal of Experimental Child Psychology, 33*, 87-110.

Boyd, T. L., Skedsvold, P., & Rossiter L. (1986). The control of contextual extinction effects during a fear-incubation procedure. *Behaviour Research and Therapy, 24*, 613-617.

Bradley, T. B. (1983). Remediation of cognitive deficits: A critical appraisal of the Feuerstein model. *Journal of Mental Deficiency Research, 27*, 79-92.

Brailsford, A. (1981). *The relationship between cognitive strategy training and performance on tasks of reading comprehension with a learning disabled group of children.* Unpublished masters thesis, University of Alberta, Edmonton, Canada.

Bransford, J., Sherwood, R., Vye, N., & Rieser, J. (1986). Teaching thinking and problem solving. *American Psychologist, 41*, 1078-1089.

Brickner, D. D. (1982). *Interventions with at risk and handicapped infants.* Baltimore, MD: University Park Press.

Brown, A. L. (1975). The development of memory: Knowing, knowing about knowing, and knowing how to know. In H. W. Reese (Ed.), *Advances in child development and behavior* (Vol. 10) (pp. 103-151). New York: Academic Press.

Brown, A. L. (1978). Knowing when, where and how to remember: A problem of metacognition. In R. Glaser (Ed.), *Advances in instructional psychology* (pp. 77-143). New Jersey: Erlbaum.

Brown, A. L., Armbruster, B. B., & Baker, L. (1986). The role of metacognition in reading and studying. In J. Orasanu (Ed.), *Reading comprehension: From research to practice* (pp. 49-78). Hillsdale, NJ: Erlbaum.

Brown, A. L., & Barclay, C. R. (1976). The effects of training specific mnemonics on the metamnemonic efficiency of retarded children. *Child Development, 47*, 71-80.

Brown, A. L., Bransford, J. D., Ferrara, R. A., & Campione, J. C. (1983). Learning, remembering and understanding. In P. Mussen (Ed.), *Handbook of child psychology: Cognitive development* (Vol. 3) (pp. 77-166). New York: John Wiley.

Brown, A. L., & Campione, J. C. (1982). Modifying intelligence or modifying cognitive skills: More than a semantic quibble? In D. K. Detterman & R. J. Sternberg (Eds.), *How and how much can intelligence be increased* (pp. 215-229). Norwood, NJ: ABLEX.

Brown, A. L., & Campione, J. C. (1986). Psychological theory and the study of learning disabilities. *American Psychologist, 14*, 1059-1068.

REFERENCES

Brown, A. L., Campione, J. C., & Barclay, C. R. (1979). Training self-checking routines for estimating test readiness: Generalization from list learning to prose recall. *Child Development*, *50*, 501-512.

Brown, A. L., & Palincsar, A. S. (1982). *Inducing strategic learning from texts by means of informed, self-control training* (Tech. Rep. No. 262). Champaign, Ill: University of Illinois at Urbana-Champaign, Center for the Study of Reading.

Brown, A. L., & Palincsar, A. (1986). *Guided, co-operative learning and individual knowledge acquisition*. (Tech. Rep. No. 372). Urbana: University of Illinois, Center for the Study of Reading.

Bryant, P. E. (1985). The distinction between knowing when to do a sum and knowing how to do it. *Educational Psychology*, *5*, 207-215.

Burger, A. L., Blackman, L. S., & Clark, H. T. (1981). Generalization of verbal abstraction strategies by EMR children and adolescents. *American Journal of Mental Deficiency*, *85*, 611-618.

Burger, A. L., Blackman, L. S., Clark, H. T., & Reis, E. (1982). Effects of hypothesis testing and variable format training on generalization of a verbal abstraction strategy by EMR learners. *American Journal of Mental Deficiency*, *86*, 405-413.

Burns, M. B., Haywood, H. C., & Delclos, V. R. (1987). Young children's problem-solving strategies: An observational study. *Journal of Applied Developmental Psychology*, *8*, 113-121.

Burns, R. B., & Lash, A. A. (1986). A comparison of activity structures during basic skills and problem-solving instruction in seventh-grade mathematics. *American Educational Research Journal*, *23*, 393-414.

Burton, A. (Ed.) (1982). *The pathology and psychology of cognition*. London: Methuen.

Butterfield, E. C. (1983). To cure cognitive deficits of mentally retarded persons. In F. J. Menolascino, R. Neman, & J. A. Stark (Eds.), *Curative aspects of mental retardation: Biomedical and behavioral advances* (pp. 203-221). Baltimore, MD: Paul H. Brookes.

Butterworth, G. E., & Light, P. H. (Eds.) (1982). *Social cognition: Studies of the development of understanding*. Brighton, Gt Britain: Harvester.

Byrne, R. (1981). Mental cookery: An illustration of fact retrieval from plans. *Quarterly Journal of Experimental Psychology*, *33A*, 31-37.

Byrne, R. W. (1979). *The form and use of knowledge in a decor-design task*. Unpublished manuscript, University of St. Andrews, Scotland.

233

Byrnes, M. M., & Spitz, H. H. (1977). Performance of retarded adolescents and non-retarded children on the Tower of Hanoi problem. *American Journal of Mental Deficiency, 81*, 561-569.

Campbell, D. T., & Stanley, J. C. (1963). *Experimental and quasi-experimental designs for research.* Chicago, Ill: Rand McNally.

Campione, J. C., & Brown, A. L. (1978). Towards a theory of intelligence: Contributions from research with retarded children. *Intelligence, 2*, 279-304.

Cantor, J. H., & Spiker, C. C. (1978). The problem solving strategies of kindergarten and first-grade children during discrimination learning. *Journal of Experimental Child Psychology, 26*, 341-358.

Carroll, J. B. (1978). *How shall we study individual differences in cognitive abilities? - Methodological and theoretical perspectives* (Tech. Rep. No. 1). Chapel Hill: L. L. Thurstone Psychometric Laboratory, University of North Carolina at Chapel Hill.

Cavanaugh, J. C., & Borkowski, J. G. (1979). The metamemory-memory "connection": Effects of strategy training on maintenance. *Journal of General Psychology, 101*, 161-174.

Cavanaugh, J. C., & Borkowski, J. G. (1980). Searching for metamemory-memory connections: A developmental study. *Developmental Psychology, 16*, 441-453.

Cavanaugh, J. C., & Perlmutter, M. (1982). Metamemory: A critical examination. *Child Development, 53*, 11-28.

Ceci, S. (Ed.) (1986). *Handbook of cognitive, social, and neuropsychological aspects of learning disabilities* (Vol. 1). Hillsdale, NJ: Erlbaum.

Chapman, J. W., Silva, P. A., & Williams, S. (1984). Academic self-concept: A study of academic and emotional correlates in nine-year old children. *British Journal of Educational Psychology, 54*, 284-292.

Chase, W. G., & Chi, M. T. H. (1980). Cognitive skills: Implications for spatial skill in large-scale environment. In J. Harvey (Ed.), *Cognition, social behavior, and the environment* (pp. 111-136). Potomac, MD: Erlbaum.

Cline, R. (1981). Principals' attitudes and knowledge about handicap. *Exceptional Children, 48*, 172-174.

Cohen, R. L. (1983). Reading disabled children are aware of their cognitive deficits. *Journal of Learning Disabilities, 16*, 286-289.

Cohen, R. L., & Nealon, J. (1979). An analysis of short-term memory differences between retardates and nonretardates. *Intelligence, 3*, 65-72.

Conway, R. N. F. (1981). *Maintenance and generalization of behavioural gains within and beyond a token economy.* Unpublished Masters thesis, University of Newcastle, N.S.W.

Conway, R. N. F. (1985, April). *Remediation using the information-integration model*. Paper presented at the annual meeting of the American Educational Research Association, Chicago, Illinois.

Conway, R. N. (1985). *The information processing model and the mildly developmentally delayed child: Assessment and training*. Unpublished doctoral dissertation, Macquarie University, North Ryde, Australia.

Conway, R. N. F. (1986). Teaching strategies in special education: A continual challenge in all learning environments. *The New South Wales Journal of Special Education, 6*, 11-16.

Conway, R., & Ashman, A. (1987). Process-Based Instruction: Incorporating learning skills within curriculum areas. In E. A. Bartnik, G. M. Lewis, & P. A. O'Connor (Eds.), *Technology, resources, and consumer outcomes* (pp. 133-139). Perth, WA: PE Publications.

Conway, R. N. F., & Gow, L. (in press). Mainstreaming special class students with mild handicaps through group instruction. *Remedial and Special Education*.

Corman, L., & Gottlieb, J. (1978). Mainstreaming mentally retarded children: A review of research. In N. R. Ellis (Ed.), *International review of research in mental retardation* (Vol. 9) (pp. 251-275). New York: Academic.

Cronbach, L. J. (1954). *Educational psychology*. New York: Harcourt Brace Jovanovich.

Cronbach, L. J., & Snow, R. E. (1977). *Aptitude and instructional methods*. New York: John Wiley.

Cullari, S., & Ferguson, D. G. (1981). Individual behavior change: Problems with programming in institutions for mentally retarded persons. *Mental Retardation, 19*, 267-270.

Cummins, J. P. (1979). Language functions and cognitive processing. In J. P. Das, J. Kirby, & R. F. Jarman. *Simultaneous and successive cognitive processes* (pp. 175-185). New York: Academic Press.

Cummins, J., & Das, J. P. (1977). Cognitive processing and reading difficulties: A framework for research. *Alberta Journal of Educational Research, 23*, 245-256.

Daniel, J. S. (1977). Learning styles and strategies: The work of Gordon Pask. In N. Entwistle & D. Hounsell (Eds.), *How students learn* (pp 83-92). UK: Institute for Research and Development in Post-Compulsory Education, University of Lancaster.

Das, J. P. (1985). Remedial training for the amelioration of cognitive deficits in children. In A. F. Ashman & R. S. Laura (Eds.), *The education and training of the mentally retarded: Recent advances* (pp. 215-244). London: Croom Helm.

Das, J. P., & Heemsbergen, D. (1983). Planning as a factor in the assessment of cognitive processes. *Journal of Psychoeducational Assessment, 1*, 1-15.

REFERENCES

Das, J. P., Kirby, J., & Jarman, R. F. (1979). *Simultaneous and successive cognitive processing.* New York: Academic Press.

Das, J. P., Snart, F., & Mulcahy, R. F. (1982). Reading disability and its relation to information-integration. In J. P. Das, R. F. Mulcahy, and A. E. Wall (Eds.), *Theory and research in learning disabilities* (pp. 85-109). New York: Plenum Press.

Das, J. P., & Varnhagen, C. K. (1986). Neuropsychological functioning and cognitive processing. *Child Neuropsychology, 1,* 117-140.

Davis, W. E. (1980). Public school principals' attitudes toward mainstreaming retarded pupils. *Education and Training of the Mentally Retarded, 15,* 174-178.

Day, J. D. (1983). The zone of proximal development. In M. Pressley & J. R. Levin (Eds.), *Cognitive strategy research: Psychological foundations* (pp. 155-175). New York: Springer-Verlag.

deBettencourt, L. U. (1987). Strategy training: A need for clarification. *Exceptional Children, 54,* 24-30.

Deci, E. L., & Porac, J. (1978). Cognitive evaluation theory and the study of human motivation. In M. R. Lepper & D. Greene (Eds.), *The hidden cost of reward: New perspectives on the psychology of human motivation.* Hillsdale, NJ: Erlbaum.

Dempster, F. N. (1981). Memory span: Sources of individual differences. *Psychological Bulletin, 89,* 63-100.

Derry, S. J., Hawkes, L. W., & Tsai, C. (1987). A theory of remediating problem-solving skills of older children and adults. *Educational Psychologist, 22,* 55-87.

Derry, S. J., & Murphy D. A. (1986). Designing systems that train learning ability: From theory to practice. *Review of Educational Research, 56,* 1-39.

Dixon, P. (1987) The structure of mental plans for following directions. *Journal of Experimental Psychology: Learning, Memory, and Cognition, 13,* 18-26.

Dixon, R. A., Hertzog, C., & Hultsch, D. F. (1986). The multiple relationships among metamemory in adulthood (MIA) scales and cognitive abilities in adulthood. *Human Learning, 5,* 165-177.

Doyle, W. (1983). Academic work. *Review of Educational Research, 53,* 159-199.

Drinkwater, B. A. (1976). Visual memory skills of medium contact Aboriginal children. *Australian Journal of Psychology, 30,* 33-56.

Duffy, A. T., & Nietupski, J. (1985). Acquisition and maintenance of video game initiation, sustaining and termination skills. *Education and Training of the Mentally Retarded, 20,* 157-162.

Dunn, L. M. (1968). Special education for the mildly retarded: Is much of it justifiable? *Exceptional Children, 35,* 5-22.

Ellis, E. S. (1986). The role of motivation and pedagogy on the generalization of cognitive strategy training. *Journal of Learning Disabilities, 19*, 66-70.

Ellis, E. S., Lenz, B. K., & Sabornie, E. J. (1987). Generalization and adaptation of learning strategies to natural environments: Part 1: Critical agents. *Remedial and Special Education, 8*, 6-20.

Englert, C. S., Culatta, B. E., & Horn, D. G. (1987). Influence of irrelevant information in addition word problems on problem solving. *Learning Disability Quarterly, 10*, 29-36.

Estes, W. K. (1975). The state of the field: General problems and issues of theory and metatheory. In W. K. Estes (Ed.), *Handbook of learning and cognitive processes, Vol. 1 Introduction to concepts and issues* (pp. 1-24). Hillsdale, NJ: Erlbaum.

Eyde, D. R., & Altman, R. (1978). *An exploration of metamemory processes in mildly and moderately retarded children* (Final Report). Columbia, MO: Department of Special Education, University of Missouri-Columbia.

Fardig, D. B., Algozzine, R. F., Schwartz, S. E., Hensel, J. W., & Westling, D. L. (1985). Postsecondary vocational adjustment of rural, mildly handicapped students. *Exceptional Children, 52*, 115-121

Ferguson, E. D. (1976). *Motivation: An experimental approach.* New York: Holt, Rinehart & Winston.

Feuerstein, R., Rand, Y., & Hoffman, M. (1979). *The dynamic assessment of retarded performers: The learning potential assessment device, theory, instruments, and techniques.* Baltimore, MD: University Park Press.

Feuerstein, R., Rand, Y., Hoffman, M., & Miller, R. (1980). *Instrumental Enrichment: An intervention for cognitive modifiability.* Baltimore: University Park Press.

Fixx, J. F. (1979). *Games for the super-intelligent.* London: Frederick Muller.

Flavell, J. H. (1977). Metamemory. In R. Kail & J. Hagen (Eds.), *Perspectives on the development of memory and cognition* (pp. 3-33). Hillsdale, NJ: Erlbaum.

Flavell, J. H. (1979). Metacognition and cognitive monitoring: A new area of cognitive-developmental inquiry. *American Psychologist, 34*, 906-911.

Flavell, J. H., Fredericks, A. B., & Hoyt, J. D. (1970). Developmental changes in memorization processes. *Cognitive Psychology, 1*, 324-340.

Foot, H. C., Shute, R. H., & Morgan, M. J. (1987, August). *Peer tutoring and children's memory.* Paper presented at the 2nd Practical Aspects of Memory conference, University College, Swansea, Wales.

Forness, S. R., Silverstein, A. B., & Guthrie, D. (1979). Relationship between classroom behavior and achievement of mildly mentally retarded children. *American Journal of Mental Deficiency, 84,* 260-265.

Fotheringhame, J. (1986). Transfer of training: A field study of some training methods. *Journal of Occupational Psychology, 59,* 59-71.

Fraser, B. J. (1986). *Classroom environment.* London: Croom Helm.

Fredericksen, N. (1984). Implications of cognitive theory for instruction in problem solving. *Review of Educational Research, 54,* 363-407.

Frostig, M., & Horne, D. (1964). *The Frostig program for the development of visual perception: Teacher's guide.* Chicago: Follett.

Fuchs, D., Fuchs, L. S., Benowitz, S., & Barringer, K. (1987). Norm referenced tests: Are they valid for use with handicapped students? *Exceptional Children, 54,* 263-271.

Gagné, R. M. (1980). Learnable aspects of problem solving. *Educational Psychologist, 15,* 84-92.

Gallagher, J. J., & Vietze, P. M. (Eds.) (1986). *Families of handicapped persons: Research, programs and policy issues.* Baltimore: Brooks.

Garofalo, J., & Lester, F. K. (1985). Metacognition, cognitive monitoring, and mathematical performance. *Journal of Research in Mathematics Education, 16,* 163-176.

Garrison, J. W., & MacMillan, C. J. B. (1987). Teaching research to teaching practice: A plea for theory. *Journal of Research and Development in Education, 20,* 38-43.

Gaylord-Ross, R. J. (1979). Mental retardation research, ecological validity, and the delivery of longitudinal educational programs. *Journal of Special Education, 13,* 69-80.

Gelzheiser, L. M., Shepherd, M. J., & Wozniak, R. H. (1986). The development of instruction to induce skill transfer. *Exceptional Children, 53,* 125-129.

Gentry, J. R. (1978). Early spelling strategies. *The Elementary School Journal, 79,* 88-92.

Gerber, M. M. (1983). Learning disabilities and cognitive strategies: A case for training or constraining problem solving? *Journal of Learning Disabilities, 16,* 255-260.

Gerber, M. M. (1984). Investigations of orthographic problem-solving ability in learning disabled and normally achieving students. *Learning Disability Quarterly, 7,* 157-164.

Gerber, M. M., & Hall, R. J. (1987). Information processing approaches to studying spelling deficiencies. *Journal of Learning Disabilities, 20,* 134-142.

Gick, M. L. (1985). The effect of a diagram retrieval cue on spontaneous analogical transfer. *Canadian Journal of Psychology, 39,* 460-466.

Gick, M. L., & Holyoak, K. J. (1983). Schema induction and analogical transfer. *Cognitive Psychology, 15*, 1-38.

Glidden, L. M., & Warner, D. A. (1983). Semantic processing and recall improvement of EMR adolescents. *American Journal of Mental Deficiency, 88*, 96-105.

Graham, S., & Miller, L. (1979). Spelling research and practice: A unified approach. *Focus on Exceptional Children, 12*, 1-16.

Graham. S., & Freeman, S. (1985). Strategy training and teacher- vs. student-controlled study conditions: Effects on LD students' spelling performance. *Learning Disability Quarterly, 8*, 267-274.

Greenberg, G. (1983). Psychology without the brain. *Psychological Record, 33*, 49-58.

Guilford, J. P., & Lacey, J. I. (Eds.) (1947). *Printed classification tests*. Army Air Force Aviation Psychological Research Report No. 5. Washington, DC: U.S. Government Printing Office.

Hagen, J. W., Barclay, C. R., & Newman, R. S. (1982). Metacognition, self-knowledge, and learning disabilities: Some thoughts on knowing and doing. *Topics in Learning and Learning Disabilities, 2*, 19-26.

Hanson, M., Abramson, M., & McNamara, J. (1986-87). Practical significance in special education research. *Journal of Special Education, 20*, 401-408.

Harlow, J. M. (1848). Passage of an iron rod through the head. *New England Journal of Medicine, 39*, 389-393.

Harlow, J. M. (1868). Recovery from the passage of an iron bar through the head. *Massachusetts Medical Society, 2*, 327-346.

Harman, G. S. (Ed.) (1983). *Managing structural change in education in Asia and the Pacific: A blueprint for action*. Canberra, ACT: Australian Government Publishing Service.

Harris, K. R., Graham, S., & Freeman, S. (in press). The effects of strategy training and study conditions on metamemory among LD students. *Exceptional Children*.

Harth, R. (1982). The Feuerstein perspective on modification of cognitive performance. *Focus on Exceptional Children, 15*, 1-12.

Harth, R., Johns, R., Cloud, C., & Campbell, C. (1981). Mediation: How it can improve problem solving skills. *Academic Therapy, 17*, 225-230.

Hartman, L. M. (1983). A metacognitive model of social anxiety: Implication for treatment. *Clinical Psychology Review, 3*, 435-456.

Hayes-Roth, B., & Hayes-Roth, F. (1979). A cognitive model of planning. *Cognitive Science, 3*, 275-310.

Haywood, H. C., Brooks, P., & Burns, S. (1985). *Development and evaluation of the cognitive curriculum, for young children*. Unpublished manuscript, Vanderbilt University, Nashville, Tennessee.

239

REFERENCES

Hilgard, E. R., & Bower, G. H. (1966). *Theories of learning* (3rd ed.). New York: Appleton-Century-Crofts.

Hobbs, N., Bartel, N., Dokecki, P. R., Gallagher, J. J., & Reynolds, M. C. (1977). *Exceptional teachers and exceptional learners: Instructional strategies from special education: A baker's dozen.* Nashville, TN: The Center for the Study of Families and Children, Vanderbilt Institute for Public Policy Studies, Vanderbilt University.

Horn, W. F., & Packard, T. (1985). Early identification of learning problems: A meta-analysis. *Journal of Educational Psychology, 77,* 597-607.

Horner, R. H., Bellamy, G. T., & Cohen, G. T. (1984). Responding in the presence of non-trained skill: Implications of generalization error patterns. *Journal of the Association for the Severely Handicapped, 9,* 287-295.

Howie, D. R., Thickpenny, J. P., Leaf, C. A., & Absolum, M. A. (1985). The piloting of "Instrumental Enrichment" in New Zealand with eight mildly retarded children. *Australian and New Zealand Journal of Developmental Disabilities, 11,* 3-16.

Hudson, P. J., Morsink, C. V., Branscum, G., & Boone, R. (1987). Competencies for teachers of students with learning disabilities. *Journal of Learning Disabilities, 20,* 232-236.

Humphreys, L. G. (1978). Doing research the hard way: Substituting analysis of variance for a problem in correlational analysis. *Journal of Educational Psychology, 70,* 873-876.

Jarman, R. F. (1978). Cross-modal and intra-modal matching: Relationships to simultaneous and successive synthesis and levels of performance among three intellectual groups. *Alberta Journal of Educational Research, 24,* 100-112.

Jarman, R. F., & Das, J. P. (1977). Simultaneous and successive synthesis and intelligence. *Intelligence, 1,* 151-169

Johnson, D. W., Johnson, R., & Johnson-Houlubec, E. (1984). *Circles of learning.* Alexandria, VA: Association for Supervision and Curriculum Development.

Johnson, N. F. (1986). On looking at letters within words: Do we "see" them in memory? *Journal of Memory and Language, 25,* 558-570.

Jones, H., Ridgway, J., & Bremner, J. G. (1983). The effect of encouraging self-evaluation on children's ability to transfer the use of a mnemonic strategy. *Human Learning, 2,* 327-338.

Justice, E. M. (1985). Metamemory: An aspect of metacognition in the mentally retarded. In N. R. Ellis & N. W. Bray (Eds.), *International Review of Research in Mental Retardation* (Vol. 13) (pp. 79-108). Orlando, FL: Academic.

Kagan, J., Rosman, B. L., Day, D., Albert, J., & Phillips, W. (1964). Information processing in the child: Significance of analytic and reflective attitudes. *Psychological Monographs, 78,* (1, Whole No. 578)

Karoly, P. (1984). Self-management problems in children. In E. J. Mash & L. G. Terdal (Eds.), *Behavioral assessment of childhood disorders* (pp. 79-126). New York: Guilford Press.

Kaufman, A. S. (1984). K-ABC and controversy. *Journal of Special Education, 19,* 409-444.

Kaufman, A. S., & Kaufman, N. L. (1983). *Kaufman Assessment Battery for Children (K-ABC).* Circle Pines: AGS.

Kaufman, A. S., Kaufman, N. L., & Goldsmith, B. Z. (1983). *K-SOS: Kaufman sequential or simultaneous.* Circle Pines: AGS.

Kaufman, D. (1978). *The relationship of academic performance to strategy training and remedial techniques: An information processing approach.* Unpublished doctoral dissertation, University of Alberta. Edmonton, Canada.

Kaufman, D. & Kaufman, P. (1979). Strategy training and remedial techniques. *Journal of Learning Disabilities, 12,* 416-419.

Kavale, K. A. (1987). Theoretical quandaries in learning disabilities. In S. Vaughn & C. S. Bos (Eds.), *Research in learning disabilities: Issues and future directions* (pp. 19-33). Boston: College-Hill.

Keeley, S. M., Shamberg, K. M., & Carbonell, J. (1979). Operant clinical intervention: Behavior management or beyond? Where are the data? *Behavior Therapy, 7,* 292-305.

Kendall, C. R., Borkowski, J. G., & Cavanaugh, J. C. (1980). Metamemory and the transfer of an interrogative strategy by EMR children. *Intelligence, 4,* 255-270.

Kirby, J. R., & Ashman, A. F. (1984). Planning skills and mathematics achievement: Implications regarding learning disabilities. *Journal of Psychoeducational Assessment, 2,* 9-22.

Kirby, J. R., & Robinson, G. L. W. (1987). Simultaneous and successive processing in reading disabled children. *Journal of Learning Disabilities, 20,* 243-252.

Klausmeier, H. J. & Associates (1979). *Cognitive learning and development: Information-processing and Piagetian perspective.* Cambridge, MASS: Ballinger.

Klebanoff, S. G. (1945). Psychological changes in organic brain lesions and ablations. *Psychological Bulletin, 42,* 585-623.

Koorland, M. A. (1986). Applied behavior analysis and the correction of learning disabilities. In J. K. Torgesen & B. Y. L. Wong (Eds.), *Psychological and educational perspectives on learning disabilities* (pp. 297-328). Orlando, FL: Academic Press.

Kramer, J. J., & Engle, R. W. (1981). Teaching awareness of strategic behavior in combination with strategy training: Effects on children's memory performance. *Journal of Experimental Child Psychology, 32,* 513-530.

REFERENCES

Kramer, J. J., Nagle, R. J., & Engle, R. W. (1980). Recent advances in mnemonic strategy training with mentally retarded persons: Implications for educational practice. *American Journal of Mental Deficiency, 85*, 306-314.

Kreitler, S., & Kreitler, H. (1986). Individuality in planning: Meaning patterns of planning styles. *International Journal of Psychology, 21*, 565-587.

Kreutzer, M. A., Leonard, C., & Flavell, J. H. (1975). An interview study of children's knowledge about memory. *Monographs of the Society for Research in Child Development,* (Serial No. 159, No. 1).

Krupski, A. (1979). Are retarded children more distractible? Observational analysis of retarded and nonretarded children's classroom behavior. *American Journal of Mental Deficiency, 84*, 1-10.

Krywaniuk, L. W. (1974). *Patterns of cognitive abilities of high and low achieving school children.* Unpublished doctoral dissertation, University of Alberta, Edmonton, Alberta, Canada.

Kurtz, B. F., & Borkowski, J. G. (1984). Children's metacognition: Exploring relations among knowledge, process, and motivational variables. *Journal of Experimental Child Psychology, 37*, 335-354.

Ladd, G. W. (1981). Effectiveness of a social learning method for enhancing children's social interaction and peer acceptance. *Child Development, 52*, 171-178.

Lancioni, G. E. (1982). Employment of normal third and fourth graders for training retarded children to solve problem dealing with quantity. *Education and Training of the Mentally Retarded, 17*, 93-102.

Larson, C. O., Dansereau, D. F., O'Donnell, A. M., Hythecker, V. I., Lambiotte, J. G., & Rocklin, T. R. (1985). Effects of metacognitive and elaborative activity on cooperative learning and transfer. *Contemporary Educational Psychology, 10*, 342-348.

Laura, R. S., & Ashman, A. F. (Eds.) (1985). *Moral issues in mental retardation.* London: Croom Helm.

LaVeck, B., & Brehm, S. (1978) Individual variability among children with Down's syndrome. *Mental Retardation, 16*, 135-137.

Lawson, M. J. (1980). Metamemory: Making decisions about strategies. In J. R. Kirby & J. B. Biggs (Eds.), *Cognition, development, and instruction* (pp. 145-159). New York: Academic Press.

Lawson, M. J. (1984). Being executive about metacognition. In J. R. Kirby (Ed.), *Cognitive strategies and educational performance* (pp. 89-109). New York: Academic Press.

Lawson, M. J. (1986). A framework for describing strategy use. *Mental Retardation and Learning Disability Bulletin, 14*, 2-19.

LeDoux, J. E. (1984). Cognition and emotion. In M. S. Gazzaniga (Ed.), *Handbook of cognitive neuroscience* (pp. 357-368). New York: Plenum Press.

Lenz, B. K., Schumaker, J. B., Deshler, D. D., & Beals, V. L. (1984). *Learning Strategies Curriculum: The word identification strategy.* Lawrence, KS: University of Kansas.

Leon, J. A., & Pepe, H. J. (1983). Self-instructional training: Cognitive behavior modification for remediating arithmetic deficits. *Exceptional Children, 50,* 54-60.

Leong, C. K. (1974). *An investigation of spatial-temporal information processing in children with specific reading disability.* Unpublished doctoral dissertation, University of Alberta.

Lester, F. K., & Garofalo, J. (1982, March). *Metacognitive aspects of elementary school students' performance on arithmetic tasks.* Paper presented at the meeting of the American Educational Research Association, New York.

Levine, F. M., Fasnacht, G., Funabiki, D., & Burkart, M. R. (1979). Methodological considerations regarding the evaluation of maintenance gains due to token programs. *Psychology in the Schools, 16,* 568-575.

Light, P., & Glachan, M. (1985). Facilitation of individual problem solving through peer interaction. *Educational Psychology, 5,* 217-225.

Linn, M. C., & Dalbey, J. (1985). Cognitive consequences of programming instruction: Instruction, access, and ability. *Educational Psychologist, 20,* 191-206.

Litrownik, A. J., Cleary, C. P., Lecklitner, G. L., & Franzini, L. R. (1978). Self-regulation in retarded persons: Acquisition of standards for performance. *American Journal of Mental Deficiency, 83,* 86-89.

Loper, A. B., & Hallahan, D. P. (1982). Meta-attention: The development of awareness of the attentional process. *Journal of General Psychology, 106,* 27-33.

Lovelace, E. A. (1984). Metamemory: Monitoring future recall ability during study. *Journal of Experimental Psychology: Learning, Memory, and Cognition, 10,* 756-766.

Lovitt, T., Rudsit, J., Jenkins, J., Pious, C., & Benedetti, D. (1986). Adapting science materials for regular and learning disabled seventh graders. *Remedial and Special Education, 7,* 31-39.

Ludlow, J. R., & Allen, L. M. (1979). The effect of early intervention and pre-school stimulus on the development of the Down's syndrome child. *Journal of Mental Deficiency Research, 23 ,* 29-43.

REFERENCES

Luria, A. R. (1966). *Higher cortical functions in man.* New York: Basic Books.

Luria, A. R. (1966). *Human brain and psychological processes.* New York: Harper & Row.

Luria, A. R. (1970). The functional organization of the brain. *Scientific American, 222,* 66-78.

Luria, A. R. (1973). *The working brain.* Harmondsworth, England: Penguin.

Luria, A. R. (1980). *Higher cortical functions in man* (2nd ed). New York: Basic Books.

Lyon, G. R. (1987). Learning disabilities research: False starts and broken promises. In S. Vaughn & C. S. Bos (Eds.), *Research in learning disabilities: Issues and future directions* (pp. 69-85). Boston: College-Hill.

MacCorquodale, K., & Meehl, P. E. (1948). On a distinction between hypothetical constructs and intervening variables. *Psychological Review, 55,* 95-107.

McDermott, D. (1978). Planning and acting. *Cognitive Science, 2,* 71-109.

McGee, G. G., Krantz, P. J., & McClannahan, L. E. (1986). An extension of incidental teaching procedures to reading instruction for autistic children. *Journal of Applied Behavior Analysis, 19,* 147-158.

McGraw, K. O. (1978). The detrimental effects of reward on performance: A literature review and a prediction model. In M. A. Lepper & D. Greene (Eds.), *The hidden cost of reward: New perspectives on the psychology of human motivation* (pp. 33-60). Hillsdale, NJ: Erlbaum.

McKinney, J. D., & Feagans, L. (1984). Academic and behavioral characteristics of learning disabled children and average achievers. *Learning Disability Quarterly, 7,* 251-265.

McLaskey, J., Rieth, H. J., & Polsgrove, L. (1980). The implications of response generalization for improving the effectiveness of programs for learning disabled children. *Journal of Learning Disabilities, 13,* 287-290.

McRae, C. R. (1929). *Psychology and education.* Melbourne: Whitcombe & Tombs.

McRae, S. G. (1986). Sequential-simultaneous processing and reading skills in primary grade children. *Journal of Learning Disabilities, 19,* 509-511.

Mahoney, M. J. (1977). Reflections on the cognitive learning trend in psychotherapy. *American Psychologist, 32,* 5-13.

Mahoney, M. J., & Nezworski, M. T. (1985). Cognitive-behavioral approaches to children's problems. *Journal of Abnormal Child Psychology, 13,* 467-476.

Malamuth, Z. N. (1979). Self-management training for children with reading problems: Effects on reading performance and sustained attention. *Cognitive Therapy and Research, 3*, 279-289.

Mandell, C. J., & Gold, V. (1984). *Teaching handicapped students.* St. Paul, MN: West.

Manion, I. G., & Bucher, B. (1986). Generalization of a sign language rehearsal strategy in mentally retarded and hearing deficient children. *Applied Research in Mental Retardation, 7,* 133-148.

Manzo, A. V. (1968). *Improvement of reading comprehension through reciprocal questioning.* Unpublished doctoral dissertation, Syracuse University, New York.

Marsh, G. E., Price, B. J., & Smith, T. E. C. (1983). *Teaching mildly handicapped children: Methods and materials.* St Louis: C. V. Mosby.

Martin, D. S. (1984). Infusing cognitive strategies into teacher preparation programs. *Educational Leadership, 42,* 68-72.

Maslow, A. H. (1954). *Motivation and personality.* New York: Harper.

Meichenbaum, D. (1972). Cognitive modification of test anxious college students. *Journal of Consulting and Clinical Psychology, 39,* 370-380.

Meichenbaum, D. (1974). Self-instruction methods. In F. G. Kanfer & A. P. Goldstein (Eds.), *Helping people change* (pp. 357-392). London: Pergamon Press.

Meichenbaum, D. (1977). *Cognitive behavior modification: An integrative approach.* New York: Plenum Press.

Meichenbaum, D. (1980). *Teaching thinking: A cognitive-behavioral perspective.* Paper presented at NIE-IRDC Conference, Pittsburg.

Meichenbaum, D., & Asarnow, J. (1978). Cognitive-behavioral modification and metacognitive development: Implications for the classroom. In P. Kendall & S. Hollon (Eds.), *Cognitive-behavioral interventions: Theory, research and procedure* (pp. 11-36). New York: Academic Press.

Meichenbaum, D. H., & Goodman, J. (1971). Training impulsive children to talk to themselves. *Journal of Abnormal Psychology, 77,* 115-126.

Messerer, J., Hunt, E., Meyers, G., & Lerner, J. (1984). Feuerstein's Instrumental Enrichment: A new approach for activating intellectual potential in learning disabled youth. *Journal of Learning Disabilities, 17,* 322-325.

Miller, G. A., Galanter, E. H., & Pribram, K. H. (1960). *Plans and the structure of behavior.* New York: Holt, Rinehart, & Winston.

Milner, B. (1964). Some effects of frontal lobectomy in man. In J. W. Warren & K. Akert (Eds.), *The frontal granular cortex and behavior* (pp. 313-334). New York: McGraw-Hill.

REFERENCES

Minsky, S. K., Spitz, H. H., & Bessellieu, C. L. (1985). Maintenance and transfer of training by mentally retarded young adults on the Tower of Hanoi problem. *American Journal of Mental Deficiency, 90,* 190-197.

Mithaug, D. E., Horiuchi, C. N., & Fanning, P. N. (1985). A report on the Colorado statewide follow-up survey of special education students. *Exceptional Children, 51,* 397-404.

Molloy, G. N. (1973). *Age, socioeconomic status and patterns of cognitive ability.* Unpublished doctoral dissertation, University of Alberta, Edmonton, Alberta, Canada.

Molloy, G. N. (1985). Behavioral approaches to the training of the mentally retarded. In A. F. Ashman & R. L. Laura (Eds.), *The education and training of the mentally retarded: Recent advances* (pp. 43-84). London: Croom Helm.

Moore, P. J. (1983). Aspects of metacognitive knowledge about reading. *Journal of Research in Reading, 6,* 87-102.

Moore, P. J. (in press). Reciprocal teaching and reading comprehension: A review. *Journal of Research in Reading.*

Morsink, C. V., Soar, R. S., Soar, R. M., & Thomas, R. (1986). Research on teaching: Opening the door to special education classrooms. *Exceptional Children, 53,* 32-40.

Myers, M., & Paris, S. (1978). Children's metacognitive knowledge about reading. *Journal of Educational Psychology, 70,* 680-690.

Narrol, H., Silverman, H., & Waksman, M. (1982). Developing cognitive potential in vocational high school students. *Journal of Educational Research, 76,* 107-112.

National Joint Committee on Learning Disabilities. (1987). Learning disabilities: Issues in the preparation of professional personnel. *Journal of Learning Disabilities, 20,* 229-231.

Nelson, C. M., & Polsgrove, L. (1984). Behavior analysis in special education: White rabbit or white elephant. *Remedial and Special Education, 5,* 6-17.

Newcomer, P. L. (1977). Special education services for the "mildly handicapped": Beyond a diagnostic and remedial model. *Journal of Special Education, 11,* 153-165.

Newell, A., & Simon, H. A. (1972). *Human problem solving.* Englewood Cliffs, NJ: Prentice-Hall.

Palincsar, A. S. (1986). Metacognitive strategy instruction. *Exceptional Children, 53,* 118-124.

Palincsar, A. S., & Brown, A. L. (1982). Inducing strategic learning from texts by means of informed, self-control training. *Topics in Learning and Learning Disabilities, 2,* 1-17.

Palincsar, A. S., & Brown, A. L. (1983). *Reciprocal teaching of comprehension-monitoring activities* (Tech. Rep. No. 269). Champaign, Ill: University of Illinois at Urbana-Champaign, Center for the Study of Reading.

Palincsar, A. S., & Brown, A. L. (1984). Reciprocal teaching of comprehension-fostering and comprehension-monitoring activities. *Cognition and Instruction, 1*, 117-175.

Palincsar, A. S., & Brown, A. L. (1984). Reciprocal teaching of comprehension fostering and monitoring activities. *Cognition and Instruction, 1*, 117-175.

Paris, S. G., Newman, R. S., & McVey, K.A. (1982). Learning the functional significance of mnemonic actions: A microgenetic study of strategy acquisition. *Journal of Experimental Child Psychology, 34*, 410-509.

Paris, S. G., & Oka, E. R. (1986). Self-regulated learning among exceptional children. *Exceptional Children, 53*, 103-108.

Paris, S. G., Saarnio, D. A., & Cross, D. R. (1986). A metacognitive curriculum to promote children's reading and learning. *Australian Journal of Psychology, 38*, 107-123.

Parmenter, T. R. (1984). *An investigation of the strategic behaviour of mildly intellectually handicapped adolescents in acquiring reading skills.* Unpublished doctoral dissertation, Macquarie University, North Ryde, NSW, Australia.

Parrill-Burnstein, M. (1978). Teaching kindergarten children to solve problems: An information processing approach. *Child Development, 49*, 700-706.

Pask, G. (1980). Developments in conversational theory - Part 1. *International Journal of Man-Machine Studies, 13*, 357-411.

Pask, G., & Scott, B. C. E. (1972). Learning strategies and individual competence. *International Journal of Man-Machine Studies, 4*, 217-253.

Pellegreno, J. W., & Goldman, S. R. (1987). Information processing and elementary mathematics. *Journal of Learning Disabilities, 20*, 23-32.

Perlmutter, B. F. (1986). Personality variables and peer relations of children and adolescents with learning disabilities. In S. Ceci (Ed.), *Handbook of cognitive, social, and neuropsychological aspects of learning disabilities* (Vol. 1) (pp. 339-359). Hillsdale, NJ: Erlbaum.

Peterson, P. L., & Swing, S. R. (1983). Problems in classroom implementation of cognitive strategy instruction. In M. Pressley & J. R. Levin (Eds.), *Cognitive strategy research: Educational applications* (pp. 267-287). New York: Springer-Verlag.

Phillips, H. C. (1985). Return of fear in the treatment of a fear of vomiting. *Behaviour Research and Therapy, 23*, 45-52.

Pigott, H. E., Fatuzzo, J. W., & Clement, P. W. (1986). The effects of reciprocal peer tutoring and group contingencies on the academic performance of elementary school children. *Journal of Applied Behavior Analysis, 19*, 93-98.

Piper, M. C., & Pless, I. B. (1980). Early intervention for infants with Down syndrome: A controlled trial. *Pediatrics, 65* , 463-468.

Preen, B. (1976). *Schooling for the mentally retarded: A historical perspective.* St. Lucia, Q: University of Queensland Press.

Pressley, M., & Levin, J. R. (Eds.) (1983). *Cognitive strategy research: Psychological foundations* . New York: Springer-Verlag.

Pressley, M., Levin, J. R., & Bryant, S. L. (1983). Memory strategy instruction during adolescence: When is explicit instruction needed? In M. Pressley & J. R. Levin (Eds.), *Cognitive strategy research: Psychological foundations* (pp. 25-49). New York: Springer-Verlag.

Reid, G. (1980). Overt and covert rehearsal in short-term motor memory of mentally retarded and nonretarded persons. *American Journal of Mental Deficiency, 85,* 377-382.

Reynolds, C. R. (1986). Transactional models of intellectual development, yes. Deficit models of process remediation, no. *School Psychological Review, 15,* 256-260.

Robinson, G. L. (1984). *Simultaneous and successive information processing, language, and reading processes in reading disabled children.* Unpublished doctoral dissertation, University of Newcastle, NSW, Australia.

Robinson, G. L. W., & Kirby, J. R. (1987). Remedial instruction in reading: guidelines from information integration theory. *Australian Journal of Reading, 10,* 32-44.

Rogers, C. R. (1977). *Carl Rogers on personal power.* New York: Delacorte.

Rogoff, B., & Gardner, W. (1984). *Everyday cognition: Its development in social contact.* Cambridge, MA: Harvard University Press.

Rooney, K. J., & Hallahan, D. P. (1985). Future directions for cognitive behavior modification research: The quest for cognitive change. *Remedial and Special Education, 6,* 46-51.

Rose, T. L., Koorland, M. A., & Epstein, M. H. (1982). A review of applied behavior analysis interventions with learning disabled children. *Education and Treatment of Children , 5,* 41-58.

Ryan, E. B., Ledger, G. W., Short, E. J., & Weed, K. A. (1982). Promoting the use of active comprehension strategies by poor readers. *Topics in Learning and Learning Disabilities, 2,* 53-60.

Ryan, E. B., Short, E. J., & Weed, K. A. (1986). The role of cognitive strategy training in improving the academic performance of learning disabled children. *Journal of Learning Disabilities, 19,* 521-529.

Ryckman, D. B. (1981). Reading achievement, IQ, and simultaneous-successive processing among normal and learning disabled children. *Alberta Journal of Educational Research, 27,* 74-83.

248

Sarason, S. (1971). *The culture of the school and the problem of change*. Boston: Allyn and Bacon.

Savell, J. M., Twohig, P. T., & Rachford, D. L. (1986). Empirical status of Feuerstein's "Instrumental Enrichment" (FIE) technique as a method of teaching thinking skills. *Review of Educational Research, 56*, 381-409.

Schakel, J. A. (1986). Cognitive assessment of preschool children. *School Psychology Record, 15*, 200-215.

Schloss, P. J., & Schloss, C. N. (1985). Contemporary issues in social skills research with mentally retarded persons. *Journal of Special Education, 19*, 269-282.

Schoenfeld, A. H. (1981). *Episodes and executive decisions in mathematical problem solving*. Paper presented at the meeting of the American Educational Research Association, Los Angeles.

Schonell, F. J., & Schonell, F. E. (1965). *Diagnostic and attainment testing*. Edinburgh: Oliver & Boyd.

Schumaker, J. B., Denton, P. H., & Deshler, D. D. (1984). *Learning Strategies Curriculum: The paraphrasing strategy*. Lawrence, KS: University of Kansas.

Schumaker, J. B., Deshler, D. D., & Ellis, E. S. (1986). Intervention issues related to the education of LD adolescents. In J. K. Torgesen & B. Y. L. Wong (Eds.), *Psychological and educational perspectives on learning disabilities* (pp. 329-365). Orlando, FL: Academic Press.

Schumaker, J. B., & Sheldon, J. (1985). *The sentence writing strategy - Instructors' manual*. Lawrence, KS: University of Kansas.

Semel, E. M., & Wiig, E. H. (1982). *Clinical evaluation of language functions*. Columbus, OH: Merrill.

Sheinker, A., Sheinker, J. M., & Stevens, L. J. (1984). Cognitive strategies for teaching the mildly handicapped. *Focus on Exceptional Children, 17*, 1-15.

Shif, Z. I. (1969). Development of children in schools for the mentally retarded. In M. Cole & I. Maltzman (Eds.), *A handbook of contemporary Soviet Psychology* (pp. 326-353). New York: Basic Books.

Short, E. J., & Ryan, E. B. (1984). Metacognitive differences between skilled and less skilled readers: Remediating deficits through story grammar an attribution training. *Journal of Educational Psychology, 76*, 225-235.

Shuell, T. J. (1986). Cognitive conceptions of learning. *Review of Educational Research, 56*, 411-436.

Siegler, R. S. (1976). Three aspects of cognitive development. *Cognitive Psychology, 8*, 481-520.

Silverman, H. (1985). Dynamic cognitive assessment: An alternative to intelligence testing. *Canadian Journal of Special Education, 1*, 63-72.

Simon, H. A. (1973). The structure of ill-structured problems. *Artificial Intelligence, 4*, 181-201.

Simon, H. A. (1978). Information-processing theory of human problem solving. In W. K. Estes (Ed.), *Handbook of learning and cognitive processes: Vol. 5 Human information processing* (pp. 271-295). Hillsdale, NJ: Erlbaum.

Simon, H. A., & Newell, A. (1971). Human problem solving: The state of the theory in 1970. *American Psychologist, 26*, 145-159.

Skinner, B. F. (1948). *Walden Two.* New York: Macmillan.

Skinner, B. F. (1958). Teaching machines. *Science, 128*, 971.

Skinner, B. F. (1971). *Beyond freedom and dignity.* London: Jonathan Cape.

Slife, B. D., Weiss, J., & Bell, T. (1985). Separability of metacognition and cognition: Problem solving in learning disabled and regular students. *Journal of Educational Psychology, 77*, 437-445.

Smith, P. K., & Dutton, S. (1979). Play and training in direct and innovative problem solving. *Child Development, 50*, 830-836.

Smith, R. A. (1987). A teacher's views on cooperative learning. *Phi Delta Kappan, 68*, 663-666.

Snart, F. (1985). Cognitive-processing approaches to the assessment and remediation of learning problems: An interview with J. P. Das and Reuven Feuerstein. *Journal of Psychoeducational Assessment, 3*, 1-14.

Snart, F., & Swann, V. (1982). Assessment of intellectually handicapped adults: A cognitive processing model. *Applied Research in Mental Retardation, 3*, 201-212.

Snider, V. (1987). Use of self-monitoring of attention with LD students: Research and application. *Learning Disability Quarterly, 10*, 139-151.

Soar, R. S., & Soar, R. M. (1983). Context effects in the teaching-learning process. In D. Smith (Ed.), *Essential knowledge for beginning educators.* Washington, DC: American Association of Colleges for Teacher Education and ERIC Clearinghouse for Teacher Education.

Spiker, C. C., & Cantor, J. H. (1979). Factors affecting hypothesis testing in kindergarten children. *Journal of Experimental Child Psychology, 28*, 230-248.

Spitz, H. H., Minsky, S. K., & Bessellieu, C. L. (1985). Influence of planning time and first-move strategy on Tower of Hanoi problem-solving performance of mentally retarded young adults and nonretarded children. *American Journal of Mental Deficiency, 90*, 46-56.

Spitz, H. H., Webster, N. A., & Borys, S. V. (1982). Further studies of the Tower of Hanoi problem-solving performance of retarded young adults and nonretarded children. *Developmental Psychology, 18,* 922-930.

Spring, H. T. (1985). Teacher decision making: A metacognitive approach. *Reading Teacher, 39,* 290-295.

Sternberg, R. J. (1980). Sketch of a componential subtheory of human intelligence. *The Behaviour and Brain Science, 3,* 573-614.

Sternberg, R. J. (1981). Cognitive-behavioral approaches to the training of intelligence in the retarded. *Journal of Special Education, 15,* 165-183.

Sternberg, R. J. (1983). Criteria for intellectual skills training. *Educational Researcher,* 12, 6-12.

Sternberg, R. J. (1985). *Beyond IQ: A triarchic theory of human intelligence.* New York: Cambridge University Press.

Strain, P. S., & Kerr, M. M. (1981). *Mainstreaming of children in schools: Research and programmatic issues.* New York: Academic Press.

Strain, P. S., Odom, S. L., & McConnell, S. (1984). Promoting social reciprocity of exceptional children: Identification, target behavior selection, and intervention. *Remedial and Special Education, 5,* 21-28.

Stuss, D. T., & Benson, D. F. (1984). Neuropsychological studies of the frontal lobes. *Psychological Bulletin, 95,* 3-28.

Swanson, H. L. (1984). Does theory guide practice? *Remedial and Special Education, 5,* 7-16.

Swanson, H. L. (1987a). Information processing theory and learning disabilities: A commentary and future perspective. *Journal of Learning Disabilities, 20,* 155-166.

Swanson, H. L. (1987b). Information processing theory and learning disabilities: An overview. *Journal of Learning Disabilities, 20,* 3-7.

Swanson, L. (1981). Modification of comprehension deficits in learning disabled children. *Learning Disability Quarterly, 4,* 189-201.

Talbot, M. E. (1964). *Edouard Seguin: A study of an educational approach to the treatment of mentally defective children.* New York: Teachers College Press.

Tarver, S. G. (1986). Cognitive behavior modification, direct instruction and holistic approaches to the education of students with learning disabilities. *Journal of Learning Disabilities, 19,* 368-375.

Taylor, M, & Bacharach, V. R. (1981). The development of drawing rules: Metaknowledge about drawing influences performance on nondrawing tasks. *Child Development, 52,* 373-375.

Tharp, R. G., & Gallimore, R. (1985). The logical status of metacognitive training. *Journal of Abnormal Child Psychology, 13,* 455-466.

Torgesen, J. K. (1982). The learning disabled child as an inactive learner: Educational implications. *Topics in Learning and Learning Disabilities, 2*, 45-52.

Torgesen, J. K. (1987). Thinking about the future by distinguishing between issues that have resolutions and those that do not. In S. Vaughn & C. S. Bos (Eds.), *Research in learning disabilities: Issues and future directions* (pp. 55-67). Boston: College-Hill.

Turnbull, A. P., & Turnbull, III, H. R. (Eds.), (1986). *Families, professionals and exceptionality: A special partnership.* Columbus, OH: Merrill.

Turner, L. A., & Bray, N. W. (1985). Spontaneous rehearsal by mildly mentally retarded children and adolescents. *American Journal of Mental Deficiency, 90*, 57-63.

Turnure, J. E. (1986). Instruction and cognitive development: Coordinating communication and cues. In M. J. Shepard & L. Gelzheiser (Eds.), *Exceptional Children, Special Issue, Competence and instruction: Contributions from cognitive psychology, 53*, 109-117.

Turnure, J. E. (1987). Social influences on cognitive strategies and cognitive development: The role of communication and instruction. *Intelligence, 11*, 77-89.

Tyler, L. E. (1974). *Individual differences.* New York: Appleton-Century-Crofts.

Vernon, P. E., Ryba, K. A., & Lang, R. J. (1978). Simultaneous and successive processing: An attempt at replication. *Canadian Journal of Behavioural Science, 10*, 1-15.

Vietze, P., & Coates, D. (1986). Using information processing strategies for early identification of mental retardation. *Topics in Early Childhood Special Education, 6*, 72-85.

Wacker, D. P., & Berg, W. K. (1985). Use of peers to train and monitor the performance of adolescents with severe handicaps. *Education and Training of the Mentally Retarded, 20*, 109-122.

Wallin, J. E. W. (1917). *Problems of subnormality.* New York: World Book Co.

Wasserman, T. H., & Vogrin, D. J. (1979). Long term effects of a token economy on target and off-task behaviors. *Psychology in the Schools, 16*, 551-557.

Waters, H. S. (1982). Memory development during adolescence: Relationship between metamemory, strategy use, and performance. *Journal of Experimental Child Psychology, 33*, 183-195.

Watts, W. J. (1985). An error analysis on the Raven's using Feuerstein's deficient cognitive functions. *Alberta Journal of Educational Research, 21*, 41-53.

Wehman, P., Kregel, J., & Barcus, J. M. (1985). From school to work: A vocational transition model for handicapped students. *Exceptional Children, 52*, 25-37.

252

REFERENCES

Whitman, T. L. (1987). Self instruction, individual differences and mental retardation. *American Journal of Mental Deficiency, 92*, 213-233.

Whitman, T. L., & Johnson, M. B. (1983). Teaching addition and subtraction with regrouping to educable mentally retarded children: A group self-instructional training program. *Behavior Therapy, 14*, 127-143.

Wiens, J. W. (1983). Metacognition and the adolescent passive learner. *Journal of Learning Disabilities, 16*, 145-149.

Winschel, J. F., & Lawrence, E. A. (1975). Short-term memory: Curricular implications for the mentally retarded. *Journal of Special Education, 9*, 395-408.

Witkin, H. A., Moore, C. A., Goodenough, D. R., & Cox, P. W. (1977). Field-dependent and field-independent cognitive styles and their educational implications. *Review of Educational Research, 47*, 1-64.

Wong, B. Y. L. (1980). Activating the inactive learner: Use of question/prompts to enhance comprehension and retention of implied information in learning disabled children. *Learning Disability Quarterly, 3*, 29-37.

Wong, B. Y. L. (1985a). Issues in cognitive-behavioral interventions in academic skill areas. *Journal of Abnormal Child Psychology, 13*, 425-442.

Wong, B. Y. L. (1985b). Self-questioning instructional research: A review. *Review of Educational Research, 55*, 227-268.

Wong, B. Y. L. (1986a). A cognitive approach to teaching spelling. *Exceptional Children, 53*, 169-173.

Wong, B. Y. L. (1986b). Metacognition and special education: A review of a view. *Journal of Special Education, 20*, 9-30.

Wong, B. Y. L. (1987). Conceptual and methodological issues in interventions with learning-disabled children and adolescents. In S. Vaughn & C. S. Bos (Eds.), *Research in learning disabilities: Issues and future directions* (pp. 185-200). Boston: College-Hill.

Wong, B. Y. L. (1988, February). *Issues neglected in cognitive strategy training.* Paper presented at the Association for Children with Learning Disabilities, Las Vegas, NV.

Wong, B. Y. L., & Jones, W. (1982). Increasing metacomprehension in learning disabled and normally achieving students through self-questioning training. *Learning Disability Quarterly, 5*, 228-240.

Woodworth, R. S. (1938). *Experimental psychology.* New York: Henry Holt.

Author Index

255

Subject Index

Achievement,
    metacognition and, 64-68
Achievement tests, 165
Active student participation,
    important in existing
    cognitive training
        models, 60
    Instrumental Enrichment
    in, 49
Adolescents
    alternate high school
    programs, 27-28,
    high school class, 226
    information processing,
    25-28
    special needs with, 28
Aptitude by treatment
    interactions (ATIs),
    59-60, 146
Arousal,
    multi-component models
    of information, 34
As a whole thing,
    see concurrent coding,
    150
Assessment in PBI,
    application in the
    classroom, 165-176
    formal assessment, 66-
    170
    prior to teaching 166-
    174, 223

teacher constructed tests
of coding, 171-172
teacher constructed tests
of planning, 166, 173-
174
formal,
    dynamic, 170
    initial assessment,
    152
    nonstandardized,
    168-170
    on-going and final,
    174-176
    standardized tests,
    166-168
Assessment PBI phase, 154-
157
    in the classroom, 165-176
    maintaining the PBI
    sequence in, 191
Attributional belief system,
    224-225
Automated routines, 30

Behavior modification, 38
Behavioral interventions, 38
    different to cognitive, 197
    legacy in classroom
    instruction, 199
Behaviorism
    generalization, 72
    rise in special education,
    21-25, 222
    current issues, 22-23

263